ECOSYSTEM

living the 12 principles of networked business

THOMAS POWER

GEORGE JERJIAN

FT.com
FINANCIAL TIMES

PEARSON EDUCATION LIMITED

Head Office
Edinburgh Gate
Harlow CM20 2JE
Tel: +44 (0)1279 623623
Fax: +44 (0)1279 431059

London Office:
128 Long Acre
London WC2E 9AN
Tel: +44 (0)20 7447 2000
Fax: +44 (0)20 7240 5771
Website:www.businessminds.com

First published in Great Britain in 2001

ISBN 0 273 65622 8

British Library Cataloguing in Publication Data
A CIP catalogue record for this book can be obtained from the British Library.

10 9 8 7 6 5 4 3 2 1

Designed by Sue Lamble
Typeset by Pantek Arts Ltd, Maidstone, Kent
Printed and bound in the UK by Biddles Ltd of Guildford and King's Lynn

The Publishers' policy is to use paper manufactured from sustainable forests.

CONTENTS

ABOUT THE AUTHORS

THOMAS POWER, author of the *Financial Times* report 'From supply chain to value chain', is co-author of *The E-Business Advantage*, which stresses the importance of adapting your business to the new electronic economy and to the flexible and pragmatic approach that it demands.

A former managing director of the TDS Group, Thomas left to create Ecademy Ltd, an e-business learning organization.

Widely recognized for his experience, vision, energy and drive, Thomas has worked with Amstrad, Microsoft and Mercedes-Benz. He is also a director of Routecause Ltd, an internet research and consultancy.

GEORGE JERJIAN, is an author, a speaker and a chartered marketer. Over the past 20 years, he has worked in marketing in Africa, the US and the UK. His marketing career has embraced numerous sectors including export/import, real estate, financial services and now networked business.

Following an MA in journalism from New York University in 1993 and a stint at CNBC television, George won an EMMY award for his documentary *Emerging Airlines: The Kiwi Story*.

In 1996, he published *Your Money and Your Life* (*Seven Ages: Personal Financial Planning*) and in 1999, with Thomas Power, he co-authored *Battle of the Portals*. George is also a director of Routecause Ltd, an internet research and consultancy.

ABOUT THE BOOK

THIS BOOK IS A COMPANION TO *E-Business to the Power of 12*. It will give you the opportunity to see the 12 principles of networked business in action. It seeks to bring a wide array of material in networked business into focus and context. It also shows you how networked businesses work together in a living ecosystem.

In the introduction, we explain in simple and clear terms the impact of the internet on economics, finance, the law and education, inasmuch as it inevitably impacts on all businesses and organizations. After all, now that we are all connected, actions and reactions in an economy will grow ever faster, from one ecosystem to another, from one organization to another. We will introduce you to the concept of ecosystem and the 12 principles and then discuss the latter in a separate overview.

To best illustrate the ecosystem concept and its key principles in action, we interviewed 48 organizations over a six-month period, then selected 24 that would best convey the message from our journey. To make the book easy to read and use, we have broken down each chapter or principle as follows:

▶ statement of the principle

▶ two case studies, which include

   – a supplier profile
   – an interview with supplier
   – principle in action with customer

▶ executive summary of the principle.

We have structured it so that you can read the chapters in any order you wish, but we would recommend that you do not miss out the introduction and conclusion. In the conclusion, we provide a message to shareholders, employees, businesses, consumers and government and we leave you a signpost of where we are heading next.

This book is not prescriptive. Read it, absorb it, and reconfigure it for your business.

ACKNOWLEDGMENTS

WE WISH TO ACKNOWLEDGE the contribution of the following people, without whom this book would not have been possible. In the first instance, we would like to thank all those whose contribution, directly or indirectly, found its way into this book. We hope we haven't left anyone out, and if we have, it is not intentional.

We are very grateful to the following, who gave us their time, their energy and their thoughts and thereby added their flavour to the 'cooking' of our book. Tom Wheadon, Anthony Harling, Charles Johnson, Mark Edwards, Steve Bailey, Tony Fish, David Beard, Rob Wirszycz, Nicholas Brown, Ian Wilson, John Paleomylites, Mike Awford, Dave Bruce, Alan Scutt, Jim Conning, Chris Phillips, David Graham, Phil Wood, Peter Klein, David Aldridge, Matt Rushton, John Griffith, Mei Cheung, Neil Holloway, John Noakes, Andy Matson, Geoff Sutton, Jennifer Mowat, Alexis de Belloy, Neil Macehiter, and Rebekah Menezes.

We also thank the following people, whom we interviewed but whose output did not make it into this book, due to constraints outside our control. Steve Gutterman, Ian Wells, James Smith, Phil Collerton, James Cox, Bob Carter, Simon Lofthouse, Alastair Laidlaw, Jim Rose, Damon Oldcorn, Charles Walker and Matt Price. Also Nigel Atkinson, David Nabarro, Gavin Breeze, Jane Reedy, Adam Gunnell, Laurence Shafe, Julian Patterson, Greg McCrea, Ceri Jones, Eric Sidnell, Peter Landale, Paul Ellis, Russell Loarridge, Andy Tobin and John Caswell.

We would like to thank our editors, Richard Stagg and Jacqueline Cassidy, at Pearson Education and our transcribers, Nicola Haydon and

Sharon Ives-Rider, for their hard work and timely transcription of 48 interviews tapes, each taking some six hours.

Last but not least, we would like to thank our colleagues at Ecademy.Ltd for their contribution: Steve Clarke, Penny Power, Glenn Watkins, Phil Brown, Nick Davies, Mike Weber, John Bromley, Martyn Clarke and Ben Baker.

George Jerjian
Thomas Power
London, July 2001

FOREWORD

At the end of 1998 this Government set itself a visionary target of making the UK the best environment in the world for e-commerce. This embraced a far-reaching approach to getting everyone in the UK online – citizens, business and Government.

Since then, in the UK there has been a surge in businesses getting connected and significant progress has been made in the numbers of firms that are actually trading online. The challenges – and the (admittedly hazy!) language used to express them – has also moved on from e-commerce to e-business, e-enabled organisations and a host of other e-s! But there is much further to go in terms of businesses taking up new ways of working. This means not just ordering and paying online or having a website. The challenges are about how information and knowledge isused within organisations, how people work together and communicate. It also impacts upon how businesses relate to each other within supply chains: not just in placing orders but how every stage of the relationship is managed. And new approaches to customer relations management are significantly changing customers' expectations. Best practice in all the areas is only emerging as the boundaries of what is possible are pushed back.

The idea of a new emerging business ecosystem perhaps captures this sense of needing to rethink and reshape much of what we take for granted – to adapt to and prosper in a very different environment. I hope this pioneering book will stimulate further fresh thinking. By setting out some principles and illustrating them with real live cases of changing organisations I believe it has much to offer in this exciting and un-charted territory we are entering.

PATRICIA HEWITT MP
Minister for Trade & Industry

INTRODUCTION

THE MINNESOTA DEPARTMENT OF NATURAL RESOURCES
is using an ecosystem-based approach to manage the state's natural
resources. The basic idea is that you manage ecosystems rather than
specific species or disciplines. In other words, you don't manage the
pheasants as much as you manage the ecosystem the pheasants live in.
In this complex and constantly changing interaction between the
living world and its dynamic environment, it makes more sense to
look at any given situation organically or holistically rather than from
a single perspective.

Similarly, no business is an island. You cannot manage a business, let
alone a networked business, on its own. You must manage the ecosystem which your business inhabits. The 12 principles or 'the pizza' is a
catalog of the market, a framework, a language, a collaborative ecosystem, which will help you understand the big idea and how you can use
it to find your way in your ecosystem. How did we get here?

In the early 1930s, a young psychologist, Alexander Luria, was sent by
the Soviets to Uzbekistan to record how people thought before the
introduction of collectivization and formal education. Luria found that
when the pre-literate Soviet peasants were shown a round geometric
figure and asked to describe it, they said they saw a plate, a bucket or a
moon, but not a circle. Instead of a square, they saw a door, a house or
a board for drying apricots. After being shown four drawings of objects
– a hammer, a saw, a log and a hatchet – they were asked to group
them. They responded that the saw will saw and the hatchet will chop.
The research revealed that without literacy there was no necessity for
'abstract thought'.

'The emergence of an abstract category like "tool" owes much to literacy'[1] – an issue we addressed in the conclusion of our second book, *Battle of the Portals*.[2] The point we were making then, as we are now, is that just as writing changed the way we see and interpret the world about us, the same will undoubtedly happen as we travel deeper into the information age. 'The medium – not the content – is the message,' wrote Marshall McLuhan, a professor of English Literature in Canada, in 1964, referring to the impact of television on society. 'It is the medium that shapes and controls the scale and form of human association and action.'

❝the medium – not the content – is the message ❞

Similarly, and more powerfully, the emergence of the internet and the world wide web will also shape and control the scale and form of our human association and action this century. How will this come about? If 'abstract thought' emerged as the child of writing and literacy, we believe we have stumbled on its equivalent for the internet and world wide web. We have named it 'ecosystem'.

Building on the concepts we raised in *E-Business to the Power of 12*,[3] this book shows you how networked business works in a living ecosystem. It gives you a coherent strategy. Have no illusions about it: networked business is not easy. It is hard to understand and hard to implement. Just imagine how difficult it is to learn a new language, absorb a new alphabet and grasp new concepts such as abstract thought. Networked business is a new dimension and to those who seek it, it provides equal doses of excitement and exhaustion, fulfillment and failure, passion and pain.

We know this because we have lived it. What we have done, since 1994, is to aggregate all the possible types of businesses, professions and organizations that are directly involved in the internet markets. We then split them into different bins. Many of the bins shared the same qualifications, so we grouped them under what we now call 'principles'. For instance, think of a 100-piece jigsaw puzzle. You have all the pieces, you break them down into the various colors and shapes. You complete the easy ones first and then you give time to the difficult pieces. Eventually, with perseverance and agility, you complete the picture.

Of the 48 companies interviewed for this book, we selected two to illustrate each principle. The result is an overall framework with which to work out where you are in this new ecosystem. That's not all though. The 12 principles also provide a new perspective and a new language with which to communicate with your customers, shareholders, employees, partners, competitors, and the world at large.

'The Internet changes everything,' said Larry Ellison, Chief Executive Officer (CEO) of Oracle Corporation. Although it is beyond the remit of this book to delve into the massive sea-change introduced by the internet on the big issues – the macro level – we need to touch on a few of those issues that have an immediate, direct and filtering impact on networked business. Take, for instance, the impact that the internet has made and continues to make on some of the following specific disciplines that underpin networked business, such as economics, finance, law and education.

economics

Economic growth is a function of connectivity or connectedness. After the Second World War, during the administration of US President Dwight Eisenhower, the US Congress passed the 1956 Highway Act. Over the next 25 years, until 1981, 48,000 miles of highway were constructed across the United States.[4] These highways caused the gradual birth as well as the gradual death of many communities, because the growth of community and commerce is a function of being connected or linked. How many modern European communities still live on or near the original 44,000 miles of roads that the Romans built more than 1,000 years ago?[5]

Today, instead of roads, fiber optics (internet) and radio waves (mobiles/cell phones) connect us. One strand of fiber is the size of a hair on our head and it can run 40,000 telephone calls. Fiber optics are bunched together and laid under the ground and under the ocean floor and eventually connect right through to our television sets, personal computers and other devices. Just like the roads, these strands connecting our communities will inevitably cause the gradual birth of new businesses and the death of old ones.

❝all wars are said to be about economics ❞

All wars are said to be about economics. However, could it be that all economics is about war? On the one hand, when there is no more new land to fight about, fights occur on existing land that belongs to someone else. On the other hand, when there is new land, battles ensue for domination. Witness the events in history, especially the struggles of the European powers to colonize the Americas in the eighteenth century and the rest of the world in the nineteenth century. In turn, the colonized United States is swiftly colonizing the world through the power of the internet. The internet is new land, carved out of mathematics (0s and 1s). It experienced its own gold rush of the dot coms. Although it resembles the California 'gold rush' of the mid-1850s, it would be unwise to dismiss it as vapour. The internet creates efficiencies. In both ecosystem and economy, efficiency is rewarded by survival and inefficiency is punished by extinction. When the stock market correction comes – and it will – for many it will end in tears. But the internet and its electronic business proposition, like a rose garden which has been weeded and trimmed, will grow more bountiful and beautiful.

It is to this end that we have targetted our sights. Smart investors place bets on many, fully realizing that only a fraction will do well and only one may deliver exceptional returns. To better understand the financial rationales, we need to understand how financiers look at risk and reward.

finance The time value of money has changed over the centuries as society has changed. But something is wrong when 80 percent of an organization's value is not reflected in the balance sheet. In early 2000, the market capitalization of listed companies had typically reached five times book value. Even after the market carnage, the market caps are still far off the mark. In 2000 a team from Arthur Andersen, the accountancy firm, published a book called *Cracking the Value Code*.[6] In it, they posit that physical and financial assets continue to dominate balance sheets and that reporting is still primarily shaped by the industrial economy and the centuries-old measurement system that preceded it. A new language and a new set of principles are required to suit the new economy, which they call '*value dynamics*'. It aims to put value on intangible but crucial factors of modern businesses: employee assets, supplier assets, customer assets and intellectual capital. The stock market does this all the time by hunch and guesswork, but refinement is certainly needed and there is a long way to go.

People are still confused and don't understand why and how internet or new economy companies have had such alarmingly high valuations and why old economy companies have such pedestrian valuations. One credible explanation was put forward by analysts Michael Mauboussin and Bob Hiler of Credit Suisse First Boston (CSFB) in their study entitled *Cash Flow.com: Cash Economics in the New Economy*, released in March 1999.[7]

In this report, they state that 'Cash is King'. They posit that internet companies are valued on their ability to generate cash. Cash earnings for most old economy companies will typically overstate their free cash flow. To illustrate, book store Barnes and Noble generated $150 million in cash earnings for the 12 months ending October 31, 1998. However, it also had to invest more than $240 million during this period, translating into free negative cash flow of $95 million.

The internet companies analyzed all had superior cash economics to their old economy counterparts, although they generated cash in a totally different way. For instance, while Amazon.com, the online book store, incurred a cash outflow from earnings of $58 million in 1998, it generated a cash inflow of $54 million from investments – coming very close to generating positive free cash flow. This means that cash earnings for a new economy company can dramatically understate the company's total free cash flow.

The sum of the firm's cash earnings and investments drives shareholder value creation. So investors must look at both financial statements, say Mauboussin and Hiler. 'We believe that understanding these fundamental differences in the cash economics of business models will become increasingly important as the digital revolution transforms the world,' the CSFB study concludes.

Not everyone is convinced by this argument. John Ong, Managing Director of High Yield Capital Markets at BNP Paribas in London, says: 'CSFB's Cash Flow.com's argument is compelling and their models for explaining this are insightful. However, the two examples are insufficient to make the case that the technology sector, as a whole, is rationally valued, based on cash flow methods.'[8]

Perhaps the truth lies somewhere in between. Although many of the dot coms may have faltered and failed, the lesson of their superior cash economics will not have been lost on the old economy organizations.

❝raising interest rates will have the effect of further cutting off the flow of funds to innovative businesses❞

Business Week economist Michael J. Mandel, in his book *The Coming Internet Depression,*[9] likens the old economy to a car, while the new economy is likened to an airplane. To avoid an accident, a car driver simply needs to apply the brakes and the car will come to a stop. Not so for an airplane, which needs to maintain enough speed to stay in the air. Slowing a plane below the stall speed can have serious consequences. Similarly, raising interest rates will have the effect of further cutting off the flow of funds to innovative businesses, making a bad situation much worse.

While economics and finance are key, the essential ingredient for economic success must reside in the 'law'. The reason the US economy has been able to grow exponentially in its short 250-year history is because its laws and constitution protect the individual's rights to property and liberty. Without a solid legal framework, the US economy and financial health would resemble at best Europe's less entrepreneurial economy or at worst Russia's stagnant one.

the law

Law is a powerful catalyst in changing how we live. The Magna Carta, the Bill of Rights and the US Constitution have over the years initiated the pre-eminence of democracy, property rights and market forces. In each of these cases, it was the 'people' who kick-started the process. Perhaps this is why 'the law' that we have in the West cannot be easily grafted on the old Soviet economies. Similarly, the existing laws need to adapt to the inclusion of the new environment. Our historic adaptability implies that we can achieve the transformation.

'In real space, we recognize how *laws* regulate – through constitutions, statutes and other legal codes. In cyberspace we must understand how *code* regulates through software and hardware,' says Professor Lawrence Lessig of Harvard Law School. It is the codes in the software and hardware that effectively dictate how we work and what we can manipulate. 'Code is law,' says Professor Lessing in his book *Code and Other Laws of Cyberspace.*[10]

At the very start, the internet was all about 'freedom' and libertarian passion. Lessig's argument is that 'the invisible hand of cyberspace is building an architecture that is quite the opposite of what it was at cyberspace's birth.' The invisible hand, through commerce, is constructing an architecture that perfects control, an architecture that makes possible highly efficient regulation – an axis between commerce and the state. Our interview with law firm Simmons & Simmons highlights and addresses these legal issues.

There are three basic issues that emerge from this, which address the needs of the individual, the business organizations and the government. The first issue is about security and trust. If commerce is to succeed, it requires transactions to be secure. For transactions to be secure, we need to know with whom we are dealing. Can we trust them? Are they who they say they are? Trust is the cornerstone of commerce.

❝if commerce is to succeed, it requires transactions to be secure❞

The second issue is about implementing an architecture (software) to encourage commerce over the internet. Market forces encourage architectures of identity to facilitate online commerce. Governments don't need to induce this sort of development. As we stated earlier, architecture is a kind of law: it determines what people can and cannot do. By so doing, it encourages people to do business only in a certain way, the acceptable way.

The third issue is about private and public laws and the political impact. When commercial interests determine the architecture, they create a kind of privatized law. But just because there are privatized laws does not mean there can be no public laws. Public laws are above privatized laws. Just because a corporation is larger than many countries, it does not stop those countries from having laws to rein them in. The point about politics is process – by which we reason about how things ought to be. Politics is about how we decide, how that power is exercised, and by whom.[11]

Lessig ends his book on a pessimistic note. 'It is not a great time to come across revolutionary technologies. We are no more ready for this revolution than the Soviets were ready for theirs. We, like the Soviets, have been caught by a revolution. But we, unlike they, have something to lose.'[12] What we have to lose, in our view, includes our democratic system, our judicial system, our market economy, our respect for human rights, individual liberty and property rights.

We do not share Lessig's pessimism. The wise elders in pre-literate times must have felt the same doom-laden thoughts about the future of their world, but life goes on changing, changing and changing. The only assurance for human survival is its willingness to unlearn old ways and to learn the new ways.

education
'In a time of drastic change, it is the learners who inherit the future. The learned find themselves equipped to live in a world that no longer exists,' declared Eric Hoffer in *Vanguard Management* in 1989.[13]

How can skilled individuals in the old economy convert their skills to the new economy? There is a talent shortage not only in the new economy but also in the old economy. There are many jobs that remain unfilled, not because there are not enough people to fill them but because there is a shortage of people 'skilled in the new economy'. The gap between supply and demand continues to grow and this has highlighted the need for education in this market. But just to think that there is a gap between supply and demand would be to miss the point.

The $772 billion education industry was the second largest sector of the US economy in 2000, after healthcare, reveals Hambrecht + Co's 90-page report 'e-Learning Study'.[14] Corporate training amounts to $66 billion. There are changes driving the supply and demand equation. On the demand side the drivers are rapid obsolescence of knowledge and training, need for just-in-time training, search for cost-effective ways to meet learning needs of a globally distributed workforce, skills gap, and flexible access to lifelong learning. On the supply side the drivers are internet access becoming standard at home and at work, advances in interactive, media-rich content, increasing bandwidth and better delivery platforms making e-learning more attractive, growing selection of e-learning products and services, and standards facilitating compatibility and usability. Education is poised to become a lifelong experience and exercise, which indicates that it will grow relentlessly.

"education is poised to become a lifelong experience and exercise "

Another study by CSFB confirms the above. In a 250-page report entitled 'e-Learning: Power for the Knowledge Economy',[15] released in March 2000, CSFB says the e-learning industry is in its infancy but is projected to be an estimated $40 billion market by 2005. It also states: 'The economics of e-learning companies are more favourable than traditional bricks-and-mortar schools. By comparison, e-learning companies spend significantly less on hardware, maintenance and infrastructure, giving it superior cash economics.' CSFB concludes that e-learning companies will deliver 'superior educational outcomes' as well as create 'substantial shareholder value'.

If the learning experience is to deliver superior educational results, it cannot come from books alone. We learn directly from others and from our own experience. If we are simply learning from books, we do not truly understand what we are taught. Reading is a wonderful activity, but it is not everything. If we do not experience events, if we do not collide emotionally with other people, if we do not experience pain, then we cannot grow. Look back at the most painful experiences in your life and undoubtedly you will find that it was then that you grew the most. This is the emotional dimension, which is an integral part of learning and growing.

As hunter-gatherers, people could not grow because there was limited food available to support them. The deliberate cultivation of crops changed everything. It enabled them to increase the productivity of the land and escape the tyranny of the food chain. This single development makes humans ecologically different from all other species.

In *The Death of Competition: Leadership and Strategy in the Age of Business Ecosystems*,[16] author James F. Moore states:

> 'Ecology is particularly helpful in liberating our thinking . . . it
> connects us with the constantly transforming nature of reality.' In the

same manner, the deliberate cultivation of ecosystems will enable
humans to escape the tyranny of "linear and mechanistic thinking".'

the background to ecosystem – the 12 principles of networked business, 'the pizza'

Ecosystem:

1 *'a system of organisms occupying a habitat, together with those aspects*
of the physical environment with which they interact.'

The New Shorter Oxford English Dictionary (UK) ©1993

Ecosystem:

2 *'an ecological community considered together with the non-living*
factors of its environment as a unit.'

The Merriam-Webster Third New International Dictionary
of the English Language (US) ©1986

Businesses can no longer work in a singular, linear way. Once you have learned a new language, it is impossible to unlearn it. The new language is the ecosystem. It is about working in a holistic and organic way.

Business ecosystem:

'a system of websites occupying the world wide web, together with
those aspects of the real world with which they interact. It is a physical
community considered together with the non-living factors of its
environment as a unit.'

Describing an organic interaction is tough, so we've come up with the 'pizza'. The 12 principles of networked business or the 'pizza' is a multi-purpose template. John Allen Mollenhauer, a US shareholder of Ecademy, described it more lucidly as 'a catalog of the market'. We will cover this in more detail in the next chapter.

Thomas Power, the Chief Knowledge Officer of Ecademy Ltd, originally devised the 12 principles of networked business as a process rather than an organic approach. After on-the-field experiments, critics of the pizza brought forward essentially two main arguments. The first was that it was not a process and the second was that we were mixing too many disciplines to make any sense.

A process is moving through a succession of acts, events or developmental stages. In the case of our pizza, this meant that you would have to go through from principle 1 to principle 12 without skipping any number. It soon became apparent that this could not be done. However, what we discovered was that the pizza appeared to be working very well as a holistic 'framework' for networked business solutions. Some companies have even used it as a 'language', whereby their technical team could converse with their sales team and understand what they were supposed to deliver to their client.

the 12 principles are not a process but an ecosystem

Like Christopher Columbus, who sailed west looking to reach the East Indies and then ended up in the West Indies, we too were looking for something which was eluding us. Just as Columbus had used an antiquated map, which did not reflect the reality on the ground, we too were using a relic of the industrial age – the linear process. We had to think anew. We had to stop thinking in a linear fashion. We had to open our mind's eye to think in a holistic and organic way – something akin to mind mapping. Our research led us to the word 'ecosystem', which we found had entered the English language as recently as 1935. It was first used by Sir Arthur George Tansley (1871–1955), founder of the British Ecological Society and Professor of Botany at Oxford University. Further research on the concepts of 'ecology' and 'ecosystems' led us to John Seely Brown's writings.

"our research led us to the word 'ecosystem'"

John Seely Brown, former Chief Scientist at the Xerox Corporation and former director of its Palo Alto Research Center, better known as PARC (where WIMP – windows, icons, mouse and pointers – was invented) had used the terms 'knowledge ecology' and 'the ecology of learning' in his writings. He predicted that the high hit rate for radical new ideas sat between the traditional academic principles;[17] for instance, bionomics sits between biology and economics.

Michael Rothschild, President of the Bionomics Institute, wrote *Bionomics – Economy as Ecosystem* in 1992 (republished in 1995). Rothschild earned his law and MBA degrees simultaneously from Harvard University, then worked for the Boston Consulting Group. He sees the economy from a different perspective. Mainstream economics borrows concepts from Newtonian physics to view the economy in *mechanistic* terms. Bionomics, however, draws insights from evolutionary biology to view the economy in *organic* terms.

'The most difficult concept to accept about the natural world is that it runs itself. No conscious force is needed to keep the ecosystem going. Life is a self-organizing phenomenon. From the interplay of hormones in the human body to the expansions and contractions of the great Arctic caribou herds, nature's intricately linked feedback loops automatically maintain a delicate yet robust balance. Markets perform the same function in the economy. Without central planning, buyers and sellers adjust to changing prices for commodities, capital and labour. A flexible economic order emerges spontaneously from the chaos of free markets … Two centuries of economic thought, both capitalist and socialist, are based on the concept of "economy as machine" rather than "economy as ecosystem". Nonetheless, history has demonstrated that no economy behaves like a simple, cyclical machine. Like ecosystems, economies are spectacularly complex and endlessly adaptable.'[18]

Why is it so difficult for man to grasp this? Author James F. Moore quotes a seventeenth-century biologist named Albrecht von Haller, who commented on both the richness of nature and the limitations of our minds.

'Nature connected her things in a net, not a chain: but humans can follow only by chains because their language can't handle several things at once.'

If you don't adapt your thinking and your business, then like plankton, you're going to be someone else's lunch. Your organization is part of the business ecosystem in which you survive. The 12 principles will help you reconfigure your business in this new ecosystem. For most of us operating in the business environment, thinking in a 'natural' way is quite alien, so let's take a brief look at how ecology and nature are studied. Hopefully, this will give you some perspective on how business thought needs to change radically.

66the 12 principles will help you reconfigure your
business in this new ecosystem 99

Simply put, in ecology, living things can be studied at six different levels. This is called 'a hierarchy of complexity' (see Figures I.1 and I.2). Firstly, there is the *individual*, a plant or animal belonging to a particular species. A group of individuals of the same species is called a *population*. Different populations of species exist together in a *community*, and several different communities may be found together in a characteristic way, creating an *ecosystem*. Different ecosystems are found together in a single geographic zone, sharing the same climatic conditions and constituting a *biome*, such as tropical rainforest, desert or mountain. All the earth's varied biomes together make up the highest level of organization, the *biosphere*, the thin life-bearing layer that forms the outer surface of the planet.

One of the ways that we believe the internet will change how we view the world around us is in an organization's view of its stakeholders. As the internet connects more and more people, it makes it very difficult for organizations to hide information. The information we are referring to is 'corporate information'. Organizations want to send their message to the world at large and they spend enormous sums of money on doing so. Therefore, with the investment made in these messages, it is vital that people believe them – and they won't if the message is not transparent to all stakeholders.

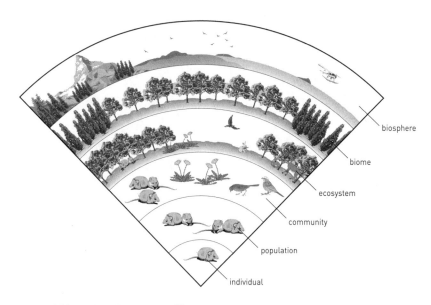

FIG I.1 A hierarchy of complexity[19]

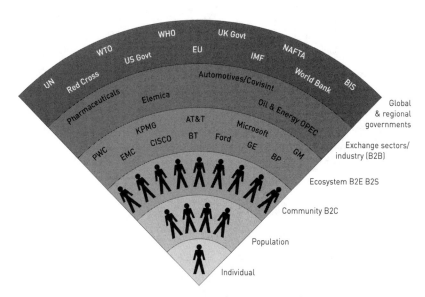

FIG I.2 A hierarchy of business complexity (George Jerjian)

Our understanding is that there are at least four stakeholders or communities to any enterprise (even the word 'company' is obsolete), as shown in Figure 1.3:

1 *A community of shareholders*, which we call B2S or business to shareholders (covering principles 1 and 2), which includes the investment community.

2 *A community of employees*, which we call B2E or business to employees (covering principles 3, 4 and 5), which includes the recruitment and education industries.

3 *A community of businesses*, both in supply chains and as sales feeders, which we call B2B or business to business (covering principles 6, 7, 8 and 9).

4 *A community of customers*, which we call B2C or business to customers (covering principles 10, 11 and 12). Every enterprise is linked to many communities and many supply chains. It is therefore imperative that organizations have a clear and transparent message to all their stakeholders and a clear understanding of where they fit in their own ecosystem.

Organizations merge and acquire other organizations, like biological organisms. In the process, they discard those businesses that are not essential to their mission. The discarded corporations, when sold, bring in monies which can be used more efficiently within the organization. These mergers-turned-mutations will increase over time. To be able to survive, play and prosper in this new environment, you need to know the new language: the 12 principles.

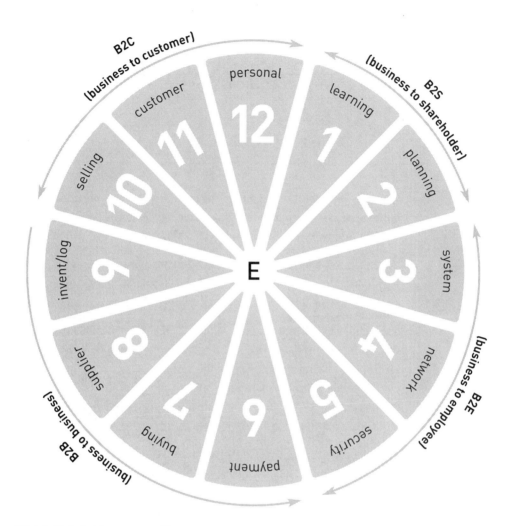

FIG I.3 Stakeholder communities

EXECUTIVE SUMMARY

▶ if 'abstract thought' emerged as the child of writing and literacy, we believe we have stumbled on its equivalent for the internet and the world wide web. We have named it 'ecosystem'

▶ the 12 principles also provide a new perspective and a new language with which to communicate with your customers, shareholders, employees, partners, competitors and the world at large

▶ economic growth is a function of connectivity or connectedness. If the 'old economy' can be likened to a car, the 'new economy' is an airplane. Slowing a plane below the stall speed can have serious consequences. Similarly, raising interest rates will have the effect of further cutting off the flow of funds to innovative businesses, making a bad situation much worse

▶ *laws* regulate the real world, through constitutions, statutes and other legal codes. In cyberspace, we must understand how *code* regulates through software and hardware. It is the codes in the software and hardware that effectively dictate how we work and what we can manipulate. Code is law and that must change how we approach and perceive business on the internet

▶ there is a talent shortage not only in the new economy but also in the old economy. There are many jobs that remain unfilled, not because there are not enough people to fill them but because there is a shortage of people 'skilled in the new economy'

▶ businesses can no longer work in a singular, linear way. Once you have learned a new language, it is impossible to unlearn it. The new language is the ecosystem. It is about working in a holistic and organic way

▶ if you don't adapt your thinking and your business, then like the plankton, you're going to be someone else's lunch. Your organization is part of the business ecosystem in which you survive

▶ it is imperative that organizations have a clear and transparent message to all their stakeholders

NOTES

1 **The Rise of the Image and the Fall of the Word**, Mitchell Stephens, Oxford University Press, New York, 1998, p.19.

2 **Battle of the Portals**, Thomas Power and George Jerjian, Ecademy Ltd, May 1999.

3 **E-Business to the Power of 12**, Thomas Power, Pearson Education, 2001.

4 'US interstate highway system', 'Dwight Eisenhower', 'Roads in the age of the automobile', 'Ancient roads of Europe', **Encyclopaedia Britannica CD 99, Multimedia and International Edition**.

5 **Battle of the Portals**, Chapter 2, p. 20.

6 **Cracking the Value Code**, Richard Boulton, Barry Libert and Steve Samek, Arthur Anderson, 2000.

7 **Cash Flow.com: Cash Economics in the New Economy**, Michael Mauboussin and Bob Hiler of Credit Suisse First Boston, study released in March 1999, pp. 3–19.

8 Transcription from telephone conversation with John Ong, Managing Director of High Yield Capital Markets at BNP Paribas in London, March 28, 2000.

9 **The Coming Internet Depression**, Michael J. Mandel, Basic Books, 2000.

10 **Code and Other Laws of Cyberspace**, Professor Lawrence Lessig, Harvard Law School, Chapter 1, p. 6.

11 **Code and Other Laws of Cyberspace**, Chapter 1, pp. 58–9.

12 **Code and Other Laws of Cyberspace**, Chapter 1, p. 234.

13 Eric Hoffer, in **Vanguard Management**, 1989, courtesy W R Hambrecht + Co., **Corporate e-Learning: exploring a new frontier**, inside cover.

14 http:/www.wrhambrecht.com/research/coverage/elearning

15 CSFB report entitled 'e-Learning: Power for the Knowledge Economy,' Gregory Cappelli, Scott Wilson and Michael Husman, released in March 2000, (http:/www.csfb.com/news/2000/february_29a_2000.html).

16 **The Death of Competition: Leadership and Strategy in the Age of Business Ecosystems**, James F. Moore, John Wiley Sons, 1996.

17 Interview with John Seely Brown, by Lawrence M. Fisher in 'Thought Leaders' in **Strategy & Business**, Fourth Quarter 1999, a Booz Allen & Hamilton publication, p. 86–95. Reprinted with permission.

18 Bionomics: **Economy as Ecosystem**, by Michael Rothschild – 'content', a graduate course at George Mason University, via the internet, by Howard Baetjer, Jr, (http:/www.virtualschool.edu/courses/Bionomics.html).

19 A Hierarchy of Complexity, What is Ecology? **Eyewitness Guides Ecology**, Steve Pollock, Dorling Kindersley Ltd, 1993, pp. 6–7.

THE 12 PRINCIPLES

BY PRINCIPLE, WE DO NOT MEAN a scientific law or a religious doctrine. We mean a general rule, a guide, a component and a constituent part of a whole. The 12 principles is not a process, it is an ecosystem of organizations, each of which has four main communities:

▶ a community of customers

▶ a community of businesses

▶ a community of shareholders

▶ a community of employees.

The 12 principles is a catalog of the whole market. All organizations fit into one of the principles, on the basis of their core activity. Some fit into several principles. Take your everyday stationery catalog. The contents are broken down by generic titles, under which you will typically have products exhibited from dozens of competing suppliers. It is in this manner that the 12 principles is a catalog. Yet it also has diverse uses in your organization. It can be used to define clearly which board member is responsible for what areas – see Figure 1. It can be used as a framework or language between the technical and the sales side of your organization as well as between your partnering organizations working on a project for the same client. It can be used to train your employees.

But the real benefit of the 12 principles for your organization is when you implement it and cross-fertilize it with, within and without your organization. You know your business better than anyone outside it

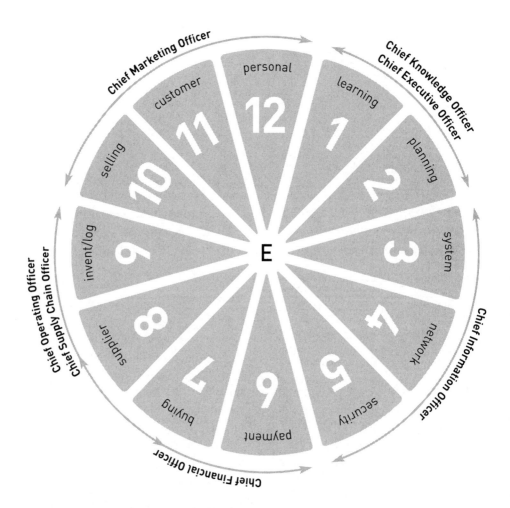

FIG 1 The 12 principles of networked business

(The Ecademy Ltd – The E-Business Education Network)

could possibly teach you. We do not know your business, but we have a template that you can use to change and grow your business into the new economy.

principle 1 – learning

To derive maximum advantage from the new economy, a complete change of perspective is required. It is a different environment after all. For many, it will mean unlearning old thinking habits in order to make room for new learning. You need to develop an inquiring and questioning mind. You must learn to forage, find and filter from information providers, research companies, investors and venture capitalist, e-commerce training companies, universities, internet lawyers, taxation and accountancy, and customer behavior. In Chapter 1, we look at the role of learning in relation to trading on the internet. We also address how the internet has changed the way we go about finding the right people or the right work.

principle 2 – planning

Choosing your partner is a critical issue. Ideally, you need to select a company that owns a strategy and will motivate your department managers and provide guidance on each of the 12 principles. The company you choose must not only understand the internet and e-commerce markets but also your business, your customers and your suppliers. The maxim 'failing to plan is planning to fail' is still valid in the new economy. Many companies have bolted an e-commerce strategy to their existing business, in what is a typical linear mental approach, only to find they have short-circuited their business flow. Your organization's expectations of itself and others will need to change, because the business itself will change. In Chapter 2, we uncover why you cannot view planning in a traditional linear plane but in a holistic ecosystem.

principle 3 – system software evaluation Organizations
need to evaluate their software infrastructure and then decide what can
be kept, consolidated and integrated or abandoned. Software enables
and controls the link between company information and its internet
site(s). It is no longer necessary to regard the website and company
information as separate systems. Software will be the tool that constantly updates prices on the main (legacy) database and simultaneously
transports them to the site so customers and suppliers are immediately
aware of the changes. This alone is an enormous task. For a company
with old systems in place, this is a very uncomfortable change. Why?
Because it will involve the whole of their system and will mean the
integration of traditionally 'stand-alone' departments, such as finance
and personnel. In Chapter 3, we show what the problems are in this
area and how they are being addressed.

principle 4 – network evaluation All the computing power
and data in the world is meaningless without a reliable and secure form
of connection to the internet and to all the areas of the company that will
be involved with it. Your company must establish at the outset how
much it is prepared to spend on hardware, what kind of website it wants
to offer, and how many visitors it anticipates. Download times are critical – online delays in e-commerce are unacceptable because the
customer will go elsewhere at a click of the mouse. We show the issues
that the communications sector is facing and how it is tackling the issue
of e-commerce for itself in Chapter 4.

principle 5 – security Both customers and organizations need the
comfort of knowing that their details are not open to abuse. Fortunately,
there are several types of security solutions such as the Public and

Private Key Infrastructure (PKI) and non-repudiation software. Passwords, verifications and digital certificates provide various layers of security that are increasingly difficult although not impossible to breach. What one has to bear in mind at all times is that there is no such thing as total security. Security is based on emotion and therefore it can cloud clarity. Is it a real security issue or is it a perceived security issue? In Chapter 5 we will look at existing solutions and cutting-edge developments in the area of security, and how they are being applied.

principle 6 – internet payments

In how many different ways or methods does your organization want to receive payments from its customers? How does it want to remit payments to its direct or indirect suppliers? Direct suppliers are those that supply core materials to the company and indirect suppliers supply ancillary materials such as office supplies. The process will vary depending on whether the company is in a business-to-business environment with monthly accounts or in a business-to-consumer market where payment is needed before delivery, and also by the size of the transaction. In Chapter 6 we look at the problems and solutions, including various payment mechanisms such as electronic data interchange (EDI) over the web, credit cards and secure electronic transactions (SET), e-wallets and micropayments.

principle 7 – buying

On the internet all companies look the same size. It is the way that they do business that makes the difference. All the company's direct suppliers should be linked to the company's website before customers begin to buy the products in order to avoid the risk of supplier shortage and inefficiency. In effect, the suppliers monitor their supplies with the company and replenish at set levels. In Chapter 7 we look at how an organization goes about putting its 'catalog' on its website and how it attempts to make it more easily navigable and more cost-effective for all parties.

principle 8 – supplier portals

A supplier portal is nothing more than a single website from which a company can buy ancillaries that provide 'the materials' the employees need to make the business work. A supplier portal will aggregate everything into one electronic catalog, where goods can be ordered on one form, paid for and delivery expedited. The cost saving is fairly obvious: there is no need for multiple telephone calls, multiple forms or multiple payments. The result is reduced inventory costs and cycle times. A supplier portal allows for near real-time price comparisons and supports multi-currency transactions, including the euro. The supplier also benefits in terms of efficiency, thus allowing them to offer better prices and better service to their customers. In Chapter 8, we illustrate that although we are in a new economy, good business is not just about price, it is about quality of supplier and service.

principle 9 – inventory and logistics

In the recent past, if companies had a surplus of slow-moving inventory, they might have organized a bricks-and-mortar sale or at worst sold it off for scrap. Today, organizations have the outlet of the internet auction. There are numerous web services that cater for business-to-business auction needs and often specialize in the type of goods sold, such as industrial and laboratory equipment, across the whole business spectrum. Cyber auctions work on the simple basis of a bidder online tapping in his bid on the keyboard. The bid is instantly recognized at the auction end, compared to other incoming bids, and a response is generated. Some auctions last an hour, some up to a week or more. In Chapter 9, we learn about 'promise to profit' and why everyone in the supply web chain has to profit. We also learn that auctions are not just about clearing inventory but about making a handsome profit where there is a shortage.

principle 10 – selling software
The internet has no unions, it has no night and day, and it has no statutory trading restrictions. It is a 24-hour-a-day, seven-days-a-week, 365-days-a-year, non-stop trading community. Past methods of selling have always had some form of restriction, either human, governmental, space or time, but the internet never closes. In this salesman's dream, however, many things can go wrong. If goods are promised and not delivered, the internet customer will not accept excuses but will go elsewhere. They will be irritated by sites that are difficult to navigate. They want to see something visually, but more importantly, they want it to be quick. In Chapter 10 we show how e-commerce software facilitates transacting on the web.

principle 11 – customer portals
A customer portal is rather like a supermarket through which a company sells. It is in effect another distribution channel. By requiring members to register, it builds up a demographic record that can develop into a valuable asset to tempt advertisers and e-merchants. What makes portals attractive to retail consumers is their ease of use. Logging on to a portal on the internet is rather like opening up a catalog of products and services. The difference is that a catalog is divided into groups of generic subjects such as business, travel, entertainment, money, news, people, health and education, shopping, politics, home and family, and much more. Under each generic category you will find hundreds, if not thousands, of sub-categories to investigate and explore. By following a hierarchical route, you can

hyperlink to millions of websites, which offer the product, service or information sought. Portals use search engine technology to help speed through the maze. They become route maps and in time customers will select a preferred portal and stick with it for pretty much everything. The customer will also be able to communicate with the portal on all devices – PC, TV, mobile phone, cable TV, bank ATM and so on. In Chapter 11, we look to msn.co.uk and eBay.com to learn from them about community, content and commerce.

principle 12 – personalization

Paradoxically, despite being the technology of the future, the web enables a return to a very old-fashioned value: personalized contact with customers. An internet site can be highly effective for monitoring and analyzing the buying habits of customers, customizing products and information to meet those habits, and responding quickly to queries   and requests. An e-commerce company can harness the power of personalization through harvesting customer profiles. Then it can generate offers that it can send down the e-mail route – known as push technology – to software that helps manage internet relationships. The power of personalization lies in its ability to create loyalty. The customer who has spent time personalizing the service at a particular site is less likely to switch to a competitor. Also, the ability of a company to provide a custom offering to its top accounts is central to the goal of cementing relationships and maximizing the benefit of an e-commerce business. We will show in Chapter 12 how individuals and organizations can profit from using 'knowledge', both internally so that employees can provide a better service and externally so that marketers can deliver better service, products or experiences to their customers.

the 12 principles are open source – they're free!

You can download Ecademy's 12 principles from its website (www.ecademy.com) and build your own learning on its framework. This offer is open to all educational institutions, business organizations and governments. Use the 12 principles as a flexible, malleable template in your business ecosystem. It will expand your horizons and liberate your thinking.

the airport analogy
It is far easier to understand the ecosystem of the new economy and the practical nature of the 12 principles as a guide to that ecosystem when we see a living example. For this purpose, we have chosen to illustrate each principle with the real-life example of London Heathrow Airport. In each principle this living example shows the principle in action – not only what it is about but also about its relationship with the other principles. This illustration also shows that the process is not a linear one. The result is not a linear process of 12 but an organic and symbiotic process of 144 (12×12). The more the relationship grows between each principle, the more improvement there is in the performance of each, through the feedback loop.

conclusion
The 12 principles is not a process, it is an ecosystem of organizations, each of which has four main communities: a community of customers, a community of businesses, a community of shareholders, and a community of employees.

> **"all organizations fit into one of the principles, on the basis of their core activity"**

The 12 principles is also a catalog of the whole market. All organizations fit into one of the principles, on the basis of their core activity. The 12 principles also have diverse uses in your organization. They can be used to define clearly which board member is responsible for what areas. They can be used as a framework or language between the technical and the sales sides of your organization as well as between your partnering organizations working on a project for the same client. They can be used to train your employees. But the real benefit of the 12 principles for your organization is when you implement it and cross-fertilize it with, within and without your organization. We have a template, so use it to change and grow your business into the new economy.

In the following chapters, we cover each of the 12 principles and explain how they relate to the others. In each chapter, we feature two organizations, an interview with a senior officer, and a case study to illustrate real issues and real solutions. Please bear in mind that the interviews and case studies are neither exhaustive nor comprehensive, they are simply to give you a flavor of what is actually happening in each principle.

PART 1

B2S
(BUSINESS TO SHAREHOLDER)

PRINCIPLE 1
LEARNING

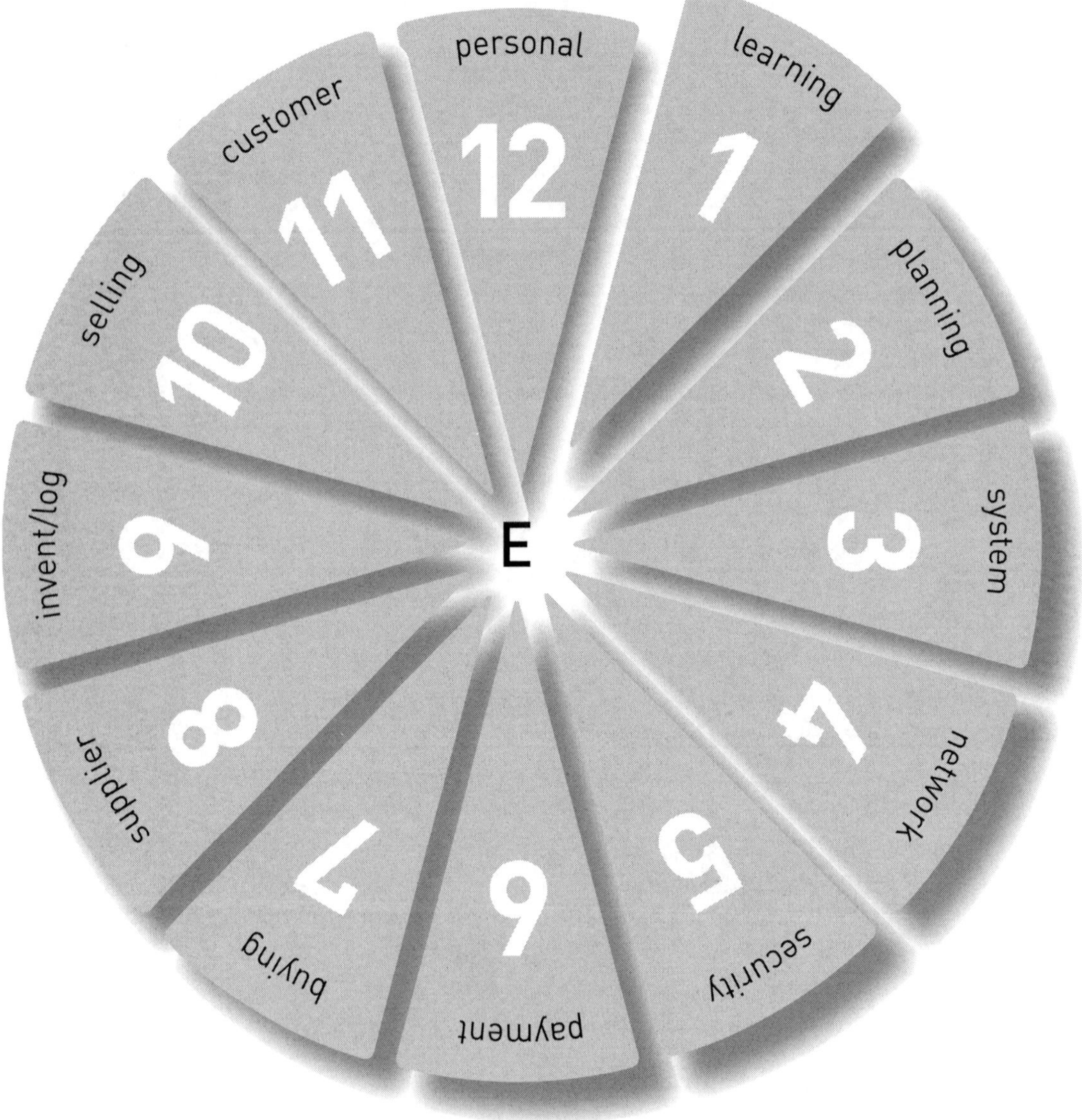

E
12
personal
1
learning
2
planning
3
system
4
network
5
security
6
payment
7
buying
8
supplier
9
invent/log
10
selling
11
customer

STATEMENT OF **PRINCIPLE 1**

THERE WAS ONCE A SMALL VILLAGE in Africa, along the banks of a great river, whose inhabitants had been in the throes of starvation for months. Then a foreigner arrived on a boat and moored beside their village. When the visitor realised that the villagers were starving because they had run out of their staple diet, he offered them a large quantity of fish from his boat's canteen. They all feasted that day and were pleased. Naturally, the next day the villagers returned expecting to receive more fish and when the visitor could not oblige them, they almost lynched the man. The visitor fled, almost as fast as fund managers flee from a company whose shares are plummetting. Within a week, the visitor was back with 100 fishing rods and began to teach the villagers how to fish and how to preserve fish. In almost no time, the villagers came back to life, grew in strength, and the village prospered.

Like the African villagers, when pre-literate people approached the idea of constructing and learning an alphabet, there were undoubtedly individuals who threw themselves into the 'new learning' and those who scoffed and carried on as though nothing was going to change. In retrospect, we all know who won that argument. But as mentioned in the introduction, learning is not just harnessing your intellect, it is also your emotions. By harnessing your emotions, you will ensure that you are absorbing not just the information but also the experience. There are no shortcuts to learning. It will be painful, if you think it is painful. By the same token, it will be fun if you allow yourself to have fun.

The 12 principles cannot simply be bolted on to your existing mental framework. You need to completely alter that framework. Your skills are still valuable, but you need to reconfigure them. Take, for instance, the different mind-set required to run a main street retail shop and one in an international airport. They are clearly different environments and different ecosystems; in order to be successful at the airport, you will need a different strategy.

In 1998, London's Heathrow Airport handled 60 million passengers. It is by far the busiest international airport in the world, with 90 airlines serving around 200 destinations. It operates 1,200 flights a day and more than 430,000 a year, and its central bus and coach station is the busiest in the UK, with more than 1,600 services each day to over 1,000 destinations.[1]

❝there are hundreds of categories of workers in the airport industry❞

With an operation of this scale, it is not only the pilots who need to learn about the flying business. Air traffic controllers, aircraft maintenance engineers, aircraft electricians, aircraft mechanics and all personnel who are directly or indirectly involved with aircraft need training. That is just the aircraft. There are hundreds of categories of workers in the airport industry: security personnel, sales and ticketing agents, and marketing personnel. And then there are the industries that subcontract to the airport, which need to train their personnel, from airline and airport catering businesses to the lawyers, accountants, financial advisers and air industry research analysts. Like its biological equivalent, each and every department, category and person impacts on the other for better or worse.

What is your organisation's role in your business or industry ecosystem? If you think there is no ecosystem, you are still thinking linearly. Think holistically and find your ecosystem. Who are your suppliers, competitors, customers and employees?

There is no substitute for your own research. The internet is a mine, full of information. FT.com, Wall Street Journal and Bloomberg, among others, provide daily news. *Explore* research companies such as Forrester and Gartner, which research organizations and industry sectors. *Speak* to investment houses and venture capitalists such as CSFB, Goldman Sachs and Robertsons Stephens, whose perspectives are available on their websites. *Listen* to recruitment organizations, such as Heidrick & Struggles, which find the most suitable individuals for a job or the most suitable job for an individual. *Find out* what courses universities and e-commerce training companies are offering. *Consult* internet law firms such as Davenport Lyons and Simmons & Simmons and ask the right questions. *Question* and seek the advice of tax specialists and accountancy specialists such as PwC. Just learning from one or two is not enough. If you are to learn networked business, you will need to immerse yourself into every facet of business that is affected by 'networks', and that means the whole business.

But the key to learning is questioning. For example, let's look at a legal aspect. If you have a global website, are your Hungarian web pages going to fall under Hungarian law? How do you reduce your risk? What options do you have? You should not be focussing on the answers. You can pay your lawyers to find them for you. What is far more important is seeking and finding the questions.

You can't have a strategy in isolation. Remember this is an ecosystem. You need to understand that every aspect in your organization is affected and how they all need to be transformed and completed in a holistic way. You need to introduce a three-dimensional approach to your questioning in your organization.

All senior managers need to understand and own the project, but the major influences in this area are the Chief Executive and the Project Manager – which may be a consultancy firm.

The following case studies give you a flavor of what is happening in terms of learning in the legal and recruiting ecosystems.

SUPPLIER PROFILE
Simmons & Simmons

law firm

SIMMONS & SIMMONS[2] (S&S) IS ONE OF THE largest international law firms. Established in the City of London more than a century ago, the firm has expanded across the globe with offices in Paris, Brussels, Lisbon, Madrid, Milan, Rome, Abu Dhabi, Hong Kong, Shanghai and New York. In addition, it has strong working relationships with other law firms specializing in 'communication' around the world. S&S has about 750 lawyers and 1,400 employees across its 11 offices.

❝telecoms, IT and media businesses are converging and becoming global concerns❞

Telecoms, IT and media businesses are converging and becoming global concerns. Recognizing this convergence and globalization, S&S has singled out the provision of legal services to communication businesses as one of the primary means of achieving its objective to develop as a premier, full-service, international law firm.

S&S's clients operate in the UK, European and international markets and include six leading incumbent telecommunications operators acting as new entrants in markets abroad. S&S advises governments, regulators, and both large and small businesses. A large proportion of its lawyers in this area have been employed in, or seconded to, industry. Drawing on the knowledge and experience which this generates is considered essential to ensure clients receive pragmatic, sector-specific, commercial advice.

Rapid growth is the salient feature of the communications sector. Its speed often restricts the ability of business people to network with contemporaries – a significant requirement, given the substantial synergies and potentials for consolidation. S&S addresses this through regular seminars, aimed at bringing regulators and industry together to focus on topical issues and, importantly, to generate new business opportunities for delegates. Issues covered recently include the opportunities offered by electronic commerce.

S&S believes that it is as vital for it to understand the commercial goals and constraints under which its clients are working as it is for its clients to understand the legal perspective. To further this, it has developed its own 'Solutions' project management system. In 1996, *The Legal 500,* an annual directory of law firms, said: 'We see Simmons & Simmons as a firm on the ascendant, and one that has become client-driven in a way that could not have been contemplated a few years ago.'

INTERVIEW WITH SUPPLIER

'Enforceability of the law on the internet is difficult. Therefore, companies and consumers must take responsibility for themselves.'

Tom Wheadon of Simmons & Simmons[3]

LIKE LAYERS AND LAYERS OF AN ONION, the complexity and stratification of the 'law' will make you weep. First, you have 'black letter' law or statute law. Then you have regulation which leads to 'very touch and feel' law, which is policy. Over and above this you have three layers of law:

▶ international law, such as that of the United Nations, which is very consensus-based and mostly about trade

▶ regional law such as that of the EU and laws enacted as a result of Nafta (North American Free Trade Agreement)

▶ national laws.

'All these laws, at each level, change over time. What complicates legal matters is that new facts (resulting directly and indirectly from the internet) are being applied to the same old law, so the precedents you had may slightly change,' says Tom Wheadon. In other words, in the pre-internet days, your lawyers could generally tell you what would happen in your case because there were previous judicial decisions.

Now, many of these decisions may not be applicable. The result is uncertainty and increased risk.

Another aspect that has added to the complexity is the liberalization of communications. The World Trade Organisation, falling into line with developments in the European Union, has given unprecedented momentum to worldwide communications liberalization. The US, followed by the UK, has liberalized the telecommunications sector by introducing privatization and competition, which have in turn radically reduced the costs of telephone calls worldwide. There is therefore sufficient evidence of the benefits that liberalization brings. The race is on for governments across the world to liberalize and introduce privatization and competition.

❝the result is uncertainty and increased risk❞

Now let's look at jurisdictional issues. Once you have set up a multi-lingual website, it is no longer your local market, explains Wheadon. Any customer can click on your website and if you have six languages available, whose law applies under each of these languages? Are your Spanish pages automatically going to fall under Spanish law? Choices of law and jurisdiction have always been extremely difficult issues. If you are to sell goods and services into a particular country, why not use terms and conditions valid to that country. The next question is, do you have any assets in that country? If the answer is yes, what happens when you get sued? There are essentially two ways to reduce risk. Wheadon advises that the first is to identify in which jurisdictions you wish to provide your goods and services, and then expressly state that in your disclaimer on the website. The second, which is probably better, is to get insurance cover.

The internet makes law enforcement difficult, perhaps even impossible. In agreement with Law Professor Lawrence Lessig of Harvard University, Wheadon says: 'This is a social issue. Take for instance copyright. We have copyright because people who have created need to have compensation for their efforts. We have criminal law, but does that stop crime? Clearly it doesn't. Do we say we shouldn't have the law at all because people keep breaking it or do we say we have to have it because society needs it?

Society makes the laws and not the other way round. Think about medicine. You have prevention and cure. If it is difficult to cure a certain disease, perhaps we need to focus on prevention. For example, on the internet, we cannot enforce copyright laws, but we can prevent people from stealing our intellectual property by allowing them to view our material for a fee and for a period of time, after which it self-destructs. You need to ask yourself, how is my organization protecting its brand, its patents or its intellectual property? How will the internet change this and what options do we have to protect our brand or property?

❝organizations are already wooing consumers because they see them as lifelong revenue streams ❞

It is because of this lack of enforceability that Wheadon thinks consumers will have to take the responsibility themselves. Today we have only manufacturers' warranties, tomorrow we will have consumer-created contracts, undoubtedly supported by portals. Organizations are already wooing consumers because they see them as lifelong revenue streams and therefore the bargaining power will be with them. Suppose you are a consumer who has received goods from an internet mail-order business and they are not what you wanted. The classic reaction is to give them back. From the business's point of view, this is an identifiable risk and it needs to be managed. One solution is to obtain insurance.

Both consumers and vendors must take great care because mistakes are inevitable while we learn how to work in the internet space. Many small mistakes and calculated risks are perfectly fine; it's the big mistakes that sink organizations. In the past, the phrase 'caveat emptor' (let the buyer beware) was touted liberally; today, one could increasingly suggest that 'caveat vendor' (let the seller beware) might be equally appropriate.

S&S long ago recognized that telecommunications, information technology and media businesses were converging and that the winds of 'liberalization' were the driving force in changing this sector. Liberalization of communications means economic warfare. It's all about trade and war in telephone calls. In 1996, the US had a net export of $4.5 billion, which meant there were more outgoing than incoming telephone calls. Why was this happening? Let's take an example. A US caller telephones a friend in Nigeria and the cost is $10 to the US telephone company. The US telephone company then pays the Nigerian telephone company $5 to terminate the call. Introducing liberalization allows the US telephone company to go into Nigeria, become a telephone company there, and terminate the call itself. The net result is that the telephone call monies, or $10 in this example, go entirely to the US telephone company.

❝each partner organization brings its own expertise to the ecosystem❞

In the past, the International Telecommunications Union (ITU) was the forum for agreeing international accounting rates for telephone calls. Today, says Wheadon, the US appears to dominate the world market in telecommunications through the unilateral imposition of 'benchmarking rates', or fixed rates for telephone call termination. The Chinese, meanwhile, have held out for so long because they do not want to lose the welcome source of funds from call termination. Because of liberalization, we have seen prices of calls go down continuously, which is clearly a positive thing. But Wheadon predicts that ultimately the US will own the entire 'spaghetti' network – satellite, terrestrial and cable – distribution and information wrapped around the world. Any organization with global ambitions must take this into account.

In order to cope with these sea-changes in the communications culture, even traditional and established law firms like Simmons & Simmons are creating their own ecosystem with partners. Each partner organization brings its own expertise to the ecosystem. Their clients have a one-stop shop. By feeding off each other, they are far more effective and beneficial to each other. Like their ocean counterparts, the tunas and flying fish, they are gathering at the feeding ground, where they know armies of plankton eagerly await them.

PRINCIPLE IN ACTION

Matchco.co.uk

MATCHCO.CO.UK[4] IS THE MODEL 'FEEDING GROUND' for a set of traditional businesses and professions which are learning about this new ecosystem. They are taking calculated risks, they are experimenting to learn. Matchco.co.uk is part of Eurobell Holdings plc, a regional telecommunications company supplying high-value telephone, television, data and internet services to residential and business customers in the South of England. Deutsche Telekom, Europe's largest telecommunications company, giving the support of world-class technology and knowledge, owns the company.

Launched in February 2000, Matchco.co.uk is an internet company partnered by leading-name businesses and professional firms to provide access to capital for entrepreneurs in the high-tech sector. It is the fastest low-cost route for people with good ideas to secure funding. 'We have combined the speed and flexibility of the internet with access to the best advice available to help entrepreneurs turn good ideas into a prosperous business,' says Malcolm Holt, Managing Director of Matchco.co.uk. 'Investors are currently swamped with poorly presented proposals from entrepreneurs. There are also countless thousands of budding entrepreneurs who don't know where to go to get best advice and how to interest funders. Matchco.co.uk will remove these barriers to enterprise. It will give investors far greater access to well-prepared and qualified applications from which to make their investment selections.'

Entrepreneurs and the City do not talk the same language. Thousands of great ideas don't even see the light of day simply because the e-entrepreneur is not properly prepared. There is a huge gap between the person with the idea and the City. In a 1999 press release, Matchco.co.uk claimed that as many as 99 percent of e-entrepreneurs seeking venture capital funding were turned down despite the fact that 81 percent of them thought that their idea could make them a million-aire. Now that dot coms are discredited in the minds of the public, it does not herald the end of 'great' ideas. On the contrary, the new weed-ing, filtering and nipping will add strength and color to good ideas.

❝now that dot coms are discredited in the minds of the public, it does not herald the end of 'great' ideas ❞

Entrepreneurs are able to enter into www.matchco.co.uk and complete 60 questions ranging across the business plan, business background, products, marketing and marketplace, operations, management, financial summary, risks and rewards, and objectives. Only when they have satis-fied the demands of each stage will a sequence of traffic light signals allow them to pass through to the next level. Throughout the process of developing their business plan, entrepreneurs are also able to discuss things with advisers, be it online or face-to-face. 'Only after every "i" has been dotted and every "t" crossed will that plan, produced in a pre-agreed format, be submitted to our funding partners,' declares Holt.

Matchco.co.uk advisers belong to one of two categories: partners and associate partners. Associates will be engaged in a normal manner and the basis of their charges will be discussed during the initial non-chargeable meeting. Partners will be engaged on the basis that an element of their fees will be payable only when and if funding is secured. The funding partners are Young Associates, Amadeus, and Reuters. The legal partners are Simmons & Simmons, Eversheds, and Field Fisher Waterhouse. The accountancy partners are KPMG and Pannel Kerr Forster. On the human resources side, the partners are Ashton Penney, Boyden and HH Group. On the marketing and public relations sphere, the partners are Bell Pottinger and Ovum. Matchco.co.uk charges a fee of £950, payable only after e-entrepreneurs have satisfactorily met pre-joining criteria, which tests the strength of their basic proposition.

Why did we choose a law firm? Organizations go to law firms to be protected from adversity, to reduce risk, to have their hand held, and to learn. Yet long-established, traditional law firms are themselves also continuously learning. They are also joining various other enterprises to create an ecosystem, a feeding ground of mutually beneficial relationships, from which they all hope to benefit.

SUPPLIER PROFILE

Heidrick & Struggles

executive search firm

THE LAW IS ABOUT REGULATING RELATIONSHIPS between people, between institutions, and between people and institutions. Without people, there is no ecosystem. It is search firms that bring people into relationships. In this new technology-driven ecosystem, all the relationships have been touched and changed, and even search firms have had to adapt.

Established in the US in 1953, Heidrick & Struggles[5] was one of the pioneers in the executive search industry. The firm expanded to Europe in 1968 and now has more than 70 offices and 700 partners in the world's major business centres. It is the only major executive search firm to operate a European board practice. Heidrick & Struggles International specializes in identifying, attracting and recruiting chief executives, directors and senior-level managers. It serves Fortune 500 companies, start-ups, universities, hospitals, family-owned businesses, not-for-profits, and others.

Heidrick & Struggles has adapted to the new environment. Its evolution has been characterized by a continuous quest for excellence and the pioneering of concepts in response to – and in advance of – its clients' needs. For example, its Search University has for many years provided thorough, ongoing training for its carefully selected and developed teams of career professionals. Its sector specialists, such as 'international technology practice' and 'financial institutions practice', have long operated on a pan-European basis, and the company is independently acknowledged as a pioneer of the speciality practice concept. *Search by research* is fundamental to its methodology and, in support of this approach, each office is linked by IT systems and an international database, which are independently cited as among the most sophisticated in the industry.

"its evolution has been characterized by
a continuous quest for excellence "

Heidrick & Struggles' technology practice was set up in Menlo Park, California in the mid-1980s on Sand Hill Road, which is now well known as the hang-out for venture capitalists. The company's search executives knew all the chief executive officers in Silicon Valley and today they do a high proportion of the CEO searches for technology companies in North America, simply because they gained prominence in that space and became successful.

Because of their rich experience in recruiting in the technology sector, they have a holistic view of what's happening in this marketplace. Anthony Harling, one of the partners in the London office, expands on this in the following case study.

INTERVIEW WITH SUPPLIER

'Today, companies have to recognize that there is a talent shortage.
They need to be more aggressive in selling themselves to the candidate.
Candidates need to be much more careful about the job search and
recruitment process. The real risk of making a mistake for an individual
is huge.'

Anthony Harling, Partner, Heidrick & Struggles[6]

RELATIONSHIPS ARE CRITICAL in any ecosystem. Organizations need 'workers' to deliver their offering to their customers. Search consultants find these workers. How they go about finding them has changed over time, and the internet has played a large part in it.

In the past, the search for 'workers' was a kind of 'old boy network'. Now it's much more of an intensive research process. Good people are always hard to find and today they are even more so. The growth of business fueled by technology has created a talent shortage. Too many organizations are chasing too few talented individuals. Where could this person be? What sort of companies might they have been in? What attributes and skills do they need for the job?

Heidrick & Struggles has a massive database embedded with 47 years of accumulated information on people. The database has an easy-to-use interrogation tool and a management tool to facilitate use across the whole organization. In spite of this, the company avoids the use of the word 'database', which it considers to be an outmoded concept. Its clients are not only always clients, they are often the company's contacts in organizations. It calls its clients its community, and its community is based on community principles, with a Chief Community Officer (CCO) who acts as guardian of the community and whose job is to serve the members.

Over the course of time, Harling reckons that the search model will change from being a search company for organizations to being an agent for individuals. It's a little bit like inviting David Beckham for an interview so he can show you his football skills. You just don't do that. You would have a conversation with his agent and you would say that you wanted to employ Beckham, what's the deal? Agents will filter all the calls and pass on only those which are truly worthwhile to their client.

❝'access' and 'speed' are essential if search companies are to deliver the most suitable candidate❞

At this point, however, a great part of the search service is still on behalf of organizations. The difference today is that 'access' and 'speed' are essential if search companies are to deliver the most suitable candidate. By the same token, organizations must react immediately to a proposed candidate. Speaking about an executive search in which he was involved recently, Harling told this story.

One of his partners in Germany called him on his mobile on a Wednesday evening. What the partner didn't realize was that Harling was actually in the same building at the time. So Harling popped upstairs to see him. The partner wanted to speak about one of his clients and he also wanted Harling to participate in a meeting as the client was looking for a managing director for its UK subsidiary. They met the client an hour later. Within 24 hours they had submitted a proposal and on Monday, they kicked off the search. The client wanted to review candidates by the following Wednesday. So Harling went to his colleagues within the practice, pooled the information, and selected the appropriate candidates.

On Thursday the clients announced they were coming to London the next day. The clients met four candidates and one of them was a nose in front in terms of being a better fit. Harling and his partner had defined what the spec was for that person. They said to the client: be pragmatic, go for your core competencies, don't go for somebody who has experience of the internet. They flew the applicant out to Munich that day and he was back in London on Sunday night with a job offer in his hand. He resigned on the Tuesday morning.

Ultimately, you need to find people who are basically very smart, have lots of mental agility, lots of breadth, and people who understand business basics. You need to be realistic. You cannot expect to find a 100 per cent fit, so you must go for the 80 per cent fit.

Of course, you won't find the 100 percent fits because the likes of Jeff Bezos of Amazon.com already have a lead position in their own organization. There are only a few organizations that have produced stellar results, despite the market gyrations affecting their market capitalization. So how do you go about finding a suitable candidate? Harling says that each role has its own set of five core competencies. Certainly, organizations regularly come up with upwards of 20 competencies for their candidates, but this just dilutes the search. Reducing it to five cuts to the chase. Examples of core competencies are:

1 specific niche industry experience

2 functional expertise

3 cultural attributes of the organization

4 leadership potential as defined by the job

5 language experience, operation experience, or multi-function management experience.

The acid test is which candidate scores the highest on these five competencies. If you find the 80 per cent-plus fit, go for it.

Apart from this need to look at core competencies in a new light, there are two trends taking place in the search and recruitment world. One is that relationships with clients have become much more interactive, particularly with the internet, and the second is that it's a candidate-driven world. In the past candidates were called applicants and the vocabulary reflected the attitude of mind. Today, companies have to be very smart to get good people. They can no longer wait for ten people to come along, because by then the business has gone. Their competitors have eaten their lunch.

❝Today, companies have to be very smart to get good people❞

The following case study illustrates how Heidrick & Struggles created its own online service for members – clients – of its community, which responds to both these market changes. The online community steps outside the company's traditional market of CEOs and boards of directors. However, LeadersOnline has positioned itself to fill an urgent need in a huge global market for mid-level management. What Heidrick & Struggles has effectively done is enlarge its organizational ecosystem.

PRINCIPLE IN ACTION

the development of LeadersOnline (Leaders!)

LIKE MANY OTHER ORGANIZATIONS that wanted to make a start on the internet, Heidrick & Struggles allowed LeadersOnline[7] (Leaders!) to develop a strategy to service a different niche market and thereby avoid cannibalization of the company's main business.

Leaders! started out as a small, garage project supported by the Menlo Park office in San Francisco. In late 1998 the office managing partner took onboard this idea and helped to incubate what has since become one of the leading business-to-business internet-based providers of recruiting solutions for mid-level management and emerging corporate leaders. The original idea offered the hope of an internet business where the software would replace a lot of the back-office functions which take up so much time and effort in the search process. As a medium, the internet affords the possibility of reaching millions of aspiring mid-level managers around the world. Where Heidrick & Struggles has built its reputation serving CEOs and boards of directors, Leaders! is ideally positioned to fill an urgent need in a huge global market for mid-level management, which is fragmented and poorly served.

In 1999, Jim Quandt, former Chief Operating Officer of Futurestep, an online recruitment agency, was appointed Chief Operating Officer of LeadersOnline. With his record of leadership and operational management experience in major corporations, Quandt brought valued management expertise and highly relevant sector experience to the challenge of building Leaders! into the dominant player in its chosen sector. This was a critical stage in the evolution of Leaders! in that it gave strength to the operational management required for the plan to succeed.

In recent years, Heidrick & Struggles has played a crucial role in appointing chief executives and senior officers into successful internet companies around the world. With this unique insight, it was quick to recognize the fundamental truth of success in the internet world: execution is everything. As Leaders! continues its expansion and rollout around the world, this will be a key focus: make sure it can deliver so that it satisfies customers and exceeds the expectations of the Heidrick & Struggles partners who introduce Leaders! to their corporate clients.

❝the fundamental truth of success in the internet world: execution is everything❞

Leaders! has been deliberately positioned at the mid-level management market. This is complementary to the positioning of Heidrick & Struggles and not in conflict with the core business. Rather than risking cannibalization of the core business, this ensures strong support and endorsement from the Heidrick & Struggles partnership and builds trust with that group as the key marketing arm of Leaders! This is not only a huge, growing market but also sits comfortably alongside the core market served by Heidrick & Struggles' traditional offering.

Other unique features which differentiate the Leaders! offering have been developed to reflect some genuine concerns felt by potential candidates in this space:

▶ the lack of candidate control, particularly with regard to confidentiality

▶ poor quality of candidate database

▶ ineffective screening/matching process by some job board-type services.

Leaders! offers candidates complete control over their confidentiality; only once a candidate has made an active decision to release their name will their details be made available to a particular company. This is a key feature of the Leaders! approach.

The unique technology platform which Leaders! has developed provides a sophisticated screening/matching process. Candidates are matched to relevant opportunities and clients are only put in touch with qualified and interested applicants.

The Leaders! community is designed to be just that – a community. Members will build a relationship with the community and will come to value that relationship. This will encourage high quality candidates to retain their involvement with Leaders! Why is that important? In a fragmented and networked world, where the individual can walk at the click of a mouse, organizations need to convert their clients into members by fostering and nurturing them, and making their communities inviting, receptive and informative, so that members will visit again and again. This concept of community is covered in greater detail in Chapter 11.

In order to deliver the quality of service which clients have come to expect from Heidrick & Struggles, Leaders! set about hiring a team of e-cruiters to accompany each project and make sure the hires are actually made. These e-cruiter teams (often former Heidrick & Struggles associates) are trained in the search process and how to effectively use the unique Leaders! technology.

Why did we choose a recruiting firm? Although cynics may scoff, the driving force in any organization is its most valuable resource: its employees. Recruiters are the repository for answers to questions such as 'what skills are required by the new economy organizations?', 'what are the skills gaps facing many of the candidates recruiters are matching for available positions?' and 'how are the skill gaps being narrowed?' Finally, Heidrick & Struggles is not only creating an internal ecosystem but also an ecosystem with client organizations into which it feeds new blood, new people, new management.

The key to the success of Leaders! lies in the effectiveness of the execution. The link with the Heidrick & Struggles partnership is proving to be highly effective in introducing Leaders! to major corporate clients who urgently need that product. The quality of execution is attributable to the high-quality, highly trained e-cruiting teams in place around the world. Ultimately, Heidrick & Struggles and Leaders! will learn much from their enlarged ecosystem and will fuse knowledge garnered from each other to improve their offering.

EXECUTIVE SUMMARY OF

PRINCIPLE 1

THE INTERNET HAS CHANGED how individuals communicate
and as a result it has changed how organizations communicate internally and externally. It has also introduced a paradox of control in
relationships between suppliers and buyers. Buyers have control
because they have more information and more choice; suppliers, on
the other hand, have a new form of control – monitoring their customers' activities as opposed to the old form of influence and
persuasion. Moreover, by creating their own ecosystems with partners,
they offer clients a one-stop shop, which saves them time and money.

► learning is not just harnessing your intellect but also your emotions.
In this way, you will ensure that you are absorbing not just the
information but the experience

► what is your organization's role in your business or industry
ecosystem? Think holistically and find your ecosystem. Who are
your suppliers, competitors, customers and employees?

► how can you enlarge your ecosystem so that you can ensure
survival and secure your place in the ecosystem, or will you work
to be part of someone else's ecosystem?

▶ *explore* research companies. *Speak* to investment houses and venture capitalists. *Listen* to recruitment organizations. *Find out* about university courses and e-commerce training workshops. *Consult* internet law firms and ask the right questions. *Question* and seek the advice of tax specialists and accountants. If you are to learn networked business, you will need to immerse yourself into every facet of business that is affected by 'networks', and that means the whole business

▶ the key to learning is questioning. You should not be focussing on the answers – you can pay your lawyers to find them for you. What is far more important is seeking and finding the questions

▶ you can't have a strategy in isolation. Remember this is an ecosystem. You need to understand that every aspect in your organization is affected and how they all need to be transformed and completed in a holistic way. You need to introduce a three-dimensional approach to your questioning in your organization

NOTES

1 BAA Heathrow, airport information, facts and figures, http:/www.baa.co.uk/domino/baa/baanet

2 http:/www.simmons-simmons.com

3 Interviews with Tom Wheadon, January 7 and January 17, 2000.

4 Case study – http:/matchco.co.uk

5 http:/heidrick.com/aboutmid.html

6 Interviews with Anthony Harling, January 25, 2000.

7 Case study – http:/leadersonline.com

PRINCIPLE 2

PLANNING

12 personal
1 learning
2 planning
3 system
4 network
5 security
6 payment
7 buying
8 supplier
9 invent/log
10 selling
11 customer

STATEMENT OF **PRINCIPLE 2**

MOST BIRDS BUILD NESTS in which they lay their eggs. Nests vary widely: they may be a scrape in the sand, a deep burrow, a hole in a tree or rock, an open cup, a globular or retort-shaped mass with a side entrance tube, or an elaborately woven hanging structure. The materials with which nests are made also vary widely. Some nests are lined with small stones, others are built of dirt or mud, with or without plant material. Sticks, leaves, algae, rootlets, and other plant fibres are used alone or in combination. Some birds seek out animal materials such as feathers, horsehair, or snakeskin. The nest materials may be held together by weaving, sewing, or felting the materials themselves or with mud or spider webs. Swifts use saliva to glue nests together and to attach the nest to the supporting structure. All this involves serious strategic planning.

All birds incubate their eggs, which can take from 11 to 80 days, depending on the size of the bird and the degree of development at hatching. Most songbirds are hatched nearly naked and helpless and are brooded until well able to regulate their body temperature. The parents feed them until they are capable of flight. The young of chickens, ducks and shorebirds are hatched with a heavy coat of down and are capable of foraging for themselves almost immediately. Feeding the young takes tactical planning.

Planning in essence has a dual nature. A broad or long-range plan is called a *strategy*. A narrow and short-range plan is called a *tactic*. Both are useful in themselves, but they are not enough to assure success. In general, you can only have one strategy, such as building a nest, but you can have as many tactics as are needed, such as finding food for the young.

Planning is of paramount importance no matter what business you are in. With networked business, the old business strategy is turned on its head. It's not a case of re-engineering, efficient though that was at the time, and neither is it just a fashionable management mantra. With principle 2, every organization is involved in a web of connections that is changing traditional roles of doing business. When a company bolts on a networked business strategy to its existing business, it is taking a short cut, which ultimately will end short of its goal. On the other hand, a company is more likely to succeed if, with proper planning from professionals, it reconfigures its entire business strategy so that the full advantages of the internet are integrated into its existing business.

Returning to our analogy of Heathrow Airport, planning is of paramount importance. Airport planners always need to consider an increase in future passenger traffic. Among many other considerations, this has an impact on land acquisition, it entails new building and runway construction, planning permissions, new roads, extension or widening of existing roads, new underground tracks and subways, and new or enlarged car parks. There are also impacts on community relations, local, national and regional governments, and the business and financial communities. Planning is what keeps the airports functioning at optimal capacity and in a financially efficient manner. In turn, this brings more airline traffic, more passenger traffic, better quality investment, better quality businesses, and better employment opportunities. All these considerations merit tactics, but Heathrow can have only one holistic strategy.[1]

In terms of your networked business strategy, it is critical that you select an organization that owns a strategy you understand and whole-heartedly embrace. This strategy should motivate your department managers and employees and provide guidance on each of the 12 principles. The organization you choose must not only understand the internet and e-commerce markets but also your business, your customers, and your suppliers. So should you start with an e-commerce or with a networked business strategy?

> **❝it is critical that you select an organization that owns a strategy you understand and wholeheartedly embrace❞**

Many organizations start with an e-commerce strategy, implement it and later realize that it cannot stand alone. It is not a piece of machinery. As an ecosystem, all parts feed into each other. It's like working on a puzzle of a warship. If you start with the most exciting part first, you may do most of that part, but you will get stuck and it will take you longer than if you had started looking at the puzzle holistically. Clearly you need to build the framework of the puzzle and then work into it. So start with networked business strategy first, then work your way into e-commerce.

Planning is hard work. Execution is made much easier if time and effort are devoted at the planning stage. This is the message in this chapter. You need to build the right system and you need to build it right. You must manage the risks; you must reduce the risks. Above all, to ensure success it is essential that your organization and its systems have resilience, availability, reliability and scalability. These issues are addressed in greater detail in the case studies.

Who are these organizations with networked business strategies?

1 the traditional consulting firms, like the Big 5, such as Arthur Andersen, PwC and KPMG

2 specialist web shops, which have focussed their skills on the internet

3   the advertising and new media agencies, which have singled out the internet as a marketing tool: they can help define a company's image and message on the web, just as it is done in any traditional area

4   the independents contracted to directly implement the instructions of a client company and construct a cohesive site and networked business policy embracing all of the 12 principles.

The Head of IT, Finance Director, Marketing Director and Operations Director will be the people who will influence the planning.

The following case studies give you a flavor of how an advertising company and a Big 5 consulting organization are grappling with planning issues in the fall-out from the internet revolution.

SUPPLIER PROFILE

AKQA

a new media and internet services company

ORGANIZATIONS WITH A NETWORKED BUSINESS strategy come in all shapes and sizes. There are traditional companies and new budding organizations. AKQA is one of the latter.

AKQA[2] is the UK's leading e-services company, with a blue-chip client list and plush offices in Central London. It was founded by four entrepreneurs: Ajaz Ahmed, Chairman, Matthew Treagus, Head of Consulting, Dan Norris-Jones, Technical Director, and James Hilton, Executive Creative Director. The combination of three unique disciplines – business, technology, and creativity – made AKQA an unstoppable force in the internet development sector.

AKQA's first major client was Coca-Cola, which wanted consulting services. A website created for recruitment firm Price Jamieson followed this; the site's interactive features were among the first in the world. AKQA's client list continued to grow and the company added Microsoft, Durex and BMW to its client list. It developed a site for car-maker BMW that was full of innovations – a used car directory (another world first), a dealer directory and a screen-saver available in nine languages. We feature BMW as the case study here. 'The site was years ahead of its time,' said Ahmed. 'It took agencies a while to understand that the web is not about putting retro-fit ads online; it's about useful and innovative services.'

By 1997, brand owners had realized that the internet was going to become an important part of business and during that year AKQA added Sainsbury's and Orange to its client list.

❝brand owners had realized that the internet was going to become an important part of business❞

AKQA's Jermyn Street offices are its fifth in five years. 'We ran out of space, so we put the boardroom table up against the wall and had nine or ten people with all the technology working around it,' said Norris-Jones. 'There were lots of late nights, eating pizzas. The established people were energizing the newer people,' said Daniel Bonner, another creative director, who joined in 1997.

Today, with more than 100 employees, AKQA has added to its list of clients the following household names: Nestlé, Land-Rover, Carlsberg, Nike, Cable & Wireless, *The Economist*, Rover, Scottish Amicable, Mini, MG, Prêt-à-Manger, and Tetley's Bitter. How did it do this? 'We're focussed on return on investment, on making sure that clients can improve their return on investment,' says Ajaz Ahmed. AKQA ploughs around 25 percent of its revenues back into the business each year in new technology and other research and development.

INTERVIEW WITH SUPPLIER

'Are you building the system right or are you building the right system?'

Matthew Treagus, Head of Consulting and Chief Operating Officer

INFORMATION TECHNOLOGY (IT) people build 'the system right'. They are operations people and they understand the technology. They have no experience of customers and so they do not understand customers. As a company, you must plan the right strategy or 'the right system' for your business before you embark on making the IT 'system right'. 'Good IT is 70 percent planning. The execution is actually quite simple. Very few people spend that level of time planning because they don't know how to do the planning. They just dive in and start,' says Matthew Treagus.[3]

It's not about documents, it's not a document-driven process. There are structured ways of spending £30 million that are not about writing documents. It's about generating ideas. It's about understanding what it is that the customer might want out of this. It's a process AKQA calls 'user experience planning'. It's all in the execution, in the subtleties of the way the technology fits with the interface. The challenge is to separate function from interface. What Treagus is saying is that websites need to make their software work in the manner that their customers would like. They type in what they want, hit the button and the software does the thinking. Call it organic software, if you like – make it very easy for the customer or surfer to obtain the information, product or service they want or need.

AKQA sees web application developments in four layers. First you have a whole bunch of servers and hardware. Second, there are business systems, sales order processing and core business systems. Third, you then build the web application and your website. Finally, on top of that you have the user interface. There will be many interfaces as people develop and deploy these systems in many channels and many contexts. In fact, the brand is communicated today not through what it looks like but through its behavior. What AKQA is building is a technology that thinks like a customer.

Treagus's background is in information technology. He used to work in a data centre. A data centre's only function is to keep whatever business functions are running on the machines alive and awake, constantly and efficiently. It's about service-level agreements, about contingency planning and what to do if the server blows up or when it's stolen or if there's a fire or a bomb drops. 'Today, you need data center mentality to make certain that your shop door is open all the time, no matter what happens,' says Treagus. This was clearly evinced when IBM ran an advertisement about why server reliability is a key customer satisfaction issue.

> **"go find yourself an environment (or an ecosystem) that nobody else is in and you work out how to be smart there "**

We asked Treagus if he thought old economy companies could migrate to the new economy. He said: 'It's about adapting to your new environment and it's about finding a space for you to exist. For instance, the whale is a mammal that shouldn't be sustainable. It is sustainable because it found itself a very large ocean and taught itself the trick of eating very small pieces of food, but billions of them at a time. It's classic Darwin. Go find yourself an environment (or an ecosystem) that nobody else is in and you work out how to be smart there.'

Why did we choose a new media company? Unlike their traditional counterparts, new media companies have experienced the agony and ectasy of being on the cutting edge of the intersection of the internet, the media and business. They bring a different mind-set to planning and solving problems, and thinking organically is a natural state of mind.

The internet is becoming increasingly populated and will soon be too dense. Like a river infested with croaking frogs, you will need to sing a new song to differentiate yourself and get noticed.

PRINCIPLE IN ACTION
BMW

LIKE A CANARY ISLAND FINCH, AKQA sang a new song and was
noticed. Its work for BMW extends far beyond managing its website
(http:\www.bmw.co.uk), crucial though it is to the car giant's UK business.[4] The relationship between the agency and the client has always
been about developing new-media strategy to build on BMW's core
values as a business, bring about a return on investment, and offer relevant information and service to enhance customer relationships.

To this end, BMW has used techniques from across the new-media
spectrum, most notably by integrating its dealer network in the
process. The entire BMW network is linked on the website, which
offers a directory allowing users to search for their nearest dealer. The
majority of BMW's leads are generated online and dealers convert
8 percent of these leads into sales.

Function is at the heart of BMW's internet activity. It takes the form of
services, such as the Approved Used Car Directory, which allows
people to interact with the company in ways that weren't possible previously. As well as the web, BMW uses e-mail for customer relationship

management (CRM), electronic kiosks, online advertising, sponsorship, screensavers and digital television. Today, BMW's site receives well in excess of 270,000 visitors a month, and that number is growing.

'The single most important medium is word of mouth,' says Ajaz Ahmed. 'If people are talking about the website and e-mailing their colleagues and friends to let them know about it, then the site is more successful. The reason for the wide-ranging approach is that we view BMW's website as the interface to the brand – it allows consumers to access all kinds of information and services, depending on where they are in the purchase cycle, from awareness and interest through to purchase and loyalty.'

Ahmed amplifies the strong focus that BMW puts on technology and innovation. Alongside the Approved Used Car Directory, you can see applications such as BMW 'body styling' and the 'wheel chooser' as well as the sophisticated pricing systems which enable the consumer to build a car to their specification. In addition, BMW is looking to make an investment in digital TV and exploring new avenues to improve its operations and delivery through applied technology. Feedback is not only critical in planning, it is organic. The better the feedback, the better the product or service will be for the customer and the better the result for the organization.

SUPPLIER PROFILE

PricewaterhouseCoopers

professional services organisation

EVERY ORGANIZATION IS INVOLVED in a web of connections within and without itself. PricewaterhouseCoopers (PwC)[5] is an example of such an organization.

As the world's largest professional services organization, PwC helps its clients build value, manage risk, and improve their performance. Drawing on the talents of more than 150,000 people in 150 countries, PwC provides a full range of advisory services to leading global, national and local companies as well as to public institutions. These services include audit, accounting, risk management and tax advice; management, information technology and human resource consulting; financial advisory services, including mergers, acquisitions and flotations, project finance, and litigation support; business process outsourcing services; and legal services through a global network of affiliated law firms.

The networked business home on PwC's website (www.e-business.pwc-global.com) is full of useful information. The site illustrates three general themes. First, how *thinking* networked business enables you to anticipate customer needs, outmaneuver competitors and become a leader in your markets. Second, how *acting* like a networked business enables you to find new customers and retain existing ones, strengthen relations with partners and deliver goods and services efficiently. Third, *becoming* a networked business involves transforming your firm into an agile, information-age competitor capable of withstanding and profitting from the rigors of this dynamic form of competition.

❝thinking e-business enables you to anticipate customer needs❞

The move into e-business is, to a large extent, exploration of new territory. How it will change your business cannot be fully anticipated or completely controlled. The move need not be a leap of blind faith, however, if you make it a planned process based on a shared vision and the support of your key decision makers. If all that seems a bit daunting, be assured that your competitors are exploring their networked business options as well. Remember, they say the best way to compete against a networked business is to become one.

A year or so ago, PwC launched the 'Emm@' assessment, which provides a 'holistic assessment of your company's' readiness'. It presents this through a series of radar diagrams depicting the extent to which good practices are observed. The nine areas covered are:

▶ strategy

▶ organization and competencies domain

▶ processes domain

▶ performance management domain

▶ systems and technology domain

▶ delivery and operations domain

▶ legal domain

▶ security domain

▶ tax domain.

Across this entire spectrum, PwC's Global Risk Management Solutions (GRMS) practice, which employs 5,000 professionals worldwide, has specialist networked business teams to look at all aspects of risk, including the risks in strategies, security operations and projects. GRMS has introduced operational resilience solutions to diagnose and improve the resilience of networked business operations, enhance performance, and deliver higher standards of service.

INTERVIEW WITH SUPPLIER

'You need to take the risk out of networked business. Being first on the internet is not enough; you must have resilience.'

Charles Johnson, E-business Director

'TRUST IS A VERY IMPORTANT FACTOR,' declares Charles Johnson. 'It is also a multifaceted subject that includes things like fulfilling service, privacy, security, and getting assurance that people you're doing business with have integrity and probity.'[6] It also means you can commit to and manage successfully the projects that take your business and evolve it step by step without bringing the whole thing crashing down. And more specifically that you are putting in place trusted systems and processes which are what we call resilient.

In the minds of the consumer and business, high dependency and continuous availability have become essential ingredients. This places conventional businesses in a difficult and expensive role. In the old economy, there are industries with a history of providing high dependency, and continuous availability, such as the emergency services, and the power and utility companies. They have to be there all the time, whenever you need them – 24 hours a day, 7 days a week, 365 days a year. The difference is that companies like British Telecom (BT) and The National Grid have a history, and so the experience, of delivering almost 100 percent availability with 100 percent coverage. They have also observed that some traditional high street retailers with experience in delivering the fulfillment part of the supplying cycle are actually doing relatively well with their internet businesses. Start-ups and retailers that are jumping into the internet without that history and that experience are finding those problems are significantly diluting the benefits of the internet channel.

People's ability to move from one provider or website to another is so much greater now, so delivering high-performance customer service is paramount. If you get this wrong, your customer churn will be enormous. Not only that, but it can get worse. Over the past two years, several organizations have seen their systems go down for many long hours, resulting in their stock market value plunging by up to 20 percent between a Friday and the following Monday.

"delivering high-performance customer service is paramount "

According to Charles Johnson, 70 percent of people who launch an internet service do so without having thoroughly trialed and tested it. PwC has worked with numerous acquisitions and floats, including the first three largest floats in the UK – Freeserve, QXL, and 365 Corporation. The company has also worked on five of the largest online banking services, learning a great deal in the process. What PwC, its clients and providers of infrastructure such as hosting centres have realized is that 'resilience, availability, reliability and scalability' are essential to ensure success.

At the moment, if you search the web, you get at least 250 million items to sludge through. That whole concept has to change. We're now seeing a combination of horizontal and vertical integration (portals and vortals) and a consolidation towards genuine commerce sites. It's a bit like high street shopping ten years ago. A high street distinguished itself by having a Marks & Spencer, a Boots and a Sainsbury's. This was replicated from town to town across the UK. It was a sign of content, not ownership, and bringing them together created demand because of the relationships. Johnson feels certain that this is what is behind the convergence – of businesses (through mergers and acquisitions) and of technologies (the internet with mobile phones) – making the headlines.

All the disasters that people have had are simply because they've done the easy bit, which is to have a good idea and throw technology together to have a presence on the web, says Johnson. 'Of course, first-mover advantage is important. But some then find to their cost and to everyone else's cost that they actually don't know how to run a net-worked business, manage a demanding operation, deliver quality customer service or provide a return on investment.'

PRINCIPLE IN ACTION

launching internet financial services

TO DELIVER ON THE PROMISES OF quality customer service, manage a demanding operation, maintain alliances with other businesses and provide a return on investment, you need to know how to run your networked business. All the promise of glamor and glitz crumbles when the promise is not delivered.

In the last quarter of 1999, PwC completed a networked business assignment for a UK bank preparing to launch its service through an internet delivery channel.[7] This case study sets out the background to the client, why PwC was asked to help, what it did, and what was the outcome of its work. The assignment provided the client with a broad risk management approach by integrating PwC's fasttrack project management, operational resilience, security and testing service offerings.

The retail banking arm of a UK financial services organization was the client. The bank had previously delivered savings and investment services through telephone banking. Reacting to market trends, it decided to implement a simple online banking transaction service to complement its existing information-only website. Wanting to be quick to market, the client faced tight implementation deadlines and had recognized the following.

key issues:

▶ it had little experience of the proposed technology

▶ it was critical that its service was secure

▶ the technology solution would need to be scalable to allow developments

▶ little consideration had been given to the strategic direction of future offerings

▶ it was unsure how current service management functions would support the new internet operation

▶ the bank was subject to a regulatory review.

PwC was called in primarily for the following reasons:

▶ experience with providing solutions to financial services clients

▶ knowledge of the requirements and expectations of the regulators

▶ the structured solution (linking technical and operational issues)

▶ the networked business experience of staff

▶ world-class skills in technical security and project management.

the solution

The services PwC delivered provided the client with significant added value in the very short time remaining prior to launch of the service.

security review and test

PwC performed a review of the application and proposed infrastructure to identify potential areas of weakness that would compromise the security of the system.

Once the issues identified within the security review had been addressed, it completed a testing exercise to ensure that the application and infrastructure were resilient to attack.

operational resilience review

PwC diagnosed areas vulnerable to disruption, and designed improvements to the way the operation would be run. This included identifying the service performance obligations, critical dependencies, defining the required service management functions, and the stress monitoring of demand and capacity.

In addition, to ensure that the client had the maximum time to address issues raised, the project management team worked closely with them throughout the assignment to manage the implementation risks.

the outcome

There were several key achievements throughout the assignments:

▶ a forward-looking networked business strategy was developed

▶ they learned that the traditional telephone banking structure was not sufficient to support the new delivery channel

▶ the necessary service management functions were defined

▶ the technical infrastructure was made more secure and matched to industry recognized standards

▶ a key dependency, an application provider, was put under proper supplier management.

PwC's work also identified critical problems, which were highlighted as 'issues to be addressed prior to launch'. So that it could address these issues in a timely manner, the client requested additional assistance from PwC, and replanned the sequence of the launch timetable as it realized the risks associated with a full-scale national launch of such a service without proper testing and trials.

❝PwC's work also identified critical problems❞

Why did we choose PwC? Where AKQA is small, agile and flexible, PwC is large, cautious and resilient. When it comes to planning, PwC has one of the best resources in the world in terms of its people, its knowledge reservoir and networks. It is a formidable ecosystem, just on its own and without its global reach.

EXECUTIVE SUMMARY OF
PRINCIPLE 2

PLANNING IS OF PARAMOUNT IMPORTANCE. It is a combination of long-term strategy and short-term tactics. The key to planning is seeking all possible options, evaluating them on the basis of risk and reward, then making a suitable choice. It's not just about ideas without profit, nor is it about profit without ideas. It's about profitable ideas, and to reach them you have to think outside the box, outside the system, outside linear thinking.

▶ What strategies and tactics has your organization put together?

▶ You must build the 'right system' and you must build the 'system right.'

▶ To ensure success it is essential that your organization and its systems have resilience, availability, reliability and scalability.

▶ An organization is more likely to succeed if, with proper planning from professionals, it reconfigures its entire business strategy so that the full advantages of the internet are integrated into its existing business.

► You cannot have a strategy in isolation. Remember this is an ecosystem. You need to understand that every aspect of your organization is affected and how they all need to be transformed and completed in a holistic way. You need to introduce a three-dimensional or 360-degree approach to planning in your organization.

NOTES

1 BAA Heathrow, airport information, facts and figures, http:/www.baa.co.uk/domino/baa/baanet

2 http:/www.akqa.com

3 Interview with Matthew Treagus, Head of Consulting and AKQA Chief Operating Officer on November 26, 1999.

4 Case study – **AKQA 1994–1999: Five Years of Innovation**, published with Revolution, October 19, 1999, p. 18.

5 http:www.pricewaterhousecoopers.co.uk/ and http:www.e-business.pwcglobal.com

6 Interview with Charles Johnson, E-business Director, PwC on December 21, 1999.

7 Case study – PwC Launching internet financial services.

PART 2

B2E

(BUSINESS TO EMPLOYEE)

3 system

4

5 network

security

PRINCIPLE 3

SYSTEM SOFTWARE
EVALUATION

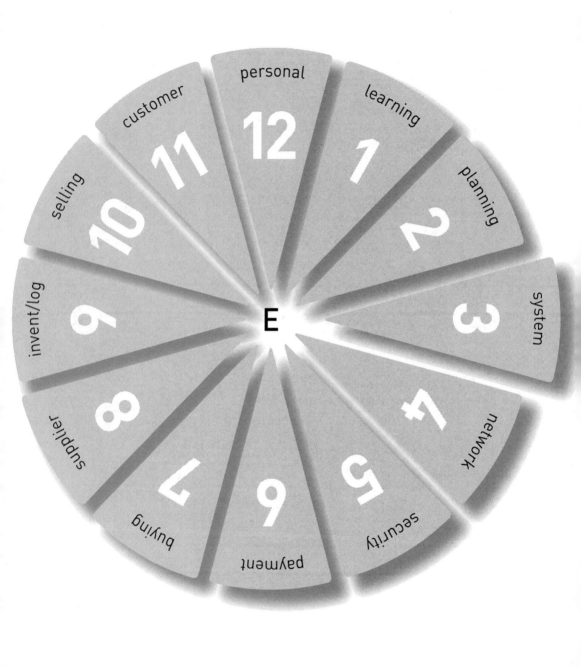

STATEMENT OF **PRINCIPLE 3**

ORGANISMS CANNOT LIVE FOR EVER; all living things die eventually and return their dead material to the earth. All the materials that every animal takes in as food also returns to the earth as waste matter. The dead material and waste matter form the diet of a group of living organisms called decomposers, such as bacteria, fungi and small animals. The latter break down nature's wastes into ever-smaller pieces until all chemicals are released into the air, the soil and the water, making them available to other living things.[1]

Evaluating your system software undergoes the same process as nature. Principle 3 is about evaluating your software infrastructure system and then deciding what can or must be kept, consolidated and integrated, and what needs to be abandoned, perished and recycled. The development of your internal or intranet portal takes place at this stage, and it's critical to bring everything together internally before making any moves on or to the outside world.

Back to Heathrow, system software evaluation is about evaluating the airport's existing facilities. It is software that runs the airport. It is software that controls the 'nervous system' of the airport, through the main computers and control tower. For example, software controls the arrivals and departures of planes and the loading and unloading of cargo and luggage. Software runs the integrated public transport, medical centers, chemists, easy baggage reclaim, stores, restaurants, cafes, leisure activities and the lost property office. Immigration and police sections, training rooms, ticketing counters linked to luggage and cargo services, purchasing and warehousing of direct and indirect goods, refrigerated warehousing of catered foods, synchronized delivery of provisions and meals to aircraft and refuse removal services from arriving aircraft could not work without software.

> **at Heathrow, £1 million is invested every day in facilities and customer service developments**

At Heathrow, £1 million is invested every day in facilities and customer service developments. It cost £450 million to place the Heathrow Express rail link connecting the airport to London's Paddington station. Investments in redeveloping terminals amounted to more than £90 million. New developments at Heathrow include the World Business Centre, extension to the Hilton International Hotel which will include a convention hall that will hold up to 1,000 people, and a £7 million perishable goods centre for British Airways.

Evaluators of airport systems need to consider not only increased future passenger traffic but also what they need to do from now to prepare and stagger new facilities over periods of time.[2]

Heathrow Airport's electronic 'nervous system', its facilities, its utilities and its transport links must be maintained, updated and upgraded so that its overall efficiency and level of service is exceptional. So too with principle 3 – system software evaluation. It's about integrating your existing business with networked business and then wiring it so that it is seamless to your customers, shareholders, employees and suppliers. How you do that will depend on many variables and once again you will need professional advice as to which way is optimal for your organization.

Software controls and enables the link between 'company information', which is essential to employees, and its 'internet site', which is essential to customers. For example, timetables of arrivals and departures at Heathrow are important not only to the control tower (employees) but also to all passengers (customers). The key to this principle is to understand this link and why it is no longer necessary to regard the website and company information as two separate systems. They are living in one ecosystem. Software is the tool that weaves the two into one. For example, software will constantly update prices on the main (legacy) database and simultaneously transport them to the website so that customers and suppliers are immediately aware of the changes. This alone is an enormous task. For a company with enterprise resource planning (ERP) systems in place, it will involve the whole of the ERP system and integration of many parts of the company, such as sales, personnel and finance. Just as the heart pumps, controls and circulates the blood around the body, software pumps, controls and circulates information around an organization. Failing to supply information to a particular part of the organization will cause that part to become 'gangrenous'.

This is the domain of the Head of IT. However, Sales and Marketing Directors will also need a general understanding of how the system will work and what software will drive it.

There are many software organizations offering a plethora of software on networked business. In the following case studies, we show you how software suppliers and user organizations have adapted their software to make it internet-enabled.

SUPPLIER PROFILE

Software AG

supplier of integrated electronic business solutions

GIVEN THAT ORGANIZATIONS LIVE IN AN ecosystem, software is the tool that weaves the various departments and divisions into a holistic and organic one. Software AG,[3] one of the largest software companies in the world, has worked for a long time to develop the building blocks of networked business.

Software AG is based in Darmstadt, Germany. It is represented in more than 60 countries by subsidiaries or partners and its products are used in more than 90 countries. It has about 5,000 clients worldwide, of which a significant number are blue-chip organizations. The company generated revenues of DM716 million in 1999, has in excess of 2,600 employees, and is in the top 100 companies in Germany. Its products and services support seamless integration of transaction-based mission-critical applications across multiple system platforms, from mainframe through to the web.

Software AG's technology expertise is based on three major business areas:

1   In database management systems it has products called *Tamino* (the XML – Extensible Mark-up Language – databank for electronic business) and *Adabas*.

2   In application development environments it has products called *Natural* and *Bolero*.

3   In middleware, it has a product called *EntireX*.

Although Software AG is active in creating products for electronic business, one of its primary goals is to protect its customers' IT investments and it continues to support and enhance its existing product lines. Software AG also has the benefit of being a profitable company with longevity within the IT sector.

INTERVIEW WITH SUPPLIER

'The real building blocks for true electronic business have only really been finished at the end of 1999. Completeness of the networked business process is upon us.'

Mark Edwards, Managing Director,

and Steve Bailey, E-Business Solutions Manager[4]

PROTECTING TRUSTED EXISTING CUSTOMERS and focussing on having the best well-engineered technology is not only very much part of German culture and philosophy but also very much the viewpoint of Software AG. How else can you retain institutions such as Chase Manhattan as clients for 30 years? Until recently, Software AG was an independent company, privately owned by a charitable foundation. It was a slumbering giant. It never really had an aggressive marketing strategy. When Dr Erwin Koenigs, a former physicist and now CEO of the company, joined Software AG in late 1996, he recognized the growth potential, refocussed the company into networked business, and initiated the IPO.

According to Steve Bailey, Dr Koenigs believes that ERP vendors are failing the industry and that the technology does not and never will lend itself to the internet and to networked business. Bailey says: 'ERP systems focus on the supply chain management and clearly efficiency in procuring goods and reducing costs is certainly an important element. However, there's been a huge push now into customer relationship management, in terms of sales and marketing initiatives, one-to-one marketing, and cross-selling of products.'

Supply chains or webs are focussed on the purchasing side of the equation. Customer relationship management is focussed on the selling side. In the past, vendors have generally sold these separately. Today, they must provide both equations in a seamless flow that a client organization needs. This is what vendors such as Software AG call 'integrated electronic business' and what we call ecosystem.

❝supply chains or webs are focussed on the purchasing side of the equation❞

Currently, companies have all their information stored in their existing systems and changing them over quickly is crucial. What can they do? Bailey says: 'Everybody's going to need high availability [meaning immediately, at the push of a button] and quick response times. What's more they're going to need to bet their business on the software they're using, because that's really all they've got. What we can promise is a high availability, high transaction, and high volume engine that allow you to do that.'

Software AG, like many other organizations, is putting its money on XML because it believes that is going to be the foundation of networked business environments. It is a common language that ensures computers and people can communicate. Language here means using common syntax and semantics. XML is only one of three key technology enablers that provide the foundations for integrated electronic business within and beyond an enterprise. The three co-existing elements are:

1 XML – a common trading language for a community, as in 'business English'

2 Http – a common electronic communicating mechanism, as in 'speaking'

3 Java – a set of tasks and rules for engaging in trading, as in 'dealing'.

In the following case study, Software AG delivered three main services to its client. It provided the software infrastructure to enable Woolwich plc to deliver a web bank, a personal account manager (Money 99), and a call center for the bank's customers. The three-layer system is flexible and allows for adding channels to customers and exploiting new competitive advantages.

PRINCIPLE IN ACTION
Woolwich PLC

personal financial services provider

IN THE HIGHLY COMPETITIVE financial services ecosystem, the Woolwich,[5] a leading UK provider of personal financial services, aims to retain existing customers and to attract new ones. To do this it regularly seeks customer feedback to assess current and future needs.

From research carried out early in 1998, the bank identified some key issues. The overwhelming message was that customers felt they did not have control over their finances. They had accounts and policies scattered across a wide variety of providers and generally had little idea of what they owned and what they owed.

> **the Woolwich believed it could address these issues through a new concept of 'anytime, anywhere, anyhow personal finances'**

The Woolwich believed it could address these issues through a new concept of 'anytime, anywhere, anyhow personal finances'. This would provide customers with the ability to manage all their finances using whichever means of communication was most convenient at the time. It included traditional methods such as branches and automated teller machines (ATMs); more recent channels such as telephone call centers; and emerging means such as the internet, digital television, and GSM (global satellite monitoring) telephone technology. This was the mission.

Open Plan Services was the name given to the new approach designed to transform the way customers would interact with the Woolwich. It would allow the bank to take advantage of the extensive information stored on the bank's mainframe, which handled account management, transactions, interest rate calculation and company financial accounting. It would also enable it to utilize the mainframe's processing capabilities.

In early 1998, the Woolwich set out to develop the vision. It faced a number of challenges. It was not viable to adapt the mainframe to new, user-friendly functionality, yet the bank could not justify redeveloping the successful mainframe-based processing system simply to accommodate new front-end functionality. Another challenge was that the new services were to be accessible 24 hours a day. This required the system to accommodate times when the mainframe was not available because it was undertaking large amounts of batch processing.

The technical remit was therefore to add a wide range of front-end functionality and to exploit the mainframe without changing it. This would involve adding a middle layer to create a three-tier architecture. As the Woolwich went through an evaluation process, it began to favor purchasing a package as opposed to in-house development. The two leading contenders were a Corba-based package and a Microsoft solution consisting of a set of tools built around the Microsoft DCOM/DNA framework.

As part of the solution Microsoft suggested Software AG's *EntireX* middleware as the link between the NT-based front end and the mainframe back end. Microsoft's recommendation was an important factor for David Ellington, technical architect of the system. Microsoft was confident of the product's performance and Software AG was prepared to guarantee the compliance and compatibility of *EntireX* with both DCOM and DNA. Just three months after the decision to establish Open Plan Services, this solution was chosen and implementation began.

Less than a year after the initial idea, the Woolwich launched Open Plan Services. The system had been built in less than six months. After the launch The *Times* newspaper described the Woolwich as 'one of the more forward-looking banks'. The *Guardian* said it was 'emerging as an intelligent and innovative performer'. The *Daily Mail* commented: 'As a retail bank it has become a leader in ideas and is providing increasingly good value to many of its customers.' Through evaluating and developing this software, Woolwich is offering added value to its customers – personal finance anytime, anywhere and anyhow – and thereby maintaining and attracting a larger customer base.

The only requirement for customer access to Open Plan Services is a current account with the Woolwich. The scalable nature of the solution is illustrated by the bank's plan to extend its services so that availability always remains ahead of customer demand. In parallel, it will add functionality such as triggering of transfers from current to deposit accounts to ensure funds above a pre-set level earn interest.

Tony O'Reilly, IT Infrastructure Manager at the Woolwich, confirmed that the bank has a leading technology which is stable and functionally rich. He also affirmed that it has delivered three main services: the web bank, Money 99, and a call center. The three-layer system has enabled Woolwich to quickly add channels to its customers and to exploit new competitive advantages.

66this is not a static process; it is organic and must therefore be constantly improved through feedback with customers 99

This is not a static process; it is organic and must therefore be constantly improved through feedback with customers. In early February 2000, the Woolwich announced that it was in partnership with

Vodafone and Nokia to be the first in the UK to offer interactive banking by WAP (wireless application protocol) mobile phone.

We chose Software AG because as a software organization it has been around for a few decades and the fact that it is a German company adds a little flavor. In spite of all its past glories, it too is adapting its software to make it internet-enabled for its wide range of customers. As an organization, it is attempting to transform itself as well as its customers. As a software organization, Software AG provides the tomato paste that covers the base of the pizza.

SUPPLIER PROFILE

EDS

a professional services firm

THERE ARE MANY ORGANIZATIONS whose services cover many aspects of the 12 principles, even though their core competence may cover one principle or perhaps straddle two. EDS[6] is one of these organizations. Unfortunately our interview under EDS cannot be featured because our interviewee left the company shortly after and EDS requested that we didn't publish it.

EDS was founded in 1962 and has been a leader in the information and technology field for more than 36 years. The company has more than 130,000 employees and serves clients in 45 countries in industries such as manufacturing, aerospace, healthcare, financial services, insurance, food, retail, travel, transportation, energy, communication and government. It registered revenues of $17 billion in 1998 and signed contracts in 1997 and 1998 that combined are valued at more than $28 billion. EDS has a backlog of client commitments of more than $70 billion and has a robust pipeline of new-business opportunities.

EDS's statement is: 'We exist to make everyone's life simpler.' Its services portfolio covers management consulting, e-solutions, business process management, and information solutions.

The company's website gives a dozen examples in which it has participated in making history. For instance, since 1994, it has been the UK Inland Revenue's IT partner, supporting 55,000 users across 600 sites. Between 1996 and 1998, EDS delivered the computerized environment for self-assessment – the largest tax change in the UK since World War II – on time and on budget. Thirty years ago, Blue Shield of California, the largest insurance plan of its kind in the nation, awarded EDS its first $1 million-a-month agreement. The relationship continues today. Currently, revenue from its healthcare business totals $500 million annually.

"the company's website gives a dozen examples in which it has participated in making history"

Lastly, with more than 17,000 stores, 7-Eleven, Inc is the world's largest convenience store retailer. But the company wanted to do even more to ensure the best items were in each store. EDS helped 7-Eleven implement a retail information system (RIS) that lets managers tailor stores and respond quickly to change. RIS even alerts them to weather forecasts that could affect inventory sales.

PRINCIPLE IN ACTION
Rolls-Royce

ROLLS-ROYCE PLC[7] IS A GLOBAL AEROSPACE, defense, marine and energy group with facilities in 15 countries.

With the company facing an increasingly competitive marketplace, a step change – achieved through improved business processes and customer service – was vital. That was why Rolls-Royce brought in EDS to work across its group of businesses, and with its US-based subsidiary, Rolls-Royce Indianapolis, which it acquired in 1995. Rolls-Royce was attracted by EDS's status as a global player, its commitment to industry best practice, and its outsourcing expertise.

Since the beginning of the partnership, Rolls-Royce and EDS have worked together to achieve key improvements for the Rolls-Royce business. Without evaluating and improving software, the following could not have been achieved:

1   Performance enhancements to core processes such as external purchasing, project management, product development and manufacturing. For example, in aerospace, an integrated product development program is reducing the cost and time of bringing the right product to market. Rolls-Royce is maximizing value from its information systems.

2 Tangible benefits include a 17 percent improvement in engineering productivity in two years, a 10 percent improvement in manufacturing productivity, and a reduction in compressor disc manufacture time from 12 weeks to four weeks, with a target of two weeks.

3 Several million dollars a year in savings in the transmission and distribution businesses, 30 percent improvement in employee productivity in the power generation businesses, and a 30 percent reduction in assembly time for the RB211 (Rolls-Royce Canada).

But how were these performance improvements achieved? Rolls-Royce aims at the world's best in everything it does. That meant that it required a business consultancy provider that could improve efficiency across the company through close partnership.

❝Rolls-Royce aims at the world's best in everything it does ❞

Rolls-Royce was also keen to ensure that its IT operations created a maximum value by implementing industry best practice. As a result, it decided to outsource systems and computing activity. Rolls-Royce's acquisition of the Allison Engine Company in Indianapolis meant that business integration was another essential element of the partnership. A key objective was to create a global enterprise, which would enable the company to balance its engineering and manufacturing capabilities between North America and Europe.

In January 1996, EDS and Rolls-Royce aerospace signed a ten-year strategic partnership, which was broadened in August 1996 to include Rolls-Royce Indianapolis. Following early success with the aerospace work, EDS was also awarded a ten-year contract with Rolls-Royce industrial businesses in late 1996. These contracts are worth a total of $2.25 billion.

The basis of this unique partnership is more than the usual outsourcing contract. To meet today's industry challenges, Rolls-Royce and EDS agreed to work together in a shared risk-and-reward relationship. The joint strategy, known as CoSourcing, pools the strengths of EDS's service portfolio to speedily deliver performance improvements for clients. This agreement involves EDS and Rolls-Royce sharing the funding of new business initiatives and rewards too. CoSourcing is key to the integration of Rolls-Royce businesses. It has brought a massive and successful restructuring of the design, manufacturing, procurement, sales and customer service processes across the enterprise.

Under the partnership agreement, Rolls-Royce, EDS, and its management consultancy, A.T. Kearney, have established dedicated teams to accelerate the improvement in business performance required by fundamentally changing the way and speed with which key business activities are carried out. EDS and A.T. Kearney consultants are working in close collaboration with Rolls-Royce management and, through comparison with industry best practice, are identifying areas of Rolls-Royce business that can be significantly improved. All the initiatives are aimed at increasing quality and improving customer service, and most require implementation of new systems. The whole program is underpinned by the application of EDS and A.T. Kearney core competencies in change management.

66almost 1,200 IT employees have transferred from
Rolls-Royce to EDS as part of the agreement 99

EDS integrates and deploys the new applications and manages the installation and operation of the entire technology infrastructure globally. Almost 1,200 IT employees have transferred from Rolls-Royce to EDS as part of the agreement. EDS's proven track record in transitioning staff was one of the factors behind Rolls-Royce's choice of the company.

One of the reasons we chose EDS for this case study is that it is a leader under this principle. Moreover, its employees work within the client organization for long periods of time. Likewise, employees from client organizations work at EDS, as cited above. This is an ecosystem in action.

In the past three-and-a-half years, Rolls-Royce and EDS together have proven that the partnership can be sustained and that the benefits can be delivered to both partners. The achievements to date have ensured a sound basis on which to build for the future. Further programs to develop the enterprise integration theme and to implement e-business across the extended supply chain will be the focus of the future.

A Rolls-Royce engine has more than 20,000 components and lasts for around 30 years, so it's a complex business. Networked business *or* e-business, where the e means 'electronic' as well as 'ecosystem' will reduce the costs, maintain quality, and increase efficiency, through constant system software evaluation and improvement.

PRINCIPLE 3: SYSTEM SOFTWARE EVALUATION

EXECUTIVE SUMMARY OF
PRINCIPLE 3

SYSTEM SOFTWARE EVALUATION is about making the work process more efficient in terms of money and time for all stakeholders in the organizations: employees, shareholders, customers, business partners, and suppliers. The main objective is to find ways to save customers time, money and hassle. This is then reconfigured to the organization and its supply web, through the internet.

▶ Principle 3 is about evaluating your system software infrastructure and then deciding what can or must be kept, consolidated and integrated, and what needs to be abandoned, taken away and recycled. Just as customer needs and wants change over time, and are accelerated by technology, software needs to mirror those expectations.

▶ Software controls and enables the link between 'company information' and its 'internet site'. The key to this principle is to understand this link of why it is no longer necessary to regard the website and company information as two separate systems. They are living in one ecosystem. Software is the tool that weaves the two into one.

▶ Business supply chains or webs are focussed on the purchasing side of the equation; customer relationship management is focussed on the selling side. In the past, vendors have generally sold these separately. Today, vendors must provide both equations in a seamless flow that a client organisation needs, or what vendors call 'integrated electronic business' and what we call 'ecosystem'.

▶ You can't have a strategy in isolation. Remember, this is an ecosystem. It is far more than simply working very closely with your partners. Just look at the above case study, where almost 1,200 IT employees were transferred from Rolls-Royce to EDS. You must transfer and cross-fertilize resources within and without your ecosystem.

NOTES

1 'Recycling to Live', **Eyewitness Guides Ecology**, Steve Pollock, Dorling Kindersley Ltd, 1993, p. 14.

2 BAA Heathrow, airport information, facts and figures, http:/www.baa.co.uk/domino/baa/baanet

3 http:/www.softwareag.com/corporat/

4 Interview with Mark Edwards, Managing Director, and Steve Bailey, E-Business Solutions Manager on December 2, 1999.

5 Case study – Woolwich plc

6 http:/www.eds.com/

7 Case study – Rolls-Royce extracted from article by EDS, 'Rolls Royce is flying high in partnership with EDS'.

PRINCIPLE 4

NETWORK EVALUATION

personal 12
learning 1
planning 2
system 3
network 4
security 5
payment 6
buying 7
supplier 8
invent/log 9
selling 10
customer 11

E

STATEMENT OF **PRINCIPLE 4**

IN THE BIOSPHERE, ENERGY FLOWS in and out, but the chemicals essential for life processes are limited. They must be constantly recycled. Water is the most common compound on earth, and all life on this planet depends on it to a greater or lesser extent. Seventy per cent of our body weight is made up of water, but its most important quality is that many chemicals will dissolve in it. Just as water also plays a vital role in the structure of living things, electricity plays a vital role in the structure of non-living things.[1]

In Chapter 3, we looked at the implications of software. In this chapter, we look at the physical infrastructure (network) which supports the software. Software without network is like electricity without cables. Principle 4, network evaluation, is in essence about your company's communications infrastructure. This includes the hardware, the intranet, the extranet, and the internet service provider. All the computing power and data in the world are meaningless without a reliable and secure form of connection to the internet and to the areas of the company that will be involved with it. Your company must also ask at the very start how much it is prepared to spend on hardware, what kind of website it wants to offer, and how many visitors it anticipates. Often companies forget their suppliers' bandwidth requirements because they are so focussed on the sales side of putting their business online.

Domestic users know the frustration of waiting for data to download through the telephone line to their PCs. Online delays in e-commerce are unacceptable because the customer will go elsewhere at a click of the mouse. The amount of data that travels through internet network connections is measured in bits per second (bps). Regular domestic bandwidth measures about 30,000 bps, while a large corporate could use a bandwidth of up to 45 Mbps. Cable modems into the home would deliver 10 Mbps in 1999. Imagine that domestic bandwidth is the size of an alleyway, then the corporate bandwidth would be a 750-lane freeway – this is an exact mathematical ratio, not a flippant exaggeration.

❝at Heathrow, the control tower is the network ❞

What is the network in your business? At Heathrow, the control tower is the network. It is the air traffic controllers, aided by radar and other electronic devices, who direct incoming and outgoing aircraft from airport control towers and control centers located some distance from the airfield. The controllers also direct all aircraft movements on the ground, guiding pilots as they taxi their planes between the loading apron and the runway. Without them, the airport ceases to function.

At large airports as many as three landing or take-off operations may occur every minute. The control of aircraft in the air is a difficult but extremely important operation. Aircraft require very large amounts of space, but at the same time the risk of collision must be set at very low, almost negligible, levels. Because aircraft are concentrated in the airspace around airports, acceptable levels of collision risk can be achieved only by strict adherence to procedures that are set out and monitored by air traffic control authorities.[2]

Just as with air traffic control, in principle 4, we look at internet networks, which must also adhere to strict procedures and monitor traffic. Examples are internet service providers (ISPs) such as BT, website hosting companies such as Intel (which is obviously much more than this) and networks. An airport control tower also needs machinery and equipment to run its operation and consequently it has suppliers which maintain and service this equipment. So must the above organizations, which are involved in the internet space. Their suppliers provide hardware servers and internet infrastructure products such as hubs, routers and bridges.

The Head of IT would be responsible for network evaluation and together with the Project Manager would be the key person with influence on this principle.

The following case studies give you a flavour of what communications and network organizations have done to convert themselves into networked businesses. They have done so by taking new software and network technologies and weaving them through their old networks, making themselves more efficient and customer focussed.

SUPPLIER PROFILE

British Telecommunications plc (BT)

world-wide communications group

BT[3] IS AN ORGANIZATION WHICH LIVES IN many ecosystems as well as encompassing many of its own ecosystems.

With assets worth about £30 billion in 1999, the accounts for that year show it had a total turnover of £18 billion, which delivered net profit after tax of about £3 billion. BT saw a 12 percent growth in demand for its products and services, which was driven by rapidly expanding internet traffic and mobile usage.

BT is organized into two main operations, BTUK and BT Global, and a number of support units in the group's headquarters which provide specialized services. BTUK comprises three divisions, business division, consumer division, and networks and systems. Business division serves the business community with 8 million lines, while consumer division serves the residential community with 20 million lines and is also responsible for BT's public payphones. On average about 100 million UK local and national calls are made every day. Networks and systems is responsible for design, operation, maintenance and development of BT's networks and technology. It is also responsible for BT's research and development facility. BT Global serves business customers who require telecommunications services around the world and is responsible for joint ventures.

The number of BT employees has fallen substantially since 1991. From figures available, we know, for instance, that in 1994 BT had around 154,000 employees and by 1998 this number had fallen to 120,000. BT declares that this has been as a result of improvements in efficiency, reduction in layers of management, and contracting out certain services. At the same time, it has increased its use of temporary contract staff.

> **"on average about 100 million UK local and national calls are made every day"**

In 1981, British Telecom (as it was then known) announced that it was to test market credit card-shaped phone cards, based on optical strip technology. Right from the start, the little green card was a massive success. Today, as technologies converge, the possibilities increase. One practical possibility being tested involves the 'downloading' of money from BT payphones on to special cards, which can then be used to pay for purchases at retail outlets. It seems as though technology is not the issue; it's the application of it.

Over the past few years BT has been working hard at forming strategic alliances to take advantage of the opportunities that the internet has offered. The company has enjoyed a feast of joint ventures (even if it is now suffering from indigestion) and subsidiary undertakings in various areas such as cable maintenance and repair, cable ownership, communication-related services and product providers, cellular and mobile systems providers and operators, and also systems integration and application developers. BT has executed joint ventures and strategic alliances in numerous countries in Europe, North America, the Far East, Australia and New Zealand. Over and above all that, BT has a global venture with AT&T in the form of Concert, which forms our case study after the interview.

INTERVIEW WITH SUPPLIER

'If you own the last mile, you'll never be forced out of the industry.
However, it may not be such an attractive business on its own.'

Tony Fish of BT Mergers & Acquisitions

THERE HAS BEEN A 90 PERCENT DROP in the cost of telephone calls in the past four years and you are likely to see another
40–50 percent drop in international traffic prices, explains Tony Fish.[4]
There is huge potential for excess capacity, so you will see a continued
degradation of price. This is all good news for the users as the cost of
connecting is falling and will continue to do so.

❝only the fleetest of foot will survive this process ❞

This assertion is confirmed by consultants Intercai Mondiale,[5] who
state that capacity will outstrip demand for the foreseeable future and
that full competition will emerge and force prices down to very low
levels indeed. Only the fleetest of foot will survive this process, and
some operators, such as the satellite companies, will have to seek
entirely new markets.

'If you take a very coarse view of the world, you would say that telephone organizations are in the transportation business. Bits and bytes
down the pipes, keeps them [customers] online and this includes talk-

ing,' says Fish. Much of the content will be localized to the culture and language. When asked if that meant Yahoo! and Excite would be considered a threat, Fish replies that perhaps in some areas, but not to the core business, because the latter do not own the physical network assets. Fish sees a 'continual consolidation in the "backbone" market in the next 18 months'.

Shareholders' faith and money is sweet music to organizations, but it can also restrict them from changing direction and morphing. It is shareholders who drive industries. On all sides, you have the influence of fund managers. Traditionally, fund managers who invest in BT have done so because BT delivers dividend income. If they were seeking capital growth in the telecoms sector, they would invest in organizations such as MCI WorldCom. Here the influencing shareholders or fund managers take a different view on risk. Capital growth is considered higher risk, whereas dividend income is considered low risk. Fund managers decide on a company's risk profile. Since its shareholders influence BT strategy, BT would tend to maintain a lower risk strategy with world-class performance. A low-risk strategy, sometimes judged as being late into markets, has worked for BT in a whole number of instances. Do not discount the slow responders as in some markets, such as mobile, says Fish – BT is a world-class leader providing risk and reward.

'Mobile' and 'mobility' are two very different things. 'Mobile' one may understand as the handset you carry; 'mobility' is a service anywhere, delivering your individual functionality. It is much more interesting than a vanilla mobile offer, particularly with developments such as Bluetooth.[6] Bluetooth is a wireless technology special interest group consisting of Ericcson, IBM, Microsoft, Nokia, Motorola and Toshiba. It provides synchronization and transfer of information functions. It allows all of your devices to be in sync. It is an enabler – where you should be, when you should be there, who you will meet and why you are there, how to get there, difficulties en route, injections to have, background information, how to pay and so on. Bluetooth essentially allows devices to talk to one another. When offered as part of an integrated service, it will allow your device to tell you just about anything.

BT's internet services are focussed on four themes, says Fish:

1 infrastructure and hosting

2 hosted services, and that's any hosted application that runs on top of the infrastructure

3 high bandwidth broadband services for entertainment

4 internet services provision in the broadest sense of what an ISP is doing and where they are going in fixed and mobile domains.

These developments will impact on the cycle of money in the supply chains. In the recent past, the big guys used to hold the little guys by the shorts by taking 90 days or more to pay them, while the little guy had to pay his supplier. In the e-commerce world, procurement, not payment, is streamlined. So now goods come on time, but how will the payment mechanism work? What's going to happen to the multiplier effect? It could speed it up, but then the net result could be to slow it down. Is there a role for the banks? Do they justify their existence by being only a trusted party?

❝in the e-commerce world, procurement, not payment, is streamlined ❞

Tony Fish believes that 'at the end of the day, people still need communication networks. It will always be there. At rock bottom, it could be a cost-plus, but I'm still going to be there. If you own the last mile, you'll never be forced out of the industry; however, it may not be such an attractive business. But we will have lots of really interesting businesses running over it.'

PRINCIPLE IN ACTION

Concert

TELEPHONE ORGANIZATIONS ARE IN THE 'communications' business (in a broader sense) and not just in the 'telephone' business (in the narrower sense).

The most important event of 1998/99 for BT was the birth of Concert,[7] the global joint venture with US telecommunications company AT&T. BT and AT&T own Concert equally. Concert effectively combines the transborder assets and operations of the two companies, including their international networks, all their international traffic, and their international products for business customers. All three operate to a common architecture to ensure provision of a seamless service to customers. Concert is now a leading global communications company serving multinational business customers, international carriers, and internet service providers worldwide. Even BT has had to evaluate its own network.

Concert provides customers with communications services on an unprecedented scale, scope and quality, with the industry's broadest portfolio of voice, data and internet services. It has a direct sales force serving around 270 multinational customers. Through its network of global distributors, it serves an additional 29,000 customers world-wide. Concert's frame relay network reaches every major city in the US and the UK, and extends to an additional 170 cities in 47 countries. Its global public network reaches directly 237 countries – more than any other existing network.

❝Concert provides customers with communications services on an unprecedented scale ❞

Spanning 21 cities in 17 countries, Concert has also built a new state-of-the-art high-speed internet protocol (IP) backbone network. Concert's IP network is interconnected with the parents' extensive domestic IP backbone networks, which distribute Concert services in critical US and UK markets. A report by Intercai Mondiale shows that due to increasing bandwidth demand the US to UK/Europe transat-lantic route of broadband cables is the busiest route. Each month 32 bunches of glass fiber are being laid physically to run along the floor of the Atlantic Ocean at a current cost of $20,000 per km, down from $50,000 per km in 1992.[8]

Here's what the leaders of the venture have said about Concert. Sir Peter Bonfield, BT's then Chief Executive, said: 'This is a new company for the new millennium addressing the massive growth in networked busi-ness in internet-enabled global economy.' Michael Armstrong, AT&T's Chairman, said: 'AT&T is committed to our growth strategy and our con-tinuing strong partnership with BT. I have no doubt the global venture will deliver on its promise.' David Dorman, Concert's Chief Executive, said: 'We've heard what our customers want – global communications made simple. Concert is the only company with the means to deliver truly global services to customers by offering the reach, connectivity, flexibility and seamlessness in network services, applications and cus-tomer support. We have a great market opportunity ahead of us and we fully intend to take advantage of it.'

Operating from multiple locations, Concert employs 6,000 people, owns fixed assets of about $3 billion, and has three profitable businesses:

1 *Global Markets*: working through a global network of distributors, Concert offers facilities-based communications solutions for multinational companies and other business customers worldwide. Global Markets is expected to generate more than 30 percent of Concert's total revenue.

2 *Global Account*: this business serves all the communication needs of most of the top multinational customers from the financial, petroleum and information technology sectors. It has its own dedicated sales and service team of 2,000 people. This year, Global Accounts is expected to generate around 35 percent of Concert's total revenue.

3 *International Carrier Services*: this business sells services, based on Concert's extensive networks, to fixed and wireless carriers and internet service providers worldwide, including AT&T and BT. In 2000, the latter's combined international voice traffic was expected to be 25 billion minutes, unmatched by any other operator. This business was expected to generate 40 percent of Concert's total revenue in 2000.

We chose BT because it is a traditional network, which owns the last mile to a large proportion of homes and businesses in the UK. As with all giant organizations, it is going through enormous pain and transition in its old businesses. In the case of its new business venture in Concert, BT is preparing a new ecosystem of its own together with AT&T to provide a seamless network service to the emerging global business ecosystems.

In 2000, Concert was expected to generate revenues of more than $7 billion and capital was expenditure expected to be around $1.5 billion.

AT&T and BT have created an international ecosystem which will feed into and out of their own national ecosystems.

SUPPLIER PROFILE

Intel Corporation

'the brains of the computer'

IF BT AND AT&T ARE THE EARS of the computer, then Intel[9] is the brain. Founded in 1968 to build semiconductor memory products, it soon made technological history with the introduction of the world's first microprocessor. The computer and the internet revolution that this technology enabled have changed the world.

Intel's mission is to be the pre-eminent building block supplier to the worldwide internet economy. Today, Intel supplies the computing industry members with the chips, boards, systems and software that are the ingredients of computer architecture and are used to create advanced computing systems.

In the ten-year period between 1989 and 1998, Intel produced a 27 percent compound annual growth rate in net revenues coupled with a 26 percent compound annual growth rate in book value per share. Intel stock rose at a 45 percent compound annual growth rate over the same period. Put another way, $100 invested in Intel for five years would be worth $805; $100 invested ten years ago would be worth $4,210 in 1998; and $100 invested 27 years ago would be worth $162,338.

Net annual revenues hover around the $30 billion level and this represents the combined effort of 65,000 employees across 30 countries. This is not all. For a number of years, Intel has been acquiring companies on a monthly basis. In February 2000 alone, Intel announced that it had acquired US technology companies Ambient Technologies and Thinkit Technologies.

❝for a number of years, Intel has been aquiring companies on a monthly basis ❞

Intel also gives back to the community. In January 2000, it announced the launch of a $100 million worldwide (20 countries) 'Technology Education Program' to train 400,000 teachers in 1,000 days. Microsoft announced it would also contribute about $350 million in software to the project. The curriculum, which consists of ten four-hour modules, is based on the Microsoft Office 2000 Professional software suite. Each of the classroom teachers and master teachers worldwide receive a free copy of the software suite and Encarta Encyclopaedia. A key element of the Intel program is its focus on keeping the knowledge in the local community through a train-the-trainer model. At a British Educational Technology Tradeshow in London in 1999, Intel unveiled details of the program's implementation in Europe.

INTERVIEW WITH SUPPLIER

'Our customers never shut, so that we means we cannot shut'

Ian Wilson, Director of E-Business and IT, Europe, Middle East and Africa.

INTEL IS ALSO TRAINING AND EDUCATING its own people.[10] It has worked hard to institute a networked business program with its direct customers. 'Our goal is to move all that business to become electronic business as fast as we can.'

There are three reasons why Intel felt compelled to evaluate its own network. First, it believed this would enable it to provide better customer service. The company had some large customers with which it had EDI already in place, but as time went by, its business grew substantially in other markets, particularly in the emerging markets of Asia-Pacific, Eastern Europe and the Middle East. Suddenly a whole bunch of customers had no ability to do business in an electronic fashion, so Intel had to move to the web.

Second, Intel found that its direct customer base was increasing, in part due to the fact that the number of its products was growing. As the complexity of running that business was mounting, so were the potential costs. The signs for Intel were clear – it had to become more productive and more efficient, and that meant moving into networked or electronic business.

Third, information exchange is very important in Intel's relationship with its customers. The latter need lots of technical information about Intel's 'very technical' products. There is also a great deal of information to be exchanged with distributors on various marketing and sales programs. One element of this is confidential information. Intel gives its customers advance technical information on products that the company does not want to be generally available. In return, customers give Intel information on their future plans and consumption forecasts, and they don't want this to fall into the hands of their competitors. In the past there were some fairly complex processes to manage this confidential exchange, which the web showed to be inefficient.

This has also had an internal impact on Intel. The company had to refocus its people to go through this new process. Intel thought customers would be au fait with the technology of the web, but what it actually found was a wide spectrum of knowledge variation, ranging from people who seemed to be naturals to others who had never used a browser to someone who had never turned on a PC before. Intel had to direct resources to train its customers' employees not just on computers but on how to surf the web.

The other issue that surfaced was to what degree a company exposes its internal business processes to the customer. Ian Wilson advised: 'What you need to make sure is you've packaged that in the right way and that it's usable to them.'

Total planning and exact budgets are not the order of the day. Intel went into this program 'with no exact ROI [return on investment] sketched out', declares Wilson. 'You know, we went into this almost as an act of faith. I'm not sure any ROI analysis would have had any validity because no one knew.'

Now from Intel's corporate website you can access a site for each European country. Intel also offers an Intel Web Outfitter Service for customers who have bought a Pentium III processor-based system. The service allows them to register for participation in this program and they will get web content specially tailored to get the benefits from Pentium III processor-based systems. To learn and to benefit from learning, calculated risks must be taken.

Clearly, you can also learn from risks already taken by others. 'Do not build the externally facing networked business system without also building and integrating all your internal systems,' recommends Wilson. 'The information flows internally and then needs to flow outside. What we actually did was a curious thing. We built the external pipeline first, and then we had to go back and kind of retrofit what we do internally so it could work. We are also building a parallel system that works with our suppliers.' You can learn only so much from the risks of others, however. In your niche business, you will need to take your own risks to learn more about how you can be more profitable.

❝in your niche business, you will need to take your own risks ❞

The internet infrastructure in Europe still has a long way to go to develop and reach the level of maturity of that in the US. 'For example, if you were to put up websites in the UK to be accessed by Italian customers, you look at the route traffic will take, it will in fact often go to the US and back again,' says Wilson. In the US, the infrastructure is homogeneous and the traffic flow is much better. The problem in Europe is we have a history of individual national telephone companies having a monopoly in each country. 'The situation gets particularly worse when you look at Eastern Europe. Take Poland, for example: any traffic that goes out of Poland to anywhere will generally go to the US first.' The situation is undoubtedly changing, but there is still a long way to go.

PRINCIPLE IN ACTION

Intel goes networked business

INTEL HAS ALREADY GONE A LONG WAY.[11] It is arguably the most technologically advanced enterprise in the world. It is the leading manufacturer of complex semiconductor products and technologies, and has been a driving force behind the ascendance of the PC platform. Its fabrication plants, which employ cutting-edge manufacturing techniques, cost billions of dollars each to build.

So what technology has Intel relied on to handle orders from its thousands of customers, distributors and business partners worldwide? For the most part, surprisingly, telephone and fax. A number of departments launched niche electronic order-handling programs during 1997. All of a sudden, Intel had gone from having no networked business system to having too many.

Clearly a solution was needed – not only to avoid the tangle of incompatible networked business systems inside the company but also to take advantage of the time and cost savings of electronic communication. 'We believe that both service and efficiency can be improved by transitioning existing business from the phone and fax to the web,' says

Sandra Morris, Director of Intel's Internet Marketing and E-Commerce. 'The web is a powerful new tool that can help us expand our market reach and strengthen our customer relationships.'

Indeed, one of the primary goals of the networked business initiative was to enhance Intel's competitive advantage by giving its customers better tools for managing transactions and data. At the same time, Intel expected web-based order handling to deliver tangible benefits closer to home. Rapid order-fulfillment, lower overhead costs, and a stream-lined process all offered significant promise.

increasing operating efficiencies

One thing was certain: Intel needed to craft a solution that could work with a broad range of customers. The companies that would be using the ordering system were dispersed all over the world and ranged in size from $10 million a year to as much as $10 billion a year. However, many of the larger customers already used established EDI systems. With these issues in mind, Intel focussed on its medium-sized customers, the majority of which operated outside the US. There was one benefit: these offshore customers were less likely to be effectively serviced by Intel's direct sales force, making the web-based order handling a valuable outreach tool.

❝first, Intel focussed on automating its order management system❞

First, Intel focussed on automating its order management system. Web-based order management made doing business with Intel easier and for customers involved in the pilot deployment, it had a compelling and immediate benefit.

The step was adding value to the web commerce link. The company began delivering personalized information to its customers throughout the organization, including management, procurement, engineering and marketing. Automated order handling and delivery also enabled Intel and its customers to allocate their resources to less repetitive tasks.

Of course, the new networked business system was designed to work within existing constraints. It had to hew to standard web technologies while remaining compatible with Intel's existing systems and ERP applications. To avoid show-stopping disconnects, Intel's IT group followed a strict policy of standardization to reduce costs and avoid complexity. Intel purchased its Pentium II processor-based servers from a single vendor, specified a single operating system, and limited the number of database and development tools used in the project.

At the same time, the IT group built in as much flexibility and forward-looking scalability as plans would allow. The ability to grow the networked business system was critical, for example, since it needed to be deployed throughout the organization. At the same time, issues of security and uptime were both paramount, since a breakdown in the system would lead to painful disruptions in service. Intel adopted strong 128-bit encryption for all transactions, a decision that required additional effort and planning since US law prohibits the export of such encryption technology. To ensure always-on service, Intel installed site level backups and established mirrored servers at alternate locations off-site.

going live, worldwide

Intel's pilot deployment went live with about 100 medium-sized original equipment manufacturers (OEMs) and distributors in about 30 countries. More than 65 percent of the networked business accounts operated outside the US, immediately reaping cost savings through reduced international phone and fax calls. The customer response to the program was immediate. Intel had set a 90-day deadline for transitioning revenue to the web, but that goal was met within just 15 days.

Thorough planning by Intel's worldwide team helped enable successful networked business deployment. While many of the benefits of a web-based e-commerce system are obvious, the challenges in delivering such a service take a lot of planning and foresight. In Intel's case, some key initiatives helped make the program a success.

focus on the customer

Intel designed its networked business system around what its customers told it they wanted. The pilot deployment focussed more on customers' needs than on Intel's short-term goals.

anticipate change

Intel approached the networked business project in much the way its processor groups handle product development – through a continuous, iterative cycle of improvement. Intel took advantage of the internet's ability to generate feedback, allowing the company to see what was getting used, receive feedback, and revise its plans and goals to suit.

test connectivity

When you are doing business in more than 30 countries, you can't assume much. Intel made sure to test the performance and reliability of customer web communications in a real production environment.

deliver personalized content

Clearly, posting cookie-cutter content was not going to do it for businesses used to personalized, point-to-point service from Intel. Therefore the networked business program had to deliver accurate, current and appropriate information for each customer.

automate authorization

Security was paramount, but a labor-intensive system for managing passwords and authorizations would limit the system's ability to scale. Intel adopted an automated process to manage passwords and entitlement to the encrypted system, enabling the company to quickly authorize customers to make use of the system.

The most valuable lesson learned from Intel's networked business deployment? The need to balance costs and risks. Creating an intelligent system that handles the tasks once performed by people is expensive, but the investment was critical if Intel was to continue to deliver lasting value to its customers.

'We were fortunate in that we were immediately successful,' says Sandra Morris. 'Many people saw the networked business deployment as a short-term win. But this kind of project should be viewed as a long-term business investment.'

Building a networked business and an ecosystem is a long-term investment. We chose Intel because it is a relatively new network organization, compared with BT. Intel has wired itself as a networked business and has hooked up all its suppliers and customers into its ecosytem. It is now ready to exploit the opportunities that will present themselves as more networked businesses migrate to their ecosystems.

EXECUTIVE SUMMARY OF
PRINCIPLE 4

WHAT THE CASE STUDIES SHOW is that network organizations need to deliver and serve internet-enabled global communications to their customers in a simple and efficient way. Markets, businesses and customers in emerging markets, who were unable to do business electronically until the arrival of the internet, are now clamoring for goods, services and information. The network organizations are compelled to train both customers and employees to go through the process. In this manner, these organizations are gaining competitive advantage by giving their customers and employees better tools for managing transactions and data.

▶ Principle 4, network evaluation, is in essence about your company's communications infrastructure. All the computing power and data in the world is meaningless without a reliable and secure form of connection to the internet and to all the areas of the company that will be involved with it.

▶ All users know the frustration of waiting for data to download through the telephone line to their PCs. Online delays in e-commerce are unacceptable because the customer will go elsewhere at a click of the mouse.

▶ Mobility is a service anywhere, anytime, any device. Bluetooth essentially allows devices to talk to each other. When offered as part of an integrated service, it will allow your device to tell you just about everything.

▶ As the complexity of running your business mounts, so will the potential costs. As your competitors become more productive and efficient, you will be compelled to move your organization on to networked or electronic business.

▶ The web is an ideal medium for better customer service, technical information exchange and confidential information between and among all customers, employees, shareholders and business partners.

▶ Do not build the externally facing networked business system without also building and integrating all your internal systems. The information flows internally and then needs to flow outside.

▶ Planning exact budgets is not always the order of the day. You may have to go into certain areas of a networked business program with no exact return on investment sketched out. You may need to take many small risks; you may need to exercise many acts of faith.

▶ You can't have a strategy in isolation. Remember, this is an ecosystem. Though you may have to take risks, you can also learn from risks already taken by others. One very important lesson is not to build the externally facing networked business system without also building and integrating all your internal systems.

NOTES

1 'The Water Cycle', **Eyewitness Guides Ecology**, Steve Pollock, Dorling Kindersley Ltd, 1993, p. 16.

2 Brittanica\BCD\Cache_15_ArticleRil.htm\Airports:Modern Airports:Air Traffic Control

3 British Telecommunications plc (BT), http:/www.bt.com, http:www.Ecommerce.bt.com

4 Interview with Tony Fish of BT Mergers & Acquisitions on December 6, 1999.

5 **Long Distance Transmission: Is the much-heralded price crash in transmission upon us?** Maria Cristina Fiocchi and Steve Hodson, consultants with Intercai Mondiale Ltd, Marlow, Bucks., p. 1.

6 http:/www.bluetooth.com

7 http:/www.concert.com and http:/www.bt.com/news

8 **Long Distance Transmission**, p. 3.

9 http:/www.intel.com and Intel Investor Fact Sheet 1999

10 Interview with Ian Wilson, Director of E-Business & IT, EMEA, on January 13, 2000.

11 Case study – Intel goes networked business.

PRINCIPLE 5

SECURITY

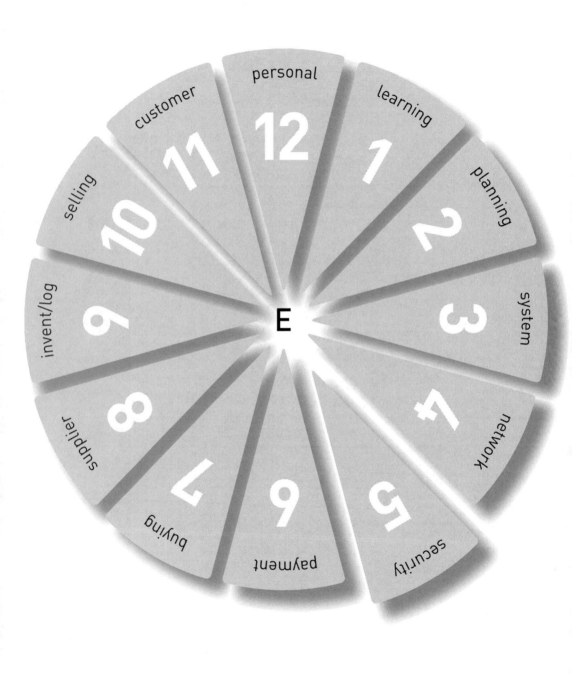

STATEMENT OF **PRINCIPLE 5**

THE HARRIS HAWK IS A TOP PREDATOR in the desert ecosystem of North America. Seeking a diet consisting mainly of reptiles, which may be thin on the ground, each individual needs a vast area as its hunting ground. An animal that eats reptiles must deal with a dinner that tends to be muscular and well equipped with teeth or fangs. The Harris hawk has powerful talons to grip its squirming prey, and long legs with protective scales to keep its body out of harm's way.[1]

The human equivalent of the Harris hawk is the hacker. The internet was designed for openness, yet security has to be bolted on to it. This principle provides comfort to organizations and their supply webs that their information is not open to abuse, and comfort to their customers that their personal details are not open to abuse by the company or a third party.

While our forefathers relied upon a wax seal to ensure confidentiality of a document in transit, so technology offers us the security we need with electronic data transfer. There are several types of security solutions, including the Public and Private Key Infrastructure (PKI) and non-repudiation software. Passwords, verifications and digital certificates provide various layers of security that are increasingly difficult but not impossible to breach. Nevertheless, all are security issues and must be addressed.

What one has to bear in mind at all times is that, just as in the natural ecosystem, there is no such thing as total security. There are several perspectives on security. One aspect is that because it is based on fear and emotion, it can cloud clarity on the issue. Is it a real security issue or is it a perceived security issue? There is a strong argument that an individual's perceived insecurity of the internet is more magnified than the real insecurity of the internet itself. Another aspect is that you cannot eliminate all risk in life. To take no risk at all is the greatest risk.

Let's look at our living example. One third of BAA employees work in security, mainly screening passengers and hand baggage after they've checked in, before the air-side departure lounge. Behind the scenes, BAA has installed systems to screen hold baggage for all international departing passengers at UK airports, at a cost of more than £175 million. Security is more than just meeting international regulation standards, it is a whole process of managing and monitoring performance. Apart from the visible passenger security, there are aspects of external security. The land-side and air-side boundary restricts movement to those with authorization both in the terminal on the access roads to the airfield roads, as well as security in the terminal and other operational areas to be managed. BAA works with airport police to maintain perimeter security.[2]

"without security, travelers would have no confidence in air travel"

Without security, travelers would have no confidence in air travel. Whether real or imagined, fears of terrorist attacks and bombs are bad for the travel business. The same applies on the internet. Without security, there is no e-commerce or any commerce at all.

The Head of IT would own this principle too and would share his influence with the Project Manager, Sales Director, Marketing Director and Finance Director.

The following case studies give you a flavor of what is happening in the leading security organizations and the transformations they promise to deliver.

SUPPLIER PROFILE

JCP/Trustbase Ltd – Sun Microsystems

enabling trusted e-commerce

THE REVOLUTION THAT JCP PROMISES in its security products was so compelling that just as we were in the process of interviewing its chief executive, Sun Microsystems was negotiating to buy the company. The interview with the chief executive was abandoned because of a non-disclosure agreement he had signed hours before.

JCP[3] is a leading provider of public key-based transactional software for financial services institutions and corporations looking to offer products and services online. JCP provides products that allow organizations to implement policy, manage access and reduce the risks online. JCP Computer Services is a wholly owned subsidiary of Trustbase Ltd.

John Paleomylites, chief executive, founded JCP in 1994. Among its illustrious clients are Barclays Bank, Deutsche Bank, UBS, BT and Sun Microsystems. Early in 2000 Sun Microsystems[4] acquired Trustbase Ltd and with it JCP, whose technology will be integrated with iPlanet Ecommerce Solutions, a Sun-Netscape alliance, offering financial institutions to one of the most complete and secure business-to-business infrastructure solutions available. In order to provide a comprehensive e-commerce solution for the net economy, America Online (AOL) and Sun Microsystems established iPlanet Ecommerce Solutions in March 1999.

JCP's technology is already being developed as part of the product offering from Identrus, a private company backed by some of the world's leading financial institutions, which we feature in the case study later. Identrus has a charter to establish the standards for and operate a global infrastructure that will accelerate high value trading between corporate customers and conclusively identify online trading partners for business-to-business transactions. The Identrus system, in addition to supporting all internet commerce authentication requirements, will potentially facilitate new corporate internet banking services such as electronic funds transfer and payment, bill presentation and payment, online procurement, cash management services and others.

> **❝Identrus has a charter to establish the standards for and operate a global infrastructure❞**

'A critical need for the development of business-to-business e-commerce is the role of the financial institutions as trusted third parties for secure transactions,' said Kristin Kupres, Chief Operating and Technology Officer for Identrus. 'The iPlanet solution will ultimately help to position financial institutions as e-commerce intermediaries, effectively removing the barriers to business-to-business e-commerce.'

The 'Trustbase' product set delivers new revenue streams and protects existing revenues by providing identity services, which reduce the risk involved in delivering financial services products online. Trustbase is available in two versions targetted at distinct communities.

1   for *financial institutions* and other organizations looking to provide a commercial authorization service, JCP offers the Trustbase Transaction Manager. This provides the infrastructure to support identity-based services, payment and insurance products, and

financing products such as invoice discounting and provision of online loan facilities. Trustbase Transaction Manager is used to run commercial services, which include identity services, information services such as address checking and credit scoring, and payment and credit products such as factoring and online loans.

2 For *corporations* looking to use entitlement services to deliver business applications online, JCP provides the Trustbase Entitlements Manager. This interoperates with web and application servers, repositories and legacy systems to manage access to business products and services, based on pre-defined policy. The manager provides a centralized console for all entitlements management. Trustbase Entitlements Manager is used with a range of applications, including online procurement systems, online catalog systems, stock control, sales order processing, cash management applications, and online broking systems.

The decision-making processes that support transactions are well established in the real world. They involve services, guarantees and facilities from a number of organizations, such as banks and credit reference agencies. However, off-line services do not fit in an automated buying and selling process. Yet these services are required to move online and be authorized in real time to electronic trading.

❝a fundamental part of managing risk is the creation of evidence❞

JCP provides software that enables organizations doing business in real time to better manage the risks that they undertake by allowing them to bring the real-world decision-making processes online. Trustbase manages entitlements based on an underlying security infrastructure.

Trustbase uses a repository of information about users, the roles to which they are assigned, and the rights assigned to those roles to take decisions about the conditions required to access business services – a customer's entitlement. Trustbase uses information about the method of user authentication, the types of transaction or service requested, and the liability or cover that will be provided by third-party financial institutions to take decisions on allowing access to business applications and placing conditions on that access.

A fundamental part of managing risk is the creation of evidence, which can be used to resolve disputes where they occur. Without the paper trail created in the real world, legal recourse online can be impossible. Trustbase provides non-repudiation services that create complete and signed digital receipts for commercial online transactions. By non-repudiation we mean a method that determines who you are and what you have done by showing evidence that cannot be challenged, denied or rejected.

PRINCIPLE IN ACTION

Identrus

A DOZEN GLOBAL FINANCIAL INSTITUTIONS came together and created Identrus LLC (Limited Liability Corporation)[5] to facilitate the growth of business-to-business e-commerce. The concept is not different to Visa and Mastercard. The institutional partners of Identrus are ABN AMRO, Bank of America, Barclays Bank, CIBC, Chase Manhattan, Citigroup, Commerzbank, Deutsche Bank, Dresdner Bank, HSBC, Industrial Bank of Japan, NatWest, Sanwa Bank, Scotia Bank and Wells Fargo.

Identrus is the first organization to establish the necessary components, both technological and operational, to enable companies worldwide to address trust and risk barriers that have until now impeded the wide adoption of e-commerce as a means of facilitating sophisticated global business transactions.

It has achieved this elusive goal by leveraging the unique positions of its participants as the traditional agents for commercial collaboration to add a legal and business framework to traditional PKI.

The Identrus solution is designed to:

▶ enable legally enforceable e-commerce transactions within a framework where all the participants can manage risk

▶ establish a uniform global system of participating rules and operating procedures that will bind both sides of any transaction (signing and relying)

▶ provide a well-defined dispute resolution process and recourse mechanism.

Identrus will facilitate the growth of e-commerce because it will issue electronic identities or certificates to its corporate customers. These new identities are the electronic equivalent of an identity card, like a passport or driver's license, and will enable customers to engage in business transactions with full confidence. One of the critical capabilities of Identrus is that it will also validate identities in real time.

The way in which Identrus will create a means for non-repudiation is that businesses will be issued with digital signatures via the Identrus network and these signatures are binding. The digital signatures are part of the digital certificate and attest to the recipient of a digitally signed communication that the sender's identity is authentic. In a typical transaction, a 'seller' might ask its financial institution to validate the digital signature and certificate of a 'buyer'. The seller's financial institution would confirm with the buyer's, and as members are certified, the financial institution will stand behind its certificate. Last but not least, as the financial institutions are regulated, local government and police authorities will also preserve their existing jurisdiction to enforce agreements between contracting parties.

❝financial institutions are the ideal providers of identification and identity risk management in the virtual world❞

Financial institutions are the ideal providers of identification and identity risk management in the virtual world. They have the experience, the infrastructure and the resources needed to facilitate global business-to-business e-commerce. They have the tradition of bridging the 'trust gap' between trading partners. They provide corporations with purchasing cards, payroll services, letters of credit and other products and services that require authorization, authentication and certification. With Identrus, financial institutions will be extending these time-honored banking practices to the internet.

The Identrus system is closed to the extent that only parties that have agreed to abide by the system's rules and regulations will be allowed to participate. However, Identrus is committed to using open standards and full interoperability to make it easy for new vendors.

Finally, on the subject of smart cards, Identrus will foster the deployment of smart cards as the principal storage devices for users' electronic identities. Smart cards are more secure than the hard drives on personal computers. They also enable users to participate in e-commerce regardless of their location or whose personal computer they are using at the time.

Why did we choose JCP/Sun Microsystems? Here we have a cutting-edge technology security company that is not only rewriting security on the internet but changing the way organizations do business with each other and with customers. Its products are creating financial ecosystems, from which it will derive future income streams.

SUPPLIER PROFILE

RSA Security

the most trusted name in e-security

TRUST AND IDENTITY VERIFICATION are cornerstones of security. RSA Security[6] is the leading organization in the field of security on the internet.

RSA Security helps organizations build secure, trusted foundations for networked business through its RSA SecurID two-factor authentication, RSA BSAFE encryption, and RSA Keon public key management systems. With more than half a billion RSA BSAFE-enabled applications in use worldwide, more than 6 million RSA SecurID users, and almost 20 years of industry experience, RSA Security has proven leadership and innovative technology to address changing security needs of networked business and to bring trust to the new online economy.

A truly global company with 7,000 customers, RSA Security is renowned for providing technologies that help organizations conduct networked business with confidence. The company's RSA SecurID enterprise authentication products are protecting information in the majority of the Fortune 100 companies today. Leading e-commerce businesses, including securities trading and banking applications, also use these products to protect against external attack and fraudulent activity. The company's RSA BSAFE line of encryption-based security technologies is embedded in more than 600 million copies of today's most successful internet applications, including web browsers, commerce servers, e-mail systems and virtual private network products. The majority of all-secure electronic commerce and communication on the internet today is conducted using RSA Security technologies. Both RSA SecurID and RSA BSAFE are considered *de facto* standards worldwide.

RSA Security now offers its customers the RSA Keon family of PKI products, a solution for enabling, managing and simplifying the public key authentication and encryption security in today's leading e-mail, web browser, web server and VPN applications. RSA Keon is the first product to combine the expertise of the entire company, from public key technology to large systems scalability and management.

❝RSA Keon is the first product to combine the expertise of the entire company ❞

Headquartered in Bedford, Massachusetts, with offices in 45 countries, RSA Security is a public company with annual revenues in excess of $200 million. Its customers span a wide range of industries, including an extensive presence in e-commerce, banking, government, telecommunications, aerospace, university and healthcare arenas. Today more than 7 million users across 7,000 organizations, including more than 60 percent of the Fortune 100, use RSA SecurID authentication products to protect corporate data. And more than 800 companies embed RSA BSAFE software in 1,000 applications, with a combined distribution of over 600 million units worldwide.

RSA Security has built its business through its commitment to interoperability. Today, the company has strategic relationships with more than 500 industry-leading companies, including 3Com, AOL, Apple, Ascend, AT&T, Nortel, Cisco, Compaq, IBM, Oracle, Microsoft, Novell and Intel, and these companies are delivering integrated RSA Security technology in more than 1,000 products.

INTERVIEW WITH SUPPLIER

'The nirvana of networked business is being able to deal securely with anybody in the world and having a trusted relationship.'

Mike Awford, UK Alliance Manager

'INTEROPERABILITY' AND 'STRATEGIC RELATIONSHIPS' have delivered market dominance and opportunities for increased revenue to RSA Security. These same two factors will drive networked business forward for all. Networked business presents enormous opportunities for companies to develop new revenue, provide added value to customers, streamline processes, and reduce costs to gain competitive advantage. However, according to Mike Awford, 'security, or lack of it, is the one recurrent barrier hindering wider adoption of e-commerce'.[7]

'Security holds the key to enabling networked business to reach its potential,' says Awford. However, he emphasizes that 'e-security is not about static, reusable passwords, which can be easily compromised. Rather, it is about strong user authentication, powerful encryption and innovative public key infrastructure. These solutions provide networked business with those essential elements that together form the basis of trust in traditional business transactions – authentication, confidentiality and non-repudiation [proof of origin, submission or receipt]. RSA operates in all three of these areas.'

Awford uses an example of an everyday situation to explain *authentication*. Strong, two-factor authentication is much stronger than passwords, which are easily stolen or hacked. Just as use of a bank's ATM machine requires something you have (your card) together with something you know (a personal identification number, or PIN), RSA offers a product called RSA SecurID that works on the same principle. You use your PIN and what we call a token or authenticator to authenticate yourself to a website or company network before being granted access. A token is something like a special key fob or credit-card-sized device that generates a random number which changes every 60 seconds. By entering that number together with a PIN, you gain access by showing that you are who you say you are, and that you are also holding the token, while unauthorized users are blocked.

While there are more than 7 million users of RSA SecurID authentication, the company actually started out as a provider of *encryption* tools to protect the confidentiality of electronic communications. Corporate and commercial software developers, to reliably incorporate security into a wide variety of applications, use the RSA BSAFE family of crypto-security development tools. It is embedded in 1,000 applications. Encryption technology is used to secure applications for e-commerce and services over the internet and intranets, enterprise security, entertainment, wireless communications, delivery of digital information over cable, and other uses.

> **"**encryption technology is used to secure applications
> for e-commerce and services over the internet **"**

Most recently, RSA Security has been addressing applications such as the need for non-repudiation in networked business. This is one of many applications that are possible through PKI. A PKI provides an online environment for establishing trustworthy identities and manages the related encryption keys that form the basis for these identities. Others include, for example, the ability to positively identify the sender of a purchase order before processing, to verify the integrity of the data in networked business applications, to use digital signatures to ensure the enforceability of contracts and encrypt confidential communications so that only the intended recipients can access them. In other words, PKI is the common foundation that serves a wide range of networked business needs.

'There are a number of companies selling PKI today, but it is not enough to be just a PKI vendor or a certificate authority' warns Awford. 'By contrast, an e-security company combines those three elements that we have discussed – encryption, authentication and PKI – to tie it all together and have an architecture of trust that we can extend right the way across the companies in this marketplace.'

Awford also advises companies 'not to get sold down a route that is proprietary. Leave your options open because standards are still evolving in this marketplace.'

PRINCIPLE IN ACTION

Beth Israel Deaconess Medical Center

THE THREE ELEMENTS – encryption, authentication and PKI – together form the key to enable networked business to work seamlessly.

When Boston's Beth Israel and Deaconess Hospitals merged, they soon realized that they needed a way to offer doctors quick, easy access to medical records from both hospitals. They came up with the notion of 'CareWeb,' an intranet providing a consolidated view of the individual systems of the merged hospitals.[8]

Before CareWeb, if doctors at one hospital needed information from another hospital, they had to wait for the information to be faxed or read to them over the phone, a process that could take hours rather than the few seconds CareWeb would use. The easier access to patient records provided by CareWeb could not only save time, it could save patients' lives.

'The problem with creating an intranet, however,' said Dr John Halamka, Executive Director, CareGroup Center for Quality and Value, 'is that the public perceived that the internet was a very bad place to store medical records. The hospital administration was wary of a headline in the local newspaper: "CareWeb Reveals Sensitive Patient Records".'

The hospital needed a network it could guarantee would be safe from break-ins. Without an airtight security solution, the project would never have got off the ground. 'We were charged with finding the best technologies – the best-of-breed – and putting them together to create a single, secure system,' said Dr Halamka.

❝the hospital needed a network it could guarantee would be safe from break-ins❞

In its quest to get it right, the hospital turned to RSA Security Inc. To ensure that only the right people were gaining access to CareWeb, the hospital supercharged user authentication by providing RSA SecurID tokens to appropriate personnel.

'We guarantee the authenticity of a user by using RSA SecurID hardware tokens,' said Dr Halamka. 'A doctor must be in possession of a hardware device in order to access pages containing patient data.' These tokens are small, hand-held, credit card-sized devices with [LCDs liquid crystal displays], containing microprocessors that calculate and display unpredictable codes. These codes change at a specified interval, typically 60 seconds.

'Our implementation requires that each user accessing CareWeb begins a session by entering a user name, a memorized PIN and the currently displayed pass-code from the RSA SecurID token.' The algorithm that the RSA SecurID token uses to generate this pass-code is synchronized with RSA's security engine, known as RSA ACE/Server. The RSA ACE/Server verifies the pass-code for a particular 60-second period when a user enters it, along with his/her PIN, to access CareWeb. Once a password is verified, the user is authenticated for the duration of the web session, or 15 minutes, whichever is less. This 'two-factor authentication' that combines a PIN with a one-time pass-code makes it virtually impossible for a hacker to access the system. Furthermore, if a token is lost or stolen, it can be immediately deactivated for the entire enterprise by disabling it at the RSA ACE/Server.

'Because the password on the token changes every minute,' said Dr Halamka, 'it makes the whole system much more secure than one which uses static passwords. Healthcare providers occasionally share user names or passwords or write them down near the computer terminal. Such practices defeat the authentication, access controls and audit trails offered by unique user names and passwords. By requiring that log-on be paired with physical possession of hardware tokens, authen tication is substantially strengthened.'

Furthermore, the data sent back and forth from the server is all encrypted using RSA's public key encryption. CareWeb deploys full-strength RSA encryption technology for data exchange, making it impossible for the information to be compromised as it is traveling over the internet. This prevents a hacker 'listening' to the data line and tapping into private information.

Although newspaper articles highlight the threat of computer break-ins by hackers from outside the organization, inappropriate healthcare data access from inside the organization is even more common. Normal human curiosity leads individuals not involved in a patient's care to look up the records of VIPs, celebrities and fellow employees. So that authenticated users are to be held accountable for actions taken while using CareWeb, retrievable audit trails have been set up that log all accesses to information. These logs include time, date, information accessed and user ID. These audit trails are available for patient review on demand.

Why did we choose RSA Security? It is the largest and most recognized brand in the technology security business. It offers organizations the full spectrum of security, which includes encryption, authentication and public key infrastructure. Because it has grown over the past 20 years and acquired other organizations, it already has an ecosystem of its own and is connected to all its client ecosystems. By virtue of the trust and security element of its technology, RSA has a much closer relationship to its client ecosystems.

EXECUTIVE SUMMARY OF
PRINCIPLE 5

MANY PEOPLE THINK THEY UNDERSTAND security, but this is a very different world. You need to understand what it is that needs protection. These two case studies show us in no uncertain terms that without security, there is no trust, and without trust, there is no business. Too little security and you risk losing your business; too much security and you risk losing your customers.

▶ Principle 5, security, is in essence about defending the assets and information of your organization's stakeholders. The internet was designed for openness, yet security has to be bolted on to it.

▶ Just as in the natural ecosystem, there is no such thing as total security; in life you cannot eliminate all risk. To take no risk at all is the greatest risk. Also, you need to differentiate between a real security issue and a perceived one.

▶ A fundamental part of managing risk is the creation of evidence, which can be used to resolve disputes where they occur. Without the paper trail created in the real world, legal recourse online can be impossible. Non-repudiation services create complete and signed digital receipts for commercial online transactions.

► Financial institutions are the ideal providers of identification and identity risk management in the virtual world. They have the experience, the infrastructure and the resources needed to facilitate global business-to-business e-commerce.

► Smart cards are more secure than the hard drives on personal computers. Smart cards also enable users to participate in e-commerce regardless of their location or whose personal computer they are using at the time.

► Just as use of a bank's ATM machine requires something you have (your card) together with something you know (a PIN), strong, two-factor authentication works on the same principle. It is also much stronger than passwords, which are easily stolen or hacked.

► Encryption tools protect the confidentiality of electronic communications. Encryption technology is used to secure applications for e-commerce and services over the internet and intranets, enterprise security, entertainment, wireless communications, delivery of digital information over cable, and other uses.

► The need for non-repudiation in networked business is possible through a technology known as public key infrastructure. A PKI provides an online environment for establishing trustworthy identities, and manages the related encryption keys, which form the basis for these identities.

► You can't have a strategy in isolation. Remember, this is an ecosystem. An e-security company combines the three elements that we have discussed – encryption, authentication and PKI – to tie it all together and have an architecture of trust. Do not go down a route that is proprietary. Leave your options open because standards are still evolving in this marketplace.

NOTES

1   'Surviving in Arid Lands,' **Eyewitness Guides Ecology**, Steve Pollock, Dorling Kindersley Ltd, 1993, p. 41.

2   BAA Heathrow, airport information, facts and figures, http:/www.baa.co.uk/domino/baa/baanet

3   JCP/Trustbase Ltd – http:/www.jcp.co.uk

4   Sun Microsystems – http:/www.sun.co.uk

5   At http:/www.identrus.com, under 'application development', Identrus presents Sun Microsystems's JCP's Trustbase as a best-of-category product showcase.

6   http:/www.rsasecurity.com

7   Interview with Mike Awford, UK Alliance Manager on January 21, 2000.

8   Case study – Beth Israel Deaconess Medical Center.

PART 3

B2B
(BUSINESS TO BUSINESS)

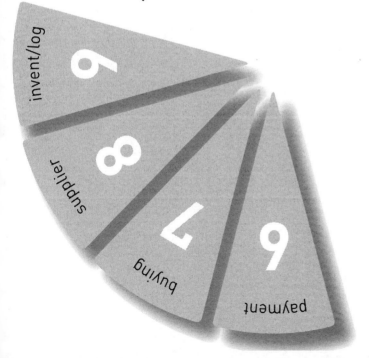

PRINCIPLE 6

INTERNET PAYMENTS

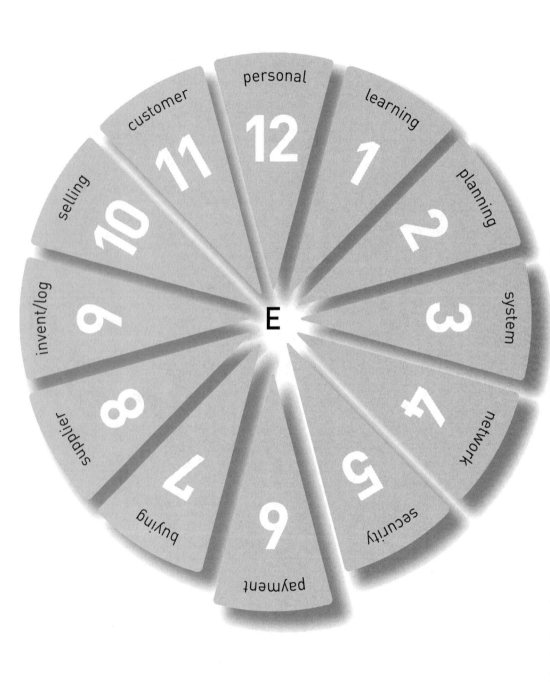

STATEMENT OF **PRINCIPLE 6**

THE SOILS ON WHICH PLANTS DEPEND are created by the interaction of living and non-living parts of the environment. Their composition is influenced by five main factors: climate and weather; geology – the underlying rocks; topography – is the land sloping or near a river; the action of living things, including humans, and time.[1] Similarly, in commerce there are many factors that influence how fertile trade will be. They include economic and political climate; all types of infrastructure; availability of talent and skills; the regional culture, and time. Payment is the conduit that weaves through all the above.

Principle 6 focuses on payments. An organization needs to choose the type of process it would like to use in order to receive payments from its customers and to remit payments to its direct or indirect suppliers. Direct suppliers are those that supply core materials to the company and indirect suppliers supply ancillary materials such as office supplies. The process will vary depending on whether the company is in a business-to-business environment with monthly accounts or whether it is in a business-to-consumer market where payment is needed before delivery, and also by the size of the transaction undertaken.

Returning to our living business example at Heathrow, leading airlines are attempting to lure customers to purchase and pay for their tickets online. Market forecasters expect travel to be the biggest-selling item over the internet between 2000 and 2005 and airline tickets could account for 60 per cent of these purchases.

British Airways (BA) is planning to invest £90 million during the two financial years from April 2000 to develop its e-commerce operations. Its aim is to increase the share of the tickets sold over the internet from less than 1 percent in 2000 to 50 per cent by March 2004. Online BA ticket sales, from all sources, currently amount to £45 million a year and this figure is expected to rise to £700 million in the next three years. Simon Harford, Head of E-Business at BA, says: 'A $5,000 ticket would currently have distribution costs of 18 percent or $900. For an online stockbroker such as Charles Schwab, a $5,000 trade has costs of $29 or 0.6 percent. This is the order of magnitude that can be achieved.'[2]

"airlines want their customers to pay for tickets through the internet because it reduces distribution costs significantly"

Airlines want their customers to pay for tickets through the internet because it reduces distribution costs significantly. This will impact on every sector, every industry, and every business. The internet has and will continue to disintermediate old distribution channels and then reintermediate new ones. In undertaking this venture, an organization needs courage, energy and vision, but also needs to manage risk. This, together with the pooling of financial resources, perhaps explains why organizations are falling over themselves to merge and acquire each other.

The Finance Director and Head of IT own this principle. Sales and Marketing Directors need authority to ensure that consideration is optimal for their customers and the Purchasing Director also needs some authority in this area to ensure that consideration is optimal for suppliers.

While new forms of payment will emerge all the time, there are currently other forms or processes for internet payments:

▶ electronic data interchange over the web

▶ credit cards and secure electronic transactions

▶ e-wallets

▶ micropayments

▶ payment by mobile phone.

The following case studies give you a flavor of what is happening in the topsoil and subsoil of the 'internet payment' ecosystems.

SUPPLIER PROFILE

Sterling Commerce

leading provider of e-commerce solutions

IMAGINE YOU ARE A FARMER, with hundreds of acres of arable land that needs to be tilled. To save you time, money and seasons – and ultimately your business – an organization offers to till your land with its monster tilling machine. In the real world, that organization would be Sterling Commerce.[3]

Sterling Commerce, based in Dallas, Texas, was established in 1974 and in 1998, with 2,500 employees in 37 offices globally, generated net revenues of $500 million. Sterling Commerce is a worldwide leader in providing networked business integration solutions for the global 5000 and their commerce communities. It is one of the 40 companies included in the Dow Jones Internet Services Index and one of the 100 companies included in the USA Today Internet 100 Stock Index. The company provides solutions to address e-business process integration, e-community management, networked business communication infrastructure, and e-sourcing.

Sterling Commerce's 'e-commerce solutions' squarely address the most important issues companies face as they make the transition to an internet-driven economy. These include how to build and manage global commerce communities, how to better integrate their business processes, and how to achieve greater competitiveness through new sales channels, improved productivity and enhanced responsiveness to customers.

The company meets these goals by focussing on four key services: community management, business process integration, e-commerce infrastructure, and outsourcing.

Community management: This service makes it possible for hundreds of thousands of companies to participate in e-commerce. For example, how does a company accommodate a barrage of new e-partners? Who sets the ground rules and manages the relationships? Sterling Commerce facilitates the flow of information among virtually all members of an e-community, prompting efficiency at unprecedented levels.

❝how does a company accommodate a barrage of new e-partners?❞

Business process integration: Another critical decision companies face is how to automate and manage the flow of information among disparate business systems within the four walls of the enterprise and across the value chain.

E-commerce infrastructure: As companies use the internet to extend their commerce communities to additional customers, suppliers, consumers and banks, they discover a growing number of applications that must work together and ever-increasing volumes of critical information to be moved and managed. To do this effectively, companies need a robust, secure and flexible e-commerce infrastructure.

Outsourcing: Enterprises are increasingly opting to focus on core competencies and turning to experts to manage their e-commerce initiatives. In response to this need, Sterling Commerce offers the industry's broadest set of options for companies of all sizes to outsource e-commerce initiatives.

By focussing on these four key services, Sterling Commerce helps its customers to make the transition to the internet-driven economy.

INTERVIEW WITH SUPPLIER

'The internet is a revolution to consumers but it's an evolution to businesses.'

Dave Bruce, Director, Northern Europe

WHAT IS THE SKILL IN MAKING the transition to the internet-driven economy? Dave Bruce[4] believes that what comes into a company, how it's processed inside and what comes out should be seamless. 'The skill is in bringing the various trading communities together,' he says. What people tend to overlook is how much of this is inside your own organization. You may capture sales data from a customer, but you need to move that around your organization, says Bruce. For example, you might be populating data warehousing applications and then using that data to do marketing programs. So it permeates the whole organization. There's a lot of talk these days about value chains and supply chains. It's not just about the stuff hitting your company from the outside or you sending stuff to the outside, it's also about the movement of all that goes on inside your company. They are all linked.

Technology has real value when married to a company with business experience and expertise; married to a company with no business experience or expertise, technology is a losing proposition. Bruce declares that the key to all of this is how successful you are. If you're building mission-critical systems, you're integrating to your internal systems and to your customers and your suppliers. What really counts is the knowledge in how to do that, not the technology; the technology changes. Sterling Commerce has been doing that for 25 years. We've been providing infrastructure, such as communications software, actual EDI networks, translation software, the tools to integrate business with processes and the expertise to do that. The value in all this is not the technology, it is that you know how to help companies interface the day-to-day production systems.

Lastly, Bruce declares: 'Most of the business-to-business applications will happen without a human interface.' The future is about your business applications talking to other business applications; computers talking to computers. 'What you want to do is to have these computerized applications exchanging data and having them do it in an automated fashion every day, day in and day out – the key is without human intervention. You want to remove the people from the process. The people sit outside those processes and they deal with the services to customers.'

❝services to customers must add value❞

Services to customers must add value. Take for instance customers' buying habits: analyze them to see how you can serve them better. People should be moving into functions that are of higher value.

PRINCIPLE IN ACTION

Charles Schwab

THE CHARLES SCHWAB CORPORATION'S success is founded
on adding higher value to its clients.[5] Through its principal operating
subsidiary, Charles Schwab & Co., Inc., it provides financial services
for 4.8 million active customer accounts, both domestically and inter-
nationally, through a nationwide network of 242 branch offices,
regional telephone service centers, automated telephone systems,
online services, and the internet.

With hundreds of internal and external customers placing their confidence in Charles Schwab's services, it is crucial that files containing
trade transactions and customer account information are processed
immediately upon receipt and accurately recorded. With more than
4 million active accounts and customer assets in excess of $354 billion,
an automated, reliable and secure data exchange strategy is a critical
requirement for the company. Significant returns on investment
depend on the timeliness and security of these transactions. Realizing
the crucial need for a robust data exchange strategy, Charles Schwab
chose Sterling Commerce to fulfil its needs.

return on investment
Charles Schwab selected Sterling Commerce's CONNECT products to serve as the cornerstone of its data exchange strategy. The CONNECT family of products offers more flexibility, functionality, security and automation than any other data exchange solution available today. Charles Schwab implemented a combination of the products, including CONNECT:Direct and CONNECT:Mailbox.

CONNECT:Direct enables Charles Schwab to exchange data with its larger banking partners, as well as application processing between its UNIX, MVS, MS-DOS and Windows NT platforms. CONNECT:Direct's powerful scheduling, scripting and checkpoint/restart capabilities help Charles Schwab automate its operations 24 × 7 – 24 hours a day, seven days a week. Eliminating manual intervention and the consequential delays saves time and money and reduces errors.

❝eliminating manual intervention and the consequential delays save time and money and reduces errors❞

CONNECT:Direct is also used to transport data to and from CONNECT:Mailbox. The latter enables data exchange with trading partners using standard communication protocols, including file transfer protocol (FTP). It also provides a secure data repository, collecting remote trading partner data and storing Charles Schwab's processed data until retrieval by the remote partners. It allows access to customer account and trade information by authorized users at specified times. Operations are verified before transfer initiation, ensuring that only authorized data transfers occur. Since CONNECT:Mailbox does not need to be installed at both ends of the transfer, it allows for an open, yet highly secure, point of entry for external networks. CONNECT:Mailbox also records all system activity in a central log file that allows Charles Schwab to maintain an audit trail of transfer activity among its trading partners and customers.

the ultimate connection

'With our thrust toward e-commerce and so many customers relying on us, we had to have a highly reliable, secure and automated data exchange solution capable of handling a high volume of internal and external multi-vendor file transfers. Minimal operator intervention, flexible cross-platform communication and tracking and monitoring capabilities were also very important. That's why we chose the CONNECT products to link us to our business partners,' said Carol Soibelman, Senior Operations Analyst at Charles Schwab.

'By using the CONNECT products, we are able to accommodate multi-platform communication with current and potential customers. Set-up time is minimal and because our operations employees find the products so easy to use, the process implementation time is also minute. This allows us to maintain our competitive advantage in the brokerage industry,' added Soibelman.

CONNECT:Mailbox and CONNECT:Direct enable maximum connectivity between heterogeneous computing platforms, operating systems, applications and network protocols. This open connectivity helps protect Charles Schwab's hardware and software investments. These features also speed automation and development by requiring little time or effort to add more remote trading partners and applications.

secure, reliable data exchange

In today's increasingly competitive financial services market, successful companies are turning to technology to assist their customers with their finances. The key to customer satisfaction is providing the right information, when and where they need it. Charles Schwab understands this key business requirement and chose CONNECT to anchor its data exchange strategy. Now, with the component for a successful data exchange framework in place, and the CONNECT family of software solutions hard at work, Charles Schwab is positioned for increased customer satisfaction, improved internal and trading partner communications, and continued growth for years to come.

Why did we choose Sterling Commerce? There are two reasons. First, it is a leading provider of e-commerce solutions, and second, it has enabled Charles Schwab to deliver and excel in what it does. Certainly Sterling Commerce had many partner organizations working with it, but that is what working in an ecosystem is about.

SUPPLIER PROFILE

ClearCommerce

the engine that drives e-commerce

ANOTHER US ORGANIZATION in the same field as Sterling Commerce is ClearCommerce.[6]

ClearCommerce based in Austin, Texas, is a leading provider of e-commerce transaction software for nearly 15,000 merchants including Apple Computer, E-Stamp, Cooking.com and Chase Merchant Services. It is a private company and has been offering innovative e-commerce solutions since 1995.

ClearCommerce software features real-time credit card processing and robust internet fraud protection, as well as online reports, back-end integration, storefront integration, shipping/tax calculation, and delivery of digital merchandise.

How does the ClearCommerce Engine work? Once the customer hits the 'buy' button, the merchant's storefront establishes a connection to the ClearCommerce Engine with SSL (Secure Sockets Layer protocol). Depending on the specific requirements of the merchant's business, modules for tax and shipping and fraud protection may be activated. The payment module then establishes contact with the credit card processor and credit card authorization is completed in real time. The state of the transaction is simultaneously logged in the database for recovery. The customer is notified via e-mail once the sale is complete and when the goods are shipped. After the credit card settlement occurs, the transaction is stored in the database and fulfillment systems may be updated. The entire transaction typically takes three to seven seconds.

"site performance and reliability are critical to the online customer experience"

Benefits of the ClearCommerce Engine are twofold. First, site perform-ance and reliability are critical to the online customer experience. Designed to keep operating costs low and profitability high, ClearCommerce software offers 24-hours, seven-days-a-week availabil-ity, data integrity, fault tolerance and scalability. In addition, its solution can support thousands of merchants on a single server and process concurrent transactions at peak performance, even during high-volume periods. Second, ClearCommerce's 'FraudShield' protects the profits of online businesses by minimizing the acceptance of fraud-ulent orders likely to result in bank charge-backs and processing fees.

INTERVIEW WITH SUPPLIER

'Within five years, you will be able to buy any service or product on the internet. It will become part of everyday life.'

Alan Scutt, European Vice-President

WITH SITE PERFORMANCE, RELIABILITY and protection as critical to online customers, Alan Scutt offers us four key points in the 'secure payments' arena that retailers must consider.[7] First, it's about online payment, exactly the same as if you walk into a store, hand over your credit card and within eight to ten seconds the transaction is cleared. Second, retailers will want the online payments integrated with their system. Third, retailers should consider 'fraud protection' as a vital issue. Fourth, which is becoming increasingly more important with the web's global reach, retailers must make it easy for their customers overseas to have the choice of payment in multiple currencies.

First, there's a very important difference between paying with a credit card in a shop, which in the business is called 'card present' transaction, and paying with a credit card over the telephone or on the internet, which is called 'card not present'. If you as a consumer have actually carried out a fraudulent transaction, such as using a stolen credit card, and the merchant accepts it, the merchant is protected by the credit card company and by his bank. There is no loss incurred by the merchant, even though he may have given you a £50 shirt.

However, with e-commerce, because it's over the internet and it's a 'card not present' transaction, it completely changes the rules. So in the previous example, for instance, the merchant will lose the £50 transaction. More than that, when the bank detects that it was a fraudulent transaction, it will charge the merchant a higher rate for processing that transaction. If the merchant accepts lots of fraudulent transactions, the bank will begin to blacklist.

The fraud checking is extensive and allows merchants to add their own rules to what's called a 'rule-based engine'. So if a merchant decides it does not want to sell to people at a certain physical address at a certain time of day or to certain e-mail addresses, it can do this. In fact, it works very much like a set of traffic lights. If an order is straightforward, it receives a *green light*, go. If an order is clearly unfit, it receives a *red light*, stop. If an order comes in at 3am and requests delivery to an area the merchant finds questionable, it can give it an *amber light* and divert it to a call center to qualify and then approve or decline, so as not to lose the sale.

> **❝**a success story for ClearCommerce was when it won the Harrods account against fairly stiff competition**❞**

A success story for ClearCommerce was when it won the Harrods account against fairly stiff competition. Alan Scutt believes it's because of the four key points we outlined at the start of the interview. Once Harrods started to do some research and analysis about who would be its potential customers (it has the Brompton Road flagship store and a few airport shops) it discovered that 30 percent might come from Japan, another 30 percent from the US, and the rest from the UK and Europe. So it now has three sites and three servers: one in the UK, one in the US and one in Japan, which rolled out in 2000.

That was just the beginning for Harrods. It is also launching a site called HOT.com or Harrods-online.com, which will cover a multitude of brands. Now if you can imagine, when you walk into Harrods today, there are a lot of departments, which they call concessions; stores within a store, like Ralph Lauren, Cartier and Hermes. Hot.com will in fact be a cyberstore. Walk through the door and go to, say, the Ralph Lauren site, not its main site but the one in Harrods, so you're still kept within the Harrods portal (just like going into the Ralph Lauren concession in the real-world store really). As this site grows, it will undoubtedly have the other El Fayed businesses such as Turnbull & Asser, the Jermyn Street shirtmakers and Fulham Football Club.

An example of what ClearCommerce developed for another client is explained in more detail in the next case study.

PRINCIPLE IN ACTION

The Street.com

BASED IN NEW YORK CITY, TheStreet.com, Inc. is the publisher of TheStreet.com, a leading web-based provider of original, timely, comprehensive and trustworthy financial news, offering both free and subscription-based online content.[8]

situation
Having initially outsourced the processing of its customer subscriptions, The Street.com decided to develop its own in-house commerce system to enable greater flexibility and control over the site's marketing and business models. The system needed to provide exceptional reliability, availability, scalability and performance to support the fast-growing site's high-volume commerce.

business solution
Deciding that no single off-the-shelf commerce solution could adequately provide for the site's requirements, The Street.com sought separate commerce and payment processing solutions that could be integrated seamlessly and scale to support the rapid growth

of its subscriber base. The company chose the ClearCommerce Merchant Engine to add payment-processing capabilities to a subscription system based on Art Technology Group's Dynamo Product Suite. The completed system's reliable 24 × 7 performance and scalability gives TheStreet.com the ability to process as many as 50,000 subscriptions per day, while providing the flexibility and control to offer customers a variety of configurable subscription packages.

benefits

The clear, straightforward Java API of the ClearCommerce Merchant Engine allowed it to be integrated quickly and easily with ATG's Java-based Dynamo Commerce Station. The result was reliable and efficient credit card processing with full fraud-detection capabilities and automatic off-line subscription renewal. With this, the system lets TheStreet.com provide efficient and reliable customer service while eliminating the cost of an outsourced solution. As The Street.com continues its rapid growth, the system will scale to handle increasing numbers of subscribers, and its open Java architecture will provide the flexibility to support new and changing requirements as the company's business model evolves.

❝because we're published entirely online, our reporters and commentators aren't shackled to print media schedules❞

TheStreet.com

Founded in 1996, TheStreet.com offers financial news and analysis in both free and paid content areas at www.thestreet.com, prepared by some of the top names in business journalism. 'Because we're published entirely online, our reporters and commentators aren't shackled to print media schedules,' says Dan Woods, the company's Vice President and Chief Technology Officer (CTO). 'We can let our readers know what's going on in the markets and around the world instantly, as it happens.'

Readers have responded enthusiastically to TheStreet.com's savvy editorial content, signing up for monthly and annual subscriptions in ever-increasing numbers. The site's subscription base grew more than 380 percent during 1998, reaching more than 51,000 by the end of March 1999; these payments now account for more than a third of the company's total revenue. To support this rapid growth while eliminating the cost of outsourcing subscription processing, TheStreet.com decided to take this function in-house.

finding the ideal solution

TheStreet.com's new commerce system needed to fulfill a very specific set of requirements. It had to process subscriptions round the clock at a variety of monthly and annual rates, renewed automatically unless instructed otherwise by the customer. The system also needed to be easily configurable to offer a variety of seasonal and special discounts and promotions, as well as to help the site convert free 30-day trial subscribers to paid subscribers through targetted e-mails and pop-up reminder messages.

From the beginning, TheStreet.com found that most commerce systems on the market were more suitable for online retailers than its own subscription-based business. Dan Woods says: 'Most of the commerce systems you buy off the shelf are the kind that allow you to buy a hard good, and deal with the fulfillment of that good. So we couldn't find anything that really fitted the bill.' Instead, TheStreet.com decided to combine separate commerce and payment processing solutions.

Following an evaluation of commerce engines, Woods selected Art Technology Group's (ATG) Dynamo Product Suite as the basis for the new subscription system. The suite's Commerce Server provides ready-made application building blocks to speed up e-commerce development, while its completely open architecture enables customers to add new functionality easily. 'We looked at a lot of different components on the market,' says Woods, 'and examining them it made it really clear that ATG had a very good system that we could use to customize a lot of what we needed to do.'

The next step was to find a payment-processing component. For this essential piece, Woods chose the ClearCommerce Merchant Engine, a solution providing online customer credit card authorizations, online order and payment processing, online internet fraud detection, and APIs to enable simple integration with other components. 'We found that ClearCommerce was a tremendously valuable plug-and-play component,' says Woods, who explains that the industry-leading reliability, availability, scalability and performance of the ClearCommerce Merchant Engine didn't come by accident. 'ClearCommerce was a product developed out of the company's early experience as a service bureau. This means we are riding on the shoulders of lots of other people who have worked to make this product successful; it has a maturity based on the fact that it has been used in practice.'

putting the pieces together

For the development of the new commerce system, TheStreet.com's internal IT staff were joined by a team of ATG consultants. The system was hosted on an Apache web server running on Sun hardware with an Oracle database. Once the Dynamo-based subscription system had been built, the ClearCommerce Merchant Engine was plugged into the Dynamo Commerce Station using the Merchant Engine's Java API.

'We found that the API was very clear and easy to understand,' recalls ATG's Anne Marie Clogston. 'Once we wrote the integration module, we just had to change the configuration and restart the system.' Because both ATG and ClearCommerce are Java-based, the system was platform-independent from the ground up.

To handle TheStreet.com's automatic subscription renewals, which are charged to credit cards off-line, the team created special error-handling routines to retry expired cards after a few days, as well as sending an e-mail notification to the subscriber, to avoid withholding access to the site unnecessarily. 'We recognized the specific errors that would come back from ClearCommerce that would indicate an expired or over-limit card, as opposed to a fraudulent card,' explains Clogston. To prepare for the latter case, the configuration of the ClearCommerce Merchant Engine allowed the team to simulate the use of fake credit cards to make certain that the system's fraud detection worked flawlessly.

All in all, the development team found the integration process remarkably simple and straightforward, taking only two weeks to complete.

ready for business
TheStreet.com's new subscription processing system went live on May 28, 1999. With the capacity to handle as many as 50,000 transactions per day, the system was well equipped for the high volume of commerce it saw right from the beginning. ATG's subscription engine and ClearCommerce's payment processing component form a tightly integrated unit that has worked flawlessly to fulfill TheStreet.com's objectives.

66the development team found the integration
process remarkably simple and straightforward 99

In addition to processing new subscriptions and renewals smoothly, the system has given TheStreet.com the flexibility to offer a variety of configurable subscription packages easily and efficiently. 'Now we have control over our own commerce system, which is a tremendous benefit,' says Woods. 'It enables us to control our own marketing. We have the freedom now to experiment with our business model.' With the demand for online financial news continuing to grow, new readers sign up for TheStreet.com every day. As its subscriber base expands, the reliability, scalability and performance of the ClearCommerce and ATG solution behind TheStreet.com's new commerce system may be the best news of all.

Why did we choose ClearCommerce? With 15,000 merchants depending on it for e-commerce transaction software, ClearCommerce has a significant advantage over its competitors in relating to us a good many successes and failures it has encountered on its journey to success.

More importantly, it has to integrate its real-time credit card process-ing, internet fraud protection, online reports, shipping/tax calculation and delivery of digital merchandise with its clients' back-end and storefront. The company also works in many ecosystems at the same time: its customers' ecosystem.

EXECUTIVE SUMMARY OF

PRINCIPLE 6

FROM THESE CASE STUDIES, it is clear that internet payments cannot be isolated from the rest of the organization. They need to be integrated in such a way that the employees, customers and suppliers can communicate, the business process can run seamlessly and efficiently, and a robust, secure and flexible e-commerce infrastructure needs to be in place for paying and receiving monies, through third parties such as Visa, and to be secure from fraud.

▶ You need to invest in order to develop your e-commerce operations. Remember the difference in distribution costs between a $5,000 airline ticket costing $900 or 18 percent and the $5,000 stock trade costing $29 or 0.6 percent. This is the order of magnitude that can be achieved.

▶ By focussing on these four key services – community management, business process integration, e-commerce infrastructure, and outsourcing – you help your customers to make the transition to the internet-driven economy.

► If you're building mission critical systems, you're integrating to your internal systems and to your customers and your suppliers. What really counts is the knowledge of how to do that, not the technology.

► Services to customers must add value. Take for instance customers' buying habits: analyze them to see how you can serve them better. People should be moving into functions that are of higher value.

► In today's increasingly competitive market, successful companies are turning to technology to assist their customers. The key to customer satisfaction is providing the right information, when and where they need it.

► There are four key points in the 'secure payments' arena that retailers must consider. First, it's about online payment. Second, retailers will want the online payments integrated with their system. Third, retailers should consider 'fraud protection' as a vital issue. Fourth, retailers must make it easy for their customers overseas to have the choice of payment in multiple currencies.

► You can't have a strategy in isolation. Remember, this is an ecosystem. For payments through the internet, you must look at the issue holistically. Integrate your suppliers, partners and customers.

NOTES

1 'The life-giving soil', **Eyewitness Guides Ecology**, Steve Pollock, Dorling Kindersley Ltd, 1993, p. 22.

2 'BA plans to cut costs through internet strategy,' Kevin Dunn, **Financial Times**, February 24, 2000.

3 http:/www.sterlingcommerce.com

4 Interview with Dave Bruce, Director, Northern Europe, on January 6, 2000.

5 Case study – Charles Schwab.

6 http:/www.clearcommerce.com

7 Interview with Alan Scutt, European Vice-President, on January 6, 2000.

8 Case study (in conjunction with Art Technology Group, http:/www.atg.com) – http:/www.thestreet.com

PRINCIPLE 7

BUYING

E

personal 12
learning 1
planning 2
system 3
network 4
security 5
payment 6
buying 7
supplier 8
invent/log 9
selling 10
customer 11

STATEMENT OF **PRINCIPLE 7**

FOR ECOLOGISTS TO UNDERSTAND how energy enters and passes through an ecosystem, they must understand the feeding relationships between the organisms in that ecosystem. In a simple food chain, a plant is eaten by a plant eater, which in its turn is eaten by a meat eater. There are many food chains, but because nature is complex, the chains are highly interconnected, creating a food web.[1] Given the benefits of the internet, we must move from thinking in supply chains to supply webs.

In looking at supply webs, it is important to understand the difference between buying (principle 7) and a supplier portal (principle 8). *Buying* ensures that all the indirect suppliers of the organization are linked to the employees' desktops. A *supplier portal* is a marketplace or exchange of all the direct suppliers for a specific industry, into which an organization would integrate its procurement system. In effect, the suppliers monitor their supplies with the buying organization and replenish at set levels agreed with them. In this way, organizations can optimize purchasing and supply.

Returning to our real-world example, airport authorities need to purchase goods, whether they are direct goods and services which are critical to run their operations or indirect goods and services, such as office stationery, which are essential to their business. Airlines are scrambling to get their procurement online.[2] British Airways is seeking to put its annual £3.5 billion purchasing budget and its relations with suppliers online. Its target is to increase the share of online purchasing from 25 percent to 80 percent, saving more than £175 million by March 2002. The number of UK suppliers will be cut from 14,000 to only 2,000 by the end of 2001.

> **❝it is not just airlines that are scambling
> to get their procurement online ❞**

It is not just airlines that are scrambling to get their procurement online. As procurement is not really a titillating subject and nor is it particularly of 'public interest', the media does not give it much attention. Yet companies that provide procurement solutions to organizations feel besieged like doctors surgeries during a winter flu epidemic. The internet has created a market and a method for organizations to interact and purchase goods and services. Suppliers which do not adapt swiftly into the new business interaction will find themselves disintermediated or out of business. Those which do adapt swiftly may well end up being acquired and re-intermediated (become part of a larger organization) but at least they will still be alive and kicking.

The Finance, Purchasing and Operations directors own this principle and the key influencer is the Project Manager. Under this principle, the following areas are covered: Enterprise Resource Planning purchasing software for direct purchasing and Maintenance, Repair and Operation purchasing software for indirect purchasing.

The following case studies show how the buying or procurement ecosystem works.

SUPPLIER PROFILE

Izodia (Infobank)

electronic commerce systems

HEADQUARTERED IN LANGLEY, BERKSHIRE, UK, Izodia[3] (Infobank Electronic Commerce Systems) is a leader in the world of e-commerce, specializing in the provision of web-based purchasing and supply solutions. Founded in 1994, it has been quoted on the Alternative Investment Market (AIM) since February 1997. Through Izodia InTrade™, its flagship e-procurement product suite, it works with corporate and government organizations to automate the process for the purchase of goods and services required for the operation of the enterprise.

Izodia aims to provide significant value to its customers by enabling them to:

► reduce the cost of purchasing

► streamline supply chains

► increase profitability

► realize the business benefits of electronic trading relationships.

Its solutions meet the needs of organizations on both sides of the online trading relationship. InTrade Purchaser supports purchases within large organizations. InTrade Supplier supports suppliers of non-production goods and services. InTrade Commerce Centre supports purchasers requiring a single directory of multiple supplier catalogs, and InTrade e-Hub supports the development of managed, electronic trading communities.

Through its extensive partnership network, Izodia ensures that its customers are provided with the necessary business knowledge and technical skills to realize the value of e-commerce. Its partners include BT, Compaq, Ernst & Young, KPMG, Hewlett-Packard, Logica, Pwc Kinesis, USWeb/CKS and Visa.

Infobank was valued at £50 million in early 1999. In early March 2000, the *Financial Times* wrote that Infobank had a market value of £1.7 billion and had positioned itself as the European rival to Ariba and Commerce One of the US. In the last quarter of 2000, even though its market value had more than halved, it was still a multiple above the original £50 million.

On April 2 2001, Infobank changed its name to Izodia (www.izodia.com) because it was not allowed to use the word 'bank' in its name in certain territories.

INTERVIEW WITH SUPPLIER

'The biggest danger for the corporates isn't a competitor, it's apathy.'

Jim Conning, Managing Director

THERE IS A LINK BETWEEN VALUATIONS and return on investment. Companies that can reduce costs substantially deliver a better return on investment, which in turn provides higher valuation, because it is worth more. On electronic procurement, the return on investment to a company is real and enormous, says Jim Conning.[4] 'We have a real customer who says that their average spend on processing a purchase order was £55 before they started using InTrade and now it's down to £10. That's a real customer who has bought our technology, implemented it, and within a month is seeing an 80 percent reduction in the cost of processing a purchase order.'

❝reducing costs makes companies more effective❞

Reducing costs makes companies more effective. The money saved goes straight to the bottom line. In other words, it's a real saving. Compare that with the sales a business has to generate to make, say, a 10 percent gross profit, which, say, delivers a 3 percent net profit, which only then goes to the bottom line, and we haven't even factored for the tax.

Studies in the US and also at Warwick University Business School in the UK show that 80 percent of a purchasing specialist's time is spent on administration. That means four days out of five, the paperwork has become their job rather than what their job actually should be, says Conning. As far as employees are concerned this isn't about redundancy, it's about redeployment.

The definition of 'supply chain' is a group of organizations which buy from each other to complete a finished good that's sold to an end user. So you can take it from the end user all the way back to raw materials. Purchasing organizations will rationalize who they buy from and they will have to aid the building of their supplier community. Large suppliers, which already have huge investments in internet supply systems, will not surrender data; they want to keep their own data. They want to own their own customer relationships. Most suppliers will not accept an intermediary in the way, who causes discontinuity in the supply chain. There will be markets where things happen quicker than in others, but ultimately, suppliers and purchasers will buy because the purchasing organizations need something that the suppliers supply.

'Everybody's talked about enterprise portals,' says Conning. 'I think there will be enterprise trading communities, where most organizations which may have an IT infrastructure but actually don't want to host this internet trading community, would put it out and host it with an internet service provider. They then create their own distinct supplier communities, who will buy from them. The real benefit is they get all their suppliers on to their community.'

As an example, Conning mentions that Izodia is talking with a construction company. Most construction companies buy from the same suppliers, so they all buy from the same group of people. Therefore you set up a buying community, which removes the IT headache and provides the content service for both supplier and buyer, at the same time giving real value by reducing costs. Izodia is talking to a large supplier in the construction industry which is looking first to create its own purchasing system and second, as soon as that's in place, to turn it inside out and provide it as a service to the rest of its community.

Apathy is the biggest threat, according to Conning. 'The winners will be the ones that are offensive, not the ones that get on the defensive. If you try to hold on to your customers, you'll lose.' In five to ten years' time, Conning foresees 'tens of thousands of vertical hubs that address a market niche in any geographical region.' Businesses of the future are basically these virtual trading communities.

66the winners will be the ones that are
offensive, not the ones that get on the defensive 99

We asked Conning to explain how the airline ecosystem such as OneWorldAlliance and OneStarAlliance worked in terms of procurement. The answer, he said, is that it gives them economic power. It starts buying fuel as one organization. It becomes a buying community in itself. Customers also win because they can transfer, get connections seamlessly, and collect membership points or air miles. For the airlines, it means less paperwork, less human involvement, easier costs, easier planning, manufacturing and supply chain management. For the oil industry, rather than dealing with ten airlines, it is now negotiating with only one. Everybody wins, just as everybody wins in the following case study of Guilbert UK.

PRINCIPLE IN ACTION
Guilbert UK

THE UK'S LARGEST AND LEADING supplier of commercial office products, Guilbert UK,[5] with an annual revenue of £300 million, has been using Izodia's InTrade to develop its new catalogs since 1999. The company has 150,000 corporate customers across seven European countries and a turnover of €980 million. In the UK, the company services the needs of 87 out of *The Times* Top 100 organizations.

Guilbert UK Ltd is a wholly-owned subsidiary of Guilbert S.A., Europe's largest office products supplier, which is itself part of the Pinault Printemps Redoute Group. The UK company supplies an extensive range of office and computer supplies, including the famous 'Niceday' brand, from its nationwide network of 22 branches and distribution centers across the whole of the UK and Eire.

With more than 20,000 orders processed daily, all of which are guaranteed for next day delivery to customers, Guilbert UK is proud of its exceedingly high-performance achievement for orders delivered correctly and on time. The company works in partnership with its customers to develop the right combination of systems, products, price and technology to provide the most efficient solution for the supply of stationery.

Andy Craig, Marketing Director, explains: 'In this industry, where it can be difficult for customers to differentiate between the various companies offering office stationery supplies, it is important for us to provide a market leading service. We achieve this by offering a package of products and services which surpasses what is available from competitive organizations. Much of our success can be attributed to the fact that Guilbert UK is constantly anticipating customer demands and responding to changes in business practices. We pride ourselves on the consistency of our product quality, technical support and customer service, but for us this is just the beginning. Much of our time is put into listening to our customers, extending the services we offer, developing existing and new product ranges and responding to the changing purchasing patterns. This enables us to continually outpace our competitors.'

❝this revolution spans both the nature of the supplier relationship and the IT systems integral to the purchasing process❞

This philosophy is clearly demonstrated by the company's commitment to offering the widest possible range of purchasing options, keeping one step ahead of the crowd by being the first to recognize the revolution in corporate purchasing culture. This revolution spans both the nature of the supplier relationship and the IT systems integral to the purchasing process. 'We work in close co-operation with our customers to develop supply partnerships which really work,' says Craig. 'This takes into account each area of the process – for example, we are able to accept orders by post, fax, e-mail, EDI, intranet or internet. We can then arrange delivery in a number of different ways: by customer, by cost center or to individual desks, if required. Our aim has been to find ways of integrating with the purchasing system in place at our customer's site, whether this is a multinational company purchasing hundreds of orders daily on a pan-European basis, or a smaller business placing one weekly order.'

The most recent addition to the range of methods by which Guilbert UK customers can place orders is through the Izodia InTrade electronic procurement system. This provides Guilbert UK with a significant competitive edge through the savings customers can make to their purchasing costs, particularly when the system is used alongside corporate purchase cards and aggregated invoicing. The facts speak for themselves, as Craig explains. 'Our average order value is approximately £85, while independent market research has found that the average cost for an organization to place an order with a supplier is upwards of £50. This means in real terms, the cost to the customer to process the order internally is almost as much as the actual cost of the goods purchased. As much as 25 percent of this purchase cost is tied up with our customers raising and authorizing the purchase order through their own internal procurement systems. We recognized that this situation clearly needed to be resolved, and with Izodia InTrade we have found the solution. Customers adopting this solution can eliminate this cost virtually overnight.'

Guilbert UK is predicting a dramatic rise in the number of organizations adopting electronic procurement systems, and it is not alone. The commitment by multinational organizations to this approach to purchasing is becoming increasingly widespread; BT, for example, stated its intention to make 95 percent of routine purchases electronic by 2000. Guilbert UK expects electronic procurement to account for 60–65 percent of all purchase transactions within the next few years, and has implemented the Izodia InTrade system to ensure its readiness for this demand.

In addition to the flexibility of service this provides to its customers when placing orders, it adds enormous value directly to its businesses by reducing the overall cost to them of receiving office supplies. Guilbert deals with thousands of businesses of all types, all of which need to drive down their procurement costs, and InTrade adds to the existing range of systems the company offers to enable its customers to achieve these goals. Electronic trading and the internet have opened up businesses to the potentially significant cost savings, but for Guilbert this goes far beyond simply providing an internet-based product catalog. 'The real value lies in the integration of back-office systems, enabling the automation of the entire purchasing process, which is the capability that Izodia InTrade enables us to provide,' says Craig.

As Europe's largest supplier of office stationery and products, the language and currency capabilities of Izodia InTrade are critical to Guilbert. The InTrade suite is designed to support electronic trade in multiple languages from multiple locations in multiple currencies from within a single system. For example, customers are able to buy in Germany from a supplier in Spain. InTrade automatically represents information in the language and currency of the buyer, at the same time as representing product orders in the language and currency of the supplier.

66customers are able to buy in Germany from a supplier in Spain 99

There is an increasing trend, through the processes of merger, acquisition and organic growth, for more companies to operate on a truly global basis. A major part of this strategy is to standardize suppliers across geographic regions, as Guilbert has found.

'We already have around 50 customers who have standardized on Guilbert for all their office product supplies throughout Europe, and this number is increasing rapidly,' says Craig. 'It is vital for us that our electronic procurement system of choice has the ability to operate on a European level. The use of InTrade is providing us with valuable experience and knowledge, which we have already put to good use in implementing the system in our Eire operation, Guilbert Ireland. Customers there are able to access our product catalog with prices automatically converted to punts and euros rather than pounds. We're looking at expanding this use to other European countries as their varying levels of use of electronic media continues to become increasingly mature and widespread.'

Craig summarizes: 'In today's highly sophisticated purchasing depart-ments it is the flexibility, creativity and collaboration which mark us out as a valuable business partner rather than simply one of a number of suppliers. Our adoption of the Izodia InTrade procurement system is a major element in our commitment to maintaining this enviable status.'

Why did we choose Izodia? Clearly because its expertise is in automat-ing the process for the purchase of goods and services required for the operation of an enterprise. More importantly, it has shown remarkable adaptability to the concept of developing its own ecosystem, evinced by its website, where each of its stakeholders has a separate door to enter.

If Infobank can be characterized as the UK's Catherine Zeta Jones, then our next case study, Commerce One, is the US's Michelle Pfeiffer.

SUPPLIER PROFILE

Commerce One

electronic procurement solutions

COMMERCE ONE[6] IS THE GLOBAL LEADER IN business-to-business electronic procurement solutions. The company, which has its headquarters in Walnut Creek, California, was founded in 1994, has more than 3,500 employees, and is growing at a frenetic pace – in the quarter ending September 1999 it grew by more than 80 percent. It is revolutionizing the way companies procure goods and services, turning a traditional cost center into a direct-line contributor to corporate profitability.

❝the Commerce One Solution provides superior cost savings❞

Unlike other procurement systems that focus on internal purchase order generation, Commerce One Solution is the only one that offers an end-to-end electronic commerce solution. The Commerce One Solution dynamically links buying and supplying organizations into real-time trading communities, giving its client the strategic advantage of simplifying and streamlining the entire process. By automating the entire indirect goods and services supply chain and enabling interactive ordering, the Commerce One Solution provides superior cost savings, reduces cycle times from days to hours, decreases inventories, and delivers the highest return on investment.

The Commerce One Solution consists of two key components. The first, Commerce One BuySite, is an intranet application which automates a company's internal procurement process from requisition to order. BuySite delivers directly to the desktop the most comprehensive suite of commerce services covering the entire purchasing cycle, from requisition to payment. This includes the procurement of goods and services, travel booking and management, and expense management.

The second, MarketSite, is the first business-to-business marketplace portal for the procurement of indirect goods and services. MarketSite automates the process of selecting, pricing, ordering and tracking to maximize cost reduction and return on investment. MarketSite provides a managed catalog content model for trading partners. It removes the burden and cost of running electronic content from both buyers and suppliers. Using a unique 'publish once' model, in any format, suppliers can quickly publish products and services to all buying organizations within the marketplace. MarketSite aggregates catalog content from multiple suppliers and provides buyer-specific contract pricing and availability. Unlike other solution providers, Commerce One will accept catalog content in the supplier's preferred format, then reformat, reorganize and map the data into the customer's preferred format.

INTERVIEW WITH SUPPLIER

'We enable an organization to establish itself at the heart of an electronic trading community.'

Chris Phillips, Director of Marketing, Europe

CHRIS PHILLIPS EXPLAINS THE DIFFERENCE between the buying process and the supplying process.[7] 'When you are presenting a self-service procurement application, you're allowing an employee to build a requisition for items they want. They need approval from different layers of management, but all this takes place within the four walls of the organization. It's important to distinguish between things like that and aspects of the process like checking stock availability with a supplier, understanding the price structure, the product information, actual transmission of the order, and the order tracking. The latter is transactional in its nature. What you are doing is linking the two sets of the business processes together – a buying process and a supplying process.'

Experience has shown Phillips three areas of issues. The first is to do with making sure that you are automating all the aspects of the process from the perspective of the employee. You've placed your purchase order and panicked because you've placed an order for a computer for a new employee who's starting on Monday and it's the Thursday before and you don't know where the computer is. What do you do? You pick up the phone and hassle the purchasing department to find where it is. They don't know and they have to fax the supplier. So the saga goes on. So one of the reasons why the portal model emerged was because it's a very good way to interact with suppliers. It gives you the electronic connectivity without falling back on the fax, the phone, maybe e-mail and more cumbersome methods.

> **"one of the reasons why the portal model emerged was because it's a very good way to interact with suppliers"**

The second issue is the need to consolidate all catalogs, so that your employees can search through one catalog. The system is no good if you are looking at 50 different websites. All catalogs are in different formats, they're riddled with errors and they use different nomenclatures. For example, 'Blk' means block in one catalog and black in another. You have to sort all this out and it is very people-intensive, grinding, donkey work. This is difficult enough when you are dealing with four catalogs, what happens when you have 50? What's emerged from this is the portal operator. The MarketSite operator can provide catalog management services in the portal. The portal operator will say, I will take all the supplier catalogs, I'll do all the donkey work, put them in the same format, clean them up and make sure they are presentable. I will do that on behalf of the whole trading community. Clearly, you also become very good at it if you are doing it all the time.

The third issue is, how do you deliver third-party services to the buying and selling process? You have enterprises that provide delivery services such as UPS and TNT. You've got people who provide payment services, trade credit services, taxation services, tax ware and travel services. These third-party services provide underpinning services to the basic trade. It's exactly the same as the real world. With these third-party services, Phillips believes it's also far more effective to use the portal structure to interact with them rather than form individual relationships.

'At the moment auctions and reverse auctions are the flavor of the month and people get carried away with it,' he says. 'People assume everything will be done by auctions. It won't. Different trading models will work for different categories of different services. There are some categories of goods that are primarily high-volume, low-value transactions, where you're going to select one strategic supplier of office stationery. Suppose I'm GM (General Motors), I will select the supplier through a reverse auction, a bid process electronically, and once selected, I'll agree a price with them, whatever the contractual mechanism, and then we'll use BuySite and MarketSite to automate the transaction against that contract.'

That was the downside. Now let's looks at the upside, which are cost reduction, better administration control and efficiency and cycle time. Confirming what Jim Conning of Infobank said, Phillips states that if you look at average figures, it's typically about $80 in terms of administration costs for each purchase order. So regardless of the value of the purchase, you could be buying something for $10 and it would actually cost you $90. You can get that cost down to around $6 by automating that process. In terms of cycle time, typically, a conservative average is seven days. Now with automation, you can drop that down to two days, which is the physical time it takes to deliver the goods to the person. It's difficult to compress that much further.

Returning to our GM example, what GM is doing is much more than e-procurement (eGM). It is establishing itself as the heart of a supply chain community and if it doesn't quite control it, it certainly has a very heavy level of influence over it. It is placing itself at the center of a business model for generating revenue. It buys on behalf of a group of buyers and takes a cut of those revenues. So GM has set up a totally new organization called TradeXchange, which runs at the GM portal, and it's far, far more profound, in terms of strategy, than e-procurement in its literal sense. It's actually a new business for GM.

In early to mid-2000, GM combined forces first with Ford and DaimlerChrysler and then with Renault and Nissan to create a portal called Covisint. This validates the trading community model of many buyers trading with many suppliers through one portal.

The following case study shows how Commerce One helped Eastman Chemical create a seamless business.

PRINCIPLE IN ACTION

Eastman Chemical

EASTMAN CHEMICAL is a global producer of fibers, plastics and chemicals, with more than 16,000 employees worldwide and annual purchases totaling more than $3 billion.[8] Eddie Page, Purchasing Manager, attests to the benefits of the Commerce One Solution because his decisions directly impact Eastman Chemical's bottom line.

Put simply, the challenges facing Eastman were threefold. First, the company needed to implement a web-based electronic procurement application while maintaining operations with and between its existing SAP ERP systems. Second, it needed to facilitate outbound ordering among approved suppliers. Third, it needed to enable a cost-effective method to manage supplier catalog content.

'Our vision,' explains Page, 'was to provide customers with the ability to search for supplies, select best value items from contracted suppliers, and easily create and submit a requisition. Further, we wanted an automated system that, once we converted to the new SAP R/3, would be able to make decisions. It would decide whether the request should go out as an SAP purchase order, whether an SAP requisition needs to be created and handled manually by purchasing professionals, or finally, whether a requisition can remain completely out of SAP and eliminate the need for invoicing and other back-end activities.'

Page's search quickly brought him to Commerce One. One of the primary concerns was finding a solution that would not only complement Eastman's SAP R/2 system but would also be able to seamlessly accept the anticipated migration to SAP R/3. The company needed a system that would grow with it and not become obsolete in a year.

In keeping with Eastman's vision, Page foresees BuySite providing automated flexibility to make choices on process handling. Configured with criteria for purchasing, based on internal company rules and policy (such as putting a cap on dollar amounts for hands-free purchasing), the system should intelligently assess multiple conditions, including whether the user has a credit card or whether the purchase is less than $2,000. With this information, BuySite should then be able to determine the best method for sending out an e-commerce purchase order so that orders can often be kept completely out of the SAP process, thereby eliminating unnecessary steps in certain transactions.

"the system should intelligently assess multiple conditions, including whether the user has a credit card "

Eastman Chemical began implementation of Commerce One's BuySite, Desktop Commerce Application at its Kingsport, Tennessee corporate headquarters with one commodity vendor (for office supplies) and 50 users. That number quickly rose to 2,509 as users witnessed BuySite's ability to enable e-commerce and automate the internal procurement process from requisition to order.

With the success of the pilot group, Eastman Chemical is now implementing BuySite on a much larger scale. The company has added a second vendor, for laboratory supplies, and has begun implementing the application across major US sites.

As BuySite extends across the Eastman enterprise, the company will continue leveraging MarketSite – the extranet portion of the solution that automates external supplier interaction through a real-time trading market – to increase its supplier base. Expansion of the Commerce One Solution in Eastman's international facilities is also planned.

Eastman Chemical previously relied on its SAP R/2 ERP system, which sends out either faxes or EDI transmissions to suppliers, to handle its procurement processes. Traditional EDI, however, does not integrate well with the systems of every vendor. Through Commerce One BuySite and MarketSite, Eastman Chemical maintains the advantage of real-time transactions without carrying the burden of multiple customizations and integration. Suppliers do not need any particular software to use MarketSite; they require only a connection to the web. Considering this, Eastman is carefully pulling out selected commodities from the SAP system and redirecting management through the Commerce One Solution to enter into the real-time trading community of the web.

Because BuySite stores data on purchase and supplier behavior patterns, it proves a useful and strategic tool for negotiating favorable vendor contracts. Its purchasing card and electronic catalog encourage employees to use only corporate-approved suppliers. As a result, Eastman Chemical has substantially decreased the volume of rogue purchasing – and orders are getting back to the preferred suppliers at the contracted prices. Because order volume is increasing with contracted suppliers and that volume is then leveraged for increased discounts, overall costs are decreasing.

Eastman Chemical is able to receive rapid responses, shorten fulfillment cycles and implement just-in-time MRO (maintenance, repair and operation) procurement strategies. The company has also improved inventory practices through its enhanced ability to gauge inventory levels that meet the real-world requirements of Eastman's departments.

Commerce One has directly improved the company's order fulfillment cycle and guaranteed best bottom-line savings. It helps Eastman streamline workflow and business processes for better order processing and tracking, bringing a tighter focus on supplier strategy and standardization of product selections. Ultimately it helps Eastman optimize overall company efficiency. Page concludes: 'The proficiency of the system was immediately apparent and it is living up to expectations. With Commerce One, we feel we have experienced a true partnership.'

❝Commerce One has directly improved the company's order fulfillment cycle❞

Why did we choose Commerce One? The obvious reason is that with Ariba, it is one of the top two organizations under this principle. The more important reason is that Commerce One was in the process of creating a business for GM, a new ecosystem called eGM. Since then, it has been creating an even bigger ecosystem called Covisint. Now there's a challenge.

EXECUTIVE SUMMARY OF
PRINCIPLE 7

WHAT THESE CASE STUDIES HIGHLIGHT is that the internet
has created markets and methods for organizations to interact to purchase goods and services. Buyers and suppliers which do not adapt
swiftly into the new business ecosystem will find themselves out-of-
business. The benefits are numerous: reduction in purchasing costs and
employee costs, increased cycle times, and optimization of supply webs.

▶ Reducing costs on purchases by up to 80 percent makes companies
   more efficient and the money saved goes straight to the bottom line.

▶ Studies in the US and also at Warwick University Business School
   show that 80 percent of a purchasing specialist's time is spent on
   administration. That means four days out of five – the paperwork
   has become their job rather than what their job actually should be.

▶ The real value lies in the integration of back-office systems,
   enabling the automation of the entire purchasing process.

▶ There are three areas of issues. The first is to do with making sure
   that you are automating all the aspects of the process from the user's
   perspective. The second is the need to consolidate all information

in one place. The third is how to incorporate third-party services such as taxation, credit and payment services to the buying and selling process.

▶ To be a leader in your sector, you must establish yourself at the heart of a supply chain community, which you will not control but will certainly have a very heavy level of influence over. By placing your organization at the center of a business model for generating revenue, you then buy on behalf of a group of buyers and take a cut of the revenues.

▶ You can't have a strategy in isolation. Remember, this is an ecosystem. Using the internet can deliver significant value to your organization by enabling it to reduce the cost of purchasing, streamline its supply chains, reduce inventory, increase profitability, and realize the business benefits of electronic trading relationships.

NOTES

1 'Food webs', **Eyewitness Guides Ecology**, Steve Pollock, Dorling Kindersley Ltd, 1993, p.12.

2 'BA plans to cut costs through internet strategy,' Kevin Dunn, **Financial Times**, February 24, 2000.

3 http:/www.izodia.com; http:/intradeonline.com and **The Guide to e-Procurement & Ecommerce**, a VNU Business publication, available from Infobank.

4 Interview with Jim Conning, Managing Director, on November 30, 1999.

5 Case study – Guilbert UK, available online at http:/www.izodia.com

6 http:/commerceone.com

7 Interview with Chris Phillips, Director of Marketing, Europe, on February 2, 2000.

8 Case study – Eastman Chemical, extracted from Commerce One customer profile article 'Eastman Chemical champions electronic procurement supply chain'.

PRINCIPLE 8

SUPPLIER PORTALS

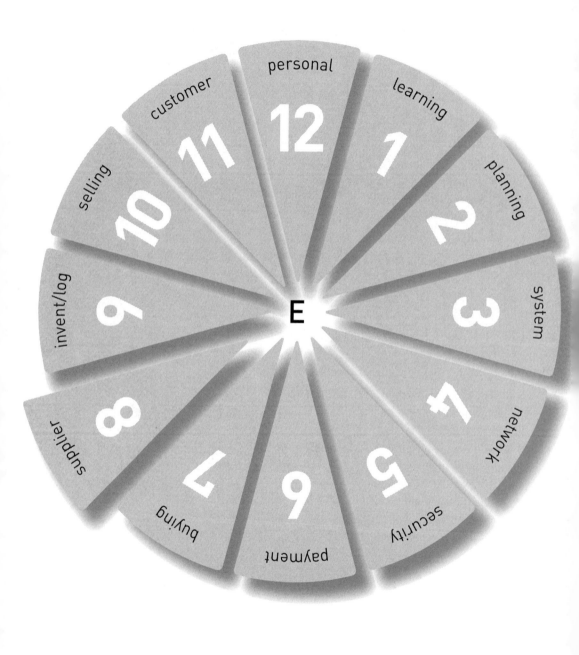

STATEMENT OF **PRINCIPLE 8**

ECOLOGICAL NICHE MEANS THE WAY in which a species uses available resources to survive, and the ways in which its existence affects the other organisms living around it. Laboratory experiments and observation of the natural world have led to the discovery that most species occupy different ecological niches. It is believed that this is to avoid competition between species when resources are limited. If two species were in direct competition, one of them would inevitably become extinct or would have to seek an alternative niche.[1] This observation of nature confirms James Moore's theory that business ecosystems will be the death of competition.[2]

❝the supplier portal or community is a child of the internet❞

The supplier portal or community is a child of the internet in that it was conceived as a business model because of the networked or web-like properties of the internet. To its users it delivers a swifter and more economic response and, if properly constructed, all parties can track any order at any time and at any place. When giant organizations in the large industrial sectors of automobile and aircraft manufacturers are converging to create their own portals, it signals that alternatives have run out and that fear and greed have merged into 'survival'. Supplier portals or communities (see the parallel in Chapter 11, Customer portals) are not limited to industries alone. Governments (regional, national or local), cities and towns will create their own supplier portals or communities. They too will have sub-communities and also links with preferred organizations, which contribute to and play a large role within the city, town or ecosystem.

The Heathrow Airport ecosystem, as with airline organizations, has thousands of suppliers on which it spends inordinate amounts of money. The internet has already shown the massive savings that businesses can make by linking electronically to their suppliers. These are not imaginary savings, they are real and substantial. These savings also go straight to the bottom line, into the company cash balance.

British Airways has set up its own supplier portal and it will not be long before the leading airlines follow the lead set by carmakers GM, Ford and DaimlerChrysler which are jointly setting up an industry portal called Covisint, with the aim of eventually supplying the entire industry. This will have a remarkable impact on lowering costs to levels well below what individual airlines can achieve on their own. Even aircraft manufacturers Boeing, Lockheed Martin, Raytheon and British Aerospace (BAe) Systems in the UK plan to place the bulk of their $71 billion of annual purchases through a new web-based trading exchange, which they plan to float as a separate entity.[3]

To avoid confusion, we repeat the difference between buying (principle 7) and a supplier portal (principle 8). *Buying* ensures that all the indirect suppliers of the organization are linked to the employees' desktops. A *supplier portal* is a marketplace or exchange of all the direct suppliers for a specific industry, into which an organization would integrate its procurement system. A supplier portal will aggregate everything into one electronic catalog, where goods can be ordered on one form and paid for, and delivery can be expedited. The cost saving is fairly obvious: there is no need for multiple telephone calls, multiple forms or multiple payments. This will result in a reduction in inventory costs and cycle times. A supplier portal will also allow for near real-time price comparisons and will support multi-currency transactions including the euro. The supplier portal also makes the suppliers more efficient, thus allowing them to offer better prices and better service to their customers.

The Finance Director and Purchasing Director own this principle. The Project Manager and Operations Director also exert their influence.

In the following case studies, we look at how supplier portals work in practice and how they can reconfigure your business, improve the circulation of information and save money for your organization.

SUPPLIER PROFILE

BuyingTeam.com

the site that saves your business money

BASED IN A LEAFY SQUARE IN LONDON, BuyingTeam.com was set up to save businesses money. It was established by The Cost Reduction Partnership (TCRP), the UK's leading purchasing consultancy, to bring to all businesses the lessons learned from its large clients, which include Asda, House of Fraser, MTV, Sotheby's and many other household names. BuyingTeam.com, realizing that most businesses don't have the time to constantly check the market for better deals, saves its customers money on cars, computing, office supplies, staff, telecoms, travel and utilities.[4]

> **BuyingTeam.com offers high-quality suppliers at competitive prices**

BuyingTeam.com offers high-quality suppliers at competitive prices. With seven years of purchasing experience behind it, it is able to choose suppliers which have the best combination of service, quality and price.

Its suppliers guarantee that the pricing on BuyingTeam.com's site is the lowest they offer. Buying is about price, quality and service, and BuyingTeam.com has negotiated deals with organizations that can offer this combination. It is also committed to driving down prices for smaller businesses and by aggregating the purchasing of all its buyers it is able to negotiate better prices through bulk buying discounts.

Using the BuyingTeam.com site will help customers to:

▶ buy at prices normally available only to larger organizations

▶ manage all purchasing from one source

▶ reach new and reliable suppliers quickly and easily

▶ keep track of when contracts need renewing and then renew at the best price

▶ save valuable time in administration by ordering and receiving quotes electronically

▶ co-ordinate purchasing for multi-site business

▶ access professional advice when buying new products or commissioning new services.

For consumers, the site also offers tariff calculators for cutting bills, an e-mail reminder service, and online ordering for consumer items. BuyingTeam.com's business site includes purchasing online from catalogs, and obtaining quotes and advice.

INTERVIEW WITH SUPPLIER

'We bludgeon suppliers on your behalf.'

David Graham, Managing Director

DAVID GRAHAM MADE THE MOVE from The Cost Reduction Partnership to BuyingTeam.com because he feared that in a few years' time The Cost Reduction Partnership would be under threat as e-commerce was fully implemented.[5] Why would anyone need it any more if they could go on the internet, find out where the best pricing was, save money, and say goodbye. If that was going to be the case, he was going to be the one destroying his business. The internet provided the tool and mechanism for them to set up an online replacement for The Cost Reduction Partnership for smaller and medium-sized companies as well as a tool to enable multisite clients to co-ordinate and aggregate their purchasing.

'It's more than just buying,' says David Graham. 'It's more than just reducing procurement costs. Buying cannot in our opinion be contained in one place, in one mode. It's much more than that. If you look at many of the B2B models, they fail to address or understand the needs of the buyers. For example, mysap.com offers me a stationer in New Zealand and other sites get you quotes for your paperclips. This is not how real buying works. I'm interested in a UK-centric buying portal backed by expert knowledge.'

'We frequently will have one or two selected suppliers in a category, whereas other buying portals have dozens,' he says. 'Now the question is, which is the better system? Having talked to suppliers, they get pretty annoyed at receiving a load of enquiries from people they don't know, which don't result in sales. They cannot be bothered to reply. We feel the more suitable method is to aggregate your buyers' needs, go to the supplier and purchase for many clients several million pounds worth of product at good prices. We then deliver that.'

❝buying is a partnership. It's all about quality of supplier and service❞

Graham declares that it isn't all about price. Buying is a partnership. It's all about quality of supplier and service. No point buying business cards at a great deal, say £20 for 250, only to find that the quality is shoddy and you are too embarrassed to use them. If you're buying a brand-name photocopier, a bidding system comes into its own on the BuyingTeam.com site, which sends the quote to several reliable suppliers. The site is effectively a portal – it is a destination for buyers to reach a full range of selected suppliers that have been carefully vetted to enable them to source and purchase all they need.

'We have developed various specific industry portals, such as one for the National Council for Voluntary Organisations, whereby the community of 'not-for-profit' bodies in the UK, such as charities, are eligible to come and access special deals for their trade body. Within this grouping, we signed a deal with The Government Buying Agency, which has 400 suppliers, whereby charities can buy at government rates through a closed user group.'

Graham recounts the background of how the company financed its internet start-up. Step one was to spend a few hundred thousand pounds in developing BuyingTeam.com. Step two was to obtain more money as the risk started becoming higher because revenues weren't so easy to come by on the internet. So it went for the first round of financing in mid-1999 and raised £2 million for 20 percent through a small venture capital house from high-net-worth individuals. It has now secured second-round financing of £15 million from Internet Capital Group, which is the leading investor in B2B companies in the world. The company is aware that if it doesn't perform it is going to have problems raising the money the next time. Having completed the first round, they started recruiting staff and had the same difficulties as everyone else in getting good people.

Graham believes it's a learning curve for everyone. 'Let's say for argument's sake that our site has cost £500,000 to develop; in the end, if we realized the final game plan, one would probably only needed to have spent one tenth, e.g. £450,000 being learning, and £50,000 was probably what we needed. No one realizes the number of designs and redesigns that have been discarded.'

❝suppliers, it appears, are frightened because of margin erosion ❞

Graham was also shocked by the attitude of suppliers who pay lip service to cost reduction, the web and e-commerce, but when it comes down to it they are not prepared to put the resources behind it. Suppliers, it appears, are frightened because of margin erosion. A major electrical wholesaler he knows still writes out everything manually in each depot, and is unwilling to commit to technology.

In the case study below, a major UK charity is now reaping the rewards of living in a supplier portal ecosystem.

PRINCIPLE IN ACTION

a major UK charity

history In June 1998 a major UK charity approached The Cost Reduction Partnership and asked it to review the charity's purchasing function.[6] The charity ran several hundred sites across the UK. All sites were predominantly autonomous in their buying and the company did not employ a professional buyer.

the review The policy was that all sites had discretion in the day-to-day running of their core business. However, this culture had crossed over into purchasing, resulting in predominantly single-site buying taking place. This created the following basic inefficiencies:

▶ no central purchasing function existed. This led to a lack of control over items purchased, suppliers used and prices paid

▶ there was little if any use of economies of scale in the buying function

▶ supplier reviews were infrequent and inadequate. On the rare occasions preferred suppliers were in place, not all sites were using them

▶ thousands of invoices were being created at a local level

▶ invoices for particular purchasing functions for some sites were issued to head office, sent to sites for authorization, then returned to head office for payment. This often resulted in lost invoices and late payments

▶ suppliers wishing to review and regrade accounts had no point of contact to discuss possible changes.

actions taken

After amalgamating the charity's buying requirements across nine basic buying areas, TCRP reviewed and renegotiated preferred suppliers contracts. Where preferred suppliers' did not exist, TCRP tendered the consolidated requirements to known third-party suppliers. All sites were informed and educated in the new arrangements. Reasons were given for the changes, along with the potential cost savings they would achieve. Controls were implemented to ensure that preferred suppliers would be used at all times.

"consolidated billing of generic areas such as utilities was arranged through head office"

Consolidated billing of generic areas such as utilities was arranged through head office. This greatly improved efficiency and eliminated the risk of sites' electricity or telephones being cut off due to loss of invoices and poor communications.

Through these actions TCRP achieved for the charity cost savings of £330,000 per annum. In addition, there were huge savings through administration and paperwork reductions.

the future

By the beginning of 2000 all sites had a PC with access to the internet and the ability to benefit from BuyingTeam.com. Discussions are under way as to how BuyingTeam.com can further reduce costs and improve efficiency at the charity. Likely potential benefits are:

- greater cost savings due to further increased buying power

- controlled expenditure through online authorization by regional managers

- reduced order times

- single monthly invoicing to head office across all purchasing functions. This will reduce the number of invoices created from thousands to hundreds

- access to live online consumption analysis for use in budgetting and live time reviews

- increased product choice.

Why did we choose BuyingTeam.com? The fact that a small supplier portal can aggregate everything into one electronic catalog for its client, effectively creating an ecosystem where goods can be ordered on one form and paid for, and delivery can be expedited. All this is an effort to reduce costs, which adds to the bottom line and improves efficiency. Although we have shown the benefits for customers, there are also benefits to suppliers. Suppliers can enter the ecosystem by forming physical and electronic relationships with organizations like BuyingTeam.com, thereby enabling them to compete in supplying to other charities.

SUPPLIER PROFILE

Oracle Corporation

the engine of e-business

IN TERMS OF DEVOURING COSTS, if BuyingTeam.com is a dolphin, Oracle Corporation[7] is a killer shark.

Founded in 1977, Oracle is the world's second largest software company, with more than 40,000 employees globally, and the leading supplier of software for enterprise information management. With annual revenues exceeding $8 billion, the company offers its database, tools and applications products, along with related consulting, education and support services, in 150 countries around the world.

66The information age has ushered in a competitive era where business opportunities are discovered and exploited more quickly than ever before 99

The information age has ushered in a competitive era where business opportunities are discovered and exploited more quickly than ever before. To thrive in this new environment, businesses are challenged to deploy information solutions that are both powerful and flexible — two characteristics that Oracle says traditionally have been competing objectives.

In response to this and leveraging the simplicity and cost effectiveness of the internet, internet computing allows organizations to shift operational and management emphasis from expensive client-centric models to focus instead on high-impact, flexible applications accessible via any web browser in a server-centric environment. A server-centric architecture places new demands on the database server with the increasingly complex applications and significantly higher usage.

Oracle's 8i is the database for internet computing. It is the most complete and comprehensive platform for building, deploying and managing internet applications. Oracle's Warehouse Technology Initiative provides customers with a complete data warehousing solution based on the industry-leading Oracle database and more than 60 complementary third-party software products and services.

Oracle Applications is a leading provider of packaged and integrated front-office and ERP solutions. Its strategy is to offer all the enterprise solution components to enable customers to execute strategies quickly and manage the risk of change. These applications comprise 45-plus software modules, which divide into the following categories: Oracle Financial, Oracle Human Resources, Oracle Projects, Oracle Manufacturing, Oracle Supply Chain and Oracle Front Office. More than 6,000 customers in 76 countries use Oracle Applications. Available in 29 languages, it lets companies operate in multiple currencies and languages, supports local business practices and legal requirements, and handles business-critical operations across borders.

For example, 6 million people in more than 160 countries have purchased products from Amazon.com, making it the world's busiest e-commerce site. The company relies on Oracle 8i to streamline order processing, house information on 5 million book titles, and supply unmatched performance.

Oracle servers, applications and tools are the standard at the US Department of Justice (DOJ). Oracle products deployed in all DOJ divisions – including the Federal Bureau of Investigation (FBI), the Drug

Enforcement Administration (DEA), the Immigration & Naturalization Service (INS) and the Bureau of Prisons – will automate, simplify and enhance information retrieval and analysis throughout the organization.

Princeton University uses Oracle WebDB, Oracle Application Server and an Oracle data warehouse to give students, faculty and a core group of administrative staff access to financial and student administration information. Princeton's 'Data Mall' provides secure, reliable data access to a broad range of the university population via a standard web browser. For example, students can view their telephone bills, payment records and other information online, saving the university from printing 12,000 pages per month in telephone bill details alone.

INTERVIEW WITH SUPPLIER

'E-business or no business?'

Phil Wood, E-Business Marketing Manager

'THE WAY COMPANIES DO BUSINESS has not changed signifi-cantly in the last 100 years,' says Phil Wood.[8] 'Accounting practices, business practices and the way in which customers link into busi-nesses and businesses to their suppliers have remained the same. Until now that is – we are at the start of a radical economic shift, and some of us haven't yet woken up and realized it.'

66becoming a networked business doesn't

just mean getting on the internet 99

Becoming a networked business doesn't just mean getting on the inter-net, it's about fundamentally changing everything that a company does, from interacting with its customers and linking all its customer-facing services, through effective sharing and managing information and applications internally, to effectively integrating suppliers into its busi-ness. As Oracle discovered, to do this requires focus in four key areas. The first of these is the requirement to change the technology being used to run the business.

technology shift

'Some companies have already spent thousands of pounds on software to run their daily business, and some of these systems may not even be fully implemented yet,' says Wood. 'But at the end of the day when it's all fully installed, they still won't be a networked business. Many of the successful networked businesses today – like Amazon – moved from nothing, and they moved quickly. For some companies, starting over again with their technology is going to enable them to become a networked business faster than their competitors. But that's a brave decision to take – to throw away all that investment.'

Internet technologies must now become an integral part of the business. 'It's no longer something that simply happens out there, on the world wide web. Customers use the internet to contact you, and your employees only have internet browsers on their desktops to interact with their business applications, and suppliers ought to interface to your systems via browsers and nothing else. The result is that you, instantly, have total integration of your business, your supply chain and your customers without the need for expensive applications or specialist software.'

business structure

The structure of the business has to change as well – the traditional hierarchical corporate structure doesn't offer the flexibility needed for a networked business. Flatter, leaner organizations, armed with technology, must tackle routine, repetitive tasks such as transaction processing, which can be performed better and faster than people. E-businesses, however, have data flowing over all parts of the organizational structure. The corporate challenge is to ensure that your new technology talks to all of the other pieces in the business – an essential feature for a networked business.

'As a customer, you are better off purchasing from someone with products across all areas,' says Wood. 'Those products might not be the best in each field, but assuming they all work together, your company will do better than with alternative options that have problems talking to each other. With Oracle applications, our customers get the best of all worlds – products that, although not number one in every case, combine to make a best-of-breed integrated solution. We have re-engineered all our products to ensure that they work together, delivering integrated functionality in a true networked business model.'

process change To accomplish this, business processes have to change too. 'All of the traditional business flows that exist today are about to change,' Wood confirms. 'They will all absolutely and radically change and businesses need to prepare, anticipate and get ready for that change.' Process change is about giving your clients self-service. One of the happiest customers is one that doesn't have to negotiate with a salesperson to get at what they want to buy. Amazon.com doesn't employ a single salesperson – it has a sophisticated computer that happily deals with more than 20 million customers. It gives information, advice, book recommendations and allows customers to buy all the books they want, plus, perhaps, a few that they didn't know they needed.

❝the ideal customer, in the e-world, is one that never visits your shop❞

The ideal customer, in this e-world, is one that never visits your shop, never phones customer service but loyally continues to purchase from you online. But customer loyalty has to be gained, it's not enough any more to simply display your wares – you have to understand their wants, needs and desires almost before they experience them. 'To sell successfully you need to have a three-dimensional view of your customer,' explains Wood. 'Traditional marketing doesn't exist on the internet, but in this strangely impersonal digital world, personal relationship marketing does, and to do that you need to glean every detail about your customers.'

Process change is also about giving your employees self-service, which results in better efficiency, greater transaction accuracy and lower costs. Oracle, like many companies, used to submit expense reports by paper at a typical processing cost of £100 per transaction and a three-week completion cycle. Now all expenses are entered directly into the system and flowed to a manager for approval, then on to the accounts payable system for electronic payment. If not approved within 24 hours, the system will hassle and prompt people to perform the necessary tasks. Now the process takes four days to complete, and costs pennies.

Another radical process change is to make suppliers compete for the business. Internet auctions are going to become commonplace, with suppliers seeing what others are bidding. No more closed rooms and secret dealings with each supplier individually to try to get the best deal. The carmaker Ford has switched to an online bid format, and on its first attempt saved $22 million against costs anticipated by its purchasing department. The winning bid came from Korea and the whole process took two-and-a-quarter hours to complete. 'More and more we are going to see consortia of buyers, rather like Ford and General Motors have established for the car industry,' says Wood. 'And these are going to be powerful players with a real impact on world purchasing, so of course they need powerful information systems like Oracle.'

business culture

Finally, in order to achieve these gains, the corporate culture has to change. 'This was the point that we, at Oracle, found most difficult,' confesses Wood. 'Oracle is the world's second-largest software company and every single person in our company is not only young but also technically savvy. It was, however, the cultural change that was the hardest for them.' For traditional businesses, which are not yet on the internet, cultural change is going to be one of the hardest challenges to meet.

Every one of these changes has to be driven from the top of the business – the CEO has to take responsibility for the direction and vision of the company. The internet is no longer about technology, it's about business. Even with the most amazing technological implementation, the project will fail if the business does not change alongside the technology. The success of this transformation is dependent on the entire process changing simultaneously, which is why the CEO must take control of the process.

❝to become a networked business you have to think web first❞

To become a networked business you have to think web first. Change your mind-set and it will actually save you money in every part of your business, not just where you interact with your customers and suppliers. To do this you need integrated applications that will support you in your vision. 'Within Oracle we have demonstrated what the return from networked business transformation using our tools and technologies can be – 20 percent on the bottom line,' says Wood. 'Internet computing allows organizations to shift operational and management emphasis from expensive client-centric computing models and focus instead on its business, using high-impact, flexible applications accessible from any web browser.'

Although Oracle powers most of the world's largest companies and is responsible for e-enabling many new businesses, it's also suitable and available for smaller companies. 'Most SMEs (small-to-medium enterprises) believe they cannot afford the outlay of time, effort and money to convert their businesses,' says Wood. 'Oracle Business Online does it for them. We host, manage and rent out the Oracle services to them, so that SMEs can get the benefit of advanced IT systems without a heavy investment in people and money.'

Oracle powers not just the world's largest companies but also world-class educational institutions, as the case study below shows.

PRINCIPLE IN ACTION

Yale University

YALE UNIVERSITY DOES MANY THINGS RIGHT. Its 10,000 students and 10,000 faculty and staff include world leaders in a full range of disciplines, and its $1.2 billion operating budget provides the resources that are basic to one of the premier places to obtain an education in the United States.[9]

It should come as no surprise that this world-class institution's foresight extends to a major modernization of its information systems. In 1997, officials evaluated the Year 2000 risks to Yale's existing systems. They considered the potential benefits of improved access to management information, reengineered business processes and reduced expenses. As a result Project X – an IT structure based on an Oracle database and an Oracle Applications software – emerged. The phased implementation began in July 1998.

Project X signals a big change for Yale. 'Imagine a city of 20,000 people with a central government, a hospital, lots of medical services, several museums, a sports complex and businesses,' explains Steve Sunderland, Project Director for the financial and human resources modernization.

'Now imagine you're putting in a financial, human resources and data warehouse information system for all of those – all the businesses, the service industries, the school systems, the medical services – all at the same time. That's what it's like doing a major modernization at a major research university.'

The Project X team includes 110 full-time workers, including consultants from Oracle and KPMG Consulting Services; in-house employees ranging from developers to major university officeholders, such as the controller; and the directors of benefits, compensation and human resources information systems. Their regular positions have been filled with temporary replacements.

The project office, which comprises a four-member group headed by Sunderland, called for significant parts of the new human resources, purchasing and accounts-payable systems to come online first. The new financial applications, including payroll and a new chart of accounts for the university, became active in the first half of 1999.

❝the scale of Project X is similar to the construction of a new wing of a building ❞

According to Joe Mullinix, Yale's Vice-President for Finance and Administration, the scale of Project X is similar to the construction of a new wing of a building, but the process is quite different. 'This is a much more creative process,' he says. 'One of the beauties of the new systems is that they allow you to create the management and process infrastructure to meet your needs and that involves a lot of creative activity on the part of the people here.

'It gives them a once-in-30-or-40-year time frame to really step back and rethink things,' he explains. 'I mean, how often do you get to change something as basic as a chart of accounts? Not that frequently.'

Project X is based on Oracle Database Server and Oracle Applications as well as Grants Management and Labour Distribution and Effort Reporting applications, which Oracle co-developed with Yale. The system runs on two IBM RS/6000 S70 Enterprise servers, configured to back each other up, and will arrive on the desks of the systems' 2,000-plus users via a fiber-optic network. The projected size of the fully implemented database is 1.2 terabytes.

The new system reflects and supports the university's reengineered business processes, aimed at cutting cost and time requirements for routine functions all across the campus. 'Numerous manual transactions took place in the university,' says Sunderland. 'For example, if a department in the school of medicine ran a DNA analysis for Internal Medicine, a manual cost transfer took place – somebody someplace filled out a piece of paper that was delivered to data entry, and a journal entry was created.'

'In the future, people will be able to requisition and effectively purchase those services from one another and the associated cost transfers will flow automatically, with Oracle Publishing, Payables and Projects.'

Oracle General Ledger, Purchasing and Payables will also simplify the reimbursement process. The university's old system required someone to fill out an expense report, refer it to a business manager for review, and send it to accounts payable, where it was reviewed again and often sent back. 'The accounts payable people had no knowledge of what that transaction was about – why a trip had been taken, for example,' says Sunderland. 'The value they were adding was cutting the check for reimbursement.'

Following reengineered business procedures, an expense report is submitted by use of the Payables module. The appropriate business manager reviews the report online and if it is approvable, passes it along to Payables, where the expense is paid and automatically recorded in the database. 'This reduces the amount of time it takes for a reimbursement by about 80 percent,' says Sunderland. 'Reducing the time and errors involved makes it less expensive. In a lot of cases, the cost of processing may have been more than the actual expense on the report.'

In addition to reaping the cumulative cost savings associated with reengineered processes, Yale stands to benefit from improved management decision making. Managers will have convenient access to information that previously was trapped in systems that departments had developed for their own use. Oracle data-warehousing technology, including Oracle Express and Oracle Financial Analyzer, will give managers an array of new tools for examining and interpreting this information quickly.

❝Yale stands to benefit from improved management decision making❞

'A research university has several lines of business, including education, research, medical services and community programs,' says Sunderland. 'If Joe Mullinix wants to conduct a financial analysis to see what the viability of these different lines of business is, Project X will allow that. Today, we can't do that because we don't have information captured about costs and revenues that would enable that senior-level analysis to take place reasonably easily.'

With Project X, the university's financial planning and management team will use the Oracle Express multidimensional database as a repository of information about their new budget system and will take advantage of Oracle's Financial Analyzer's abilities to view in several ways the information about how the university allocates resources. Oracle Express and Oracle Financial Analyzer will help the university meet its increasingly complex reporting requirements, in addition to providing the background data necessary for effective business planning.

'There has been a trend in recent years to provide more and more support services – not necessarily increasing the cost of pushing paper but raising the costs of doing business,' says Mullinix. 'The government has expectations about the kind of reporting we do to satisfy rules and regulations and everything else we should be accountable for. All those expectations essentially increase costs. We've been able to control the administrative staff growth, but we find that new requirements in a million different areas continue to add to our costs. So this is an effort to try to reduce those costs.'

From Mullinix's perspective, the improved administrative and data processes made possible by Project X add up to an enhanced ability to thrive in the modern education marketplace. 'We want to provide the highest-quality services to clinicians, researchers, faculty and students, so that we are an attractive, compelling place to work,' he says. 'And there is certainly a lot of focus on understanding and controlling costs that are associated with higher education at Yale and elsewhere. This one tool we can use to try to reduce and control those costs in the longer term, to get the biggest bang for the buck out of the money we spend.'

❝oracle continues to create a dynamic and powerful ecosystem with it's clients, which in turn grows its own internal ecosystem ❞

Why did we choose Oracle? Oracle's statement that its software powers the internet is an exaggeration to make a point. A very large percentage of e-businesses run Oracle software and as a result we could say that Oracle continues to create a dynamic and powerful ecosystem with its clients, which in turn grows its own internal ecosystem. In the above case study, we have also shown how Oracle created the Yale University ecosystem by wiring its central administration, hospital, medical services, several museums, a sports complex and businesses into a holistic and integrated unit.

EXECUTIVE SUMMARY OF
PRINCIPLE 8

A SUPPLIER PORTAL IS A SINGLE SITE that will aggregate everything into one electronic catalog. This will result in the reduction in inventory costs and cycle times; it will also allow for near real-time price comparisons and multicurrency transactions. But there is also an underlying aspect to these case studies in that they show how relationships are changing in the buyer and supplier partnership. It is no longer static and linear; it is dynamic and organic. And this means that the entire organization needs to be wired for the free flow of information.

▶ Using a supplier portal will help businesses to buy at prices normally available only to larger organizations; manage all purchasing from one source; keep track of when contracts need renewing and then renew at the best price; save valuable time in administration by ordering and receiving quotes electronically; co-ordinate purchasing for multisite business; and access professional advice when buying new products or services.

▶ It isn't all about price. It's more than just reducing procurement costs. Buying is a partnership. It's all about quality of supplier and service.

▶ Becoming a networked business doesn't just mean completing a supplier portal. It's about fundamentally changing everything that a company does. To do this, you must focus on four key areas.

1 *Technology shift.* You may have to throw away existing investment in technology. There must be a total integration of your business, your supply chain and your customers.

2 *Business structure.* The corporate challenge is to ensure that your new technology talks to all of the other pieces in the business – an essential feature for a networked business.

3 *Process change.* Process change is about giving your clients self-service, by understanding their wants, needs and desires almost before they do. It is also about giving your employees self-service, resulting in better efficiency, greater transaction accuracy and lower costs. Another radical process change is to make suppliers compete for the business through internet auctions.

4 *Business culture.* The cultural change is the hardest challenge for traditional businesses to meet. The success of this transformation is dependent on the entire process changing simultaneously, which is why the CEO must take control of the whole process.

▶ You can't have a strategy in isolation. Remember, this is an ecosystem. Most SMEs believe they cannot afford the outlay of time, effort and money to convert their businesses. Today, SMEs can host, manage and rent out the whole service, so that they can get the benefit of advanced IT systems without a heavy investment in people and money.

NOTES

1 'Ecological niche,' **Eyewitness Guides Ecology**, Steve Pollock, Dorling Kindersley Ltd, 1993, p. 26.

2 **The Death of Competition**, James F. Moore, John Wiley & Sons, 1996.

3 'Aerospace web trading exchange unveiled,' Alexander Nicoll, Kevin Done and Mark Odell, **Financial Times**, March 29, 2000.

4 http:/www.buyingteam.com; The Cost Reduction Partnership and http:/www. buy.co.uk

5 Interview with David Graham, Managing Director, on January 26, 2000.

6 Case study – a major UK charity.

7 Oracle Corporation 1999 annual report; http:/www.oracle.com/corporate

8 Interview with Phil Wood, E-Business Marketing Manager, on February 4, 2000.

9 Case study – Yale University: Modernizing a Miniature City, by Cabell Breckinridge; http:/success.oracle.../oramag; **Oracle Magazine**, September 1998.

PRINCIPLE 9

INVENTORY AND LOGISTICS

personal

learning

planning

system

network

security

payment

buying

supplier

invent/log

selling

customer

E

12 1 2 3 4 5 6 7 8 9 10 11

STATEMENT OF **PRINCIPLE 9**

IN EVERY ECOSYSTEM, ENERGY IS TRAPPED and stored by plants, the primary producers. Some of the energy is transferred to the animals that eat the plants. In turn, other animals eat these animals, and at each stage some energy is passed to the next level, where it is stored. Some energy is always lost in the transfer. Energy can never be recycled in an ecosystem; only raw materials are recycled.[1] Energy is stored, transferred and lost in much the same way in the business world. Whether it is a business acquisition, where much of the resources are transferred but some are lost, or whether it is an organization where delivery dates on orders need to be calculated in seconds, by simulating a schedule though the supplier, manufacturing and logistics facilities. By focussing on efficiencies in logistics and inventory, your organization can conserve its energy – its cash.

Principle 9 covers inventory and logistics. In the recent past, many companies which periodically have a surplus of slow-moving inventory – be it obsolete or distressed or simply overstocked – might have organized a bricks and mortar sale or at worst sold it off for scrap. Today, there is the outlet of the Internet auction.

There are numerous web services that cater for business-to-business auction needs and often specialize in the type of goods sold, such as industrial and laboratory equipment to computers and electronic parts and indeed across the whole business spectrum. One online auctioneer deals only in livestock, another auctions baseballs, several are devoted to memorabilia. There are auction sites for stamp collectors, coin collectors and even skateboards.

❝by focussing on efficiencies in logistics and inventory, your organization can conserve its energy – its cash❞

In simple terms, this is the way a cyber auction works. An online bidder taps his bid on the keyboard. The bid is recognized instantly at the auction end, compared with other incoming bids, and a response is generated. There are official closing times for online auctions, but in general terms an electronic gavel 'comes down' if there has been no bid for around two minutes. Some auctions last an hour, some up to a week or more. Internet auctions have revolutionized the world of inventory and logistics.

Returning to our example, Heathrow Airport's World Cargocenter is not an auction, but inventory and logistics play a critical role. It occupies more than 65 hectares and handles about 1.2 million tonnes of airfreight a year. For the UK, it is a crucial port, annually handling cargo worth about £50 billion. It is linked directly to all four of Heathrow's passenger terminals to assist fast clearance of bellyhold cargo from 170 aircraft stands. The Cargocenter also provides 94,000 square metres of bonded transit shed space. Most sheds are equipped with advanced mechanical handling systems, as well as cold-rooms and storage facilities for high-security and radioactive materials.

Heathrow's Cargocenter is a key component in the world's most advanced air cargo inventory computer known as CCS-UK, a comprehensive computerized cargo system which links airlines, freight forwarders and agents to the customs import clearance and export computer systems. It can track a cargo shipment through every stage of its journey and automatically handles customs and related documentation.[2]

Just as Heathrow Airport's World Cargocenter handles and stores air freight for others, there are organizations such as EMC that handle and store libraries of information for their business clients. Information, like freight, is valuable and perishable. There are many organizations like SynQuest and Opensite Technologies, featured in the following case studies, which use fresh and stored information to help their client organizations provide a more personal and more efficient service to their clients.

“information, like freight, is valuable and perishable ”

The desired result here is to auction your products either as an overall strategy or as a method of reducing your stock when it is aged or is over bought. The Operations, Sales and Finance Directors own this principle. The people with influence in this principle are the Marketing Director, for maintaining overall company image, and the Purchasing Director, for supplying information on purchasing trends and future opportunities.

In the following case studies, we show you how, under 'inventory and logistics,' a supplier organization and an industry are adapting and optimizing their businesses using the internet.

SUPPLIER PROFILE

SynQuest Inc.

optimizing supply chains

NAMED ONE OF COMPUTERWORLD'S '100 Hot Emerging Companies', SynQuest[3] is headquartered in Atlanta, Georgia, with offices worldwide. It employs hundreds of professionals dedicated to developing and implementing advanced decision-support systems that maximize the financial performance of enterprises.

SynQuest has hundreds of installations in dozens of countries at companies such as AT&T Wireless Services, The Eastman Kodak Company, Georgia Pacific, The Kellogg Company, Miller SQA, Nordstrom, Ford Motor Company, UPS and Titleist-Footjoy. Its customers come from diverse industries, but they all share a need for solutions to achieve competitive advantage by reducing cycle time, improving delivery, and reliability, and cutting costs.

Its products are used to support optimally strategic, tactical and operational management in an integrated fashion. They include a strategic module to select the most profitable number and location of suppliers, plants and warehouses; a tactical module to assign customer orders to plants and warehouses in order to meet customer demands at maximum profit; a module to optimize short-term production schedules and to track their implementation in real time; a module to generate accurate demand forecasts for any planning horizon; and a module to optimize inbound transportation decisions.

SynQuest's products offer two unique characteristics of major importance:

1 They are designed to optimize all decisions, i.e. simultaneously meet customer requirements, respecting all restrictions, while maximizing benefits to the user enterprise. This approach maximizes the enterprise's competitiveness and long-term market value.

2 They focus on optimizing performance, not merely plans: they synchronize operations by controlling, in real time, plans and execution, keeping them always very close to each other and at an optimum level. This capability also gives users early warning alarms, identifying potential performance problems and advising them on corrective actions to avoid such problems.

INTERVIEW WITH SUPPLIER

'You can build all the products you want, but if you don't understand the dynamics of your product and industry ...'

Peter Klein, Vice-President, Europe

PETER KLEIN EXPLAINS HOW the internet has changed everything in life, including business and supply chains.[4] In the pre-internet world, 'companies could sell a product even if they could not deliver on the expected date because they had the luxury of time to correct internal mistakes and get away with it. Today, there is no time to correct the problems; either you do things right or you cannot survive in networked business. To ensure your survival, you must have access to management tools that quickly provide you with the best possible solution to confront any set of circumstances, and the ability to respond to "what-if" questions always in the most profitable manner possible.'

These techniques are enabling companies to work in a lean and mean way: response times are being cut dramatically and so are transaction-processing costs and decision-support costs. They compound the effect of those benefits by collaborative management with partners. The consequence is much lower investments in inventories, facilities, and equipment, with much higher quality of customer service.

In the internet world most products will be commodities that can be differentiated mainly through service and information content. It is critical to involve customers in the process, answering their own questions and entering their own orders, for example. An increasing number of such commodities will be sold through electronic markets in which 'dynamic pricing' will increasingly be the norm; thus, prices will reflect supply and demand more effectively than before. But it will complicate the nature of decisions that will have to be made more quickly and optimally.

❝one of the first casualties of the internet
era is enterprise resource planning❞

One of the first casualties of the internet era is enterprise resource planning (ERP). This approach was originally developed in the dawn of the computer era, when super computers had a fraction of the power and speed of current laptops but cost thousands of times more. In networked business, ERP systems implemented in mainframes or client/servers are dying; their decision-support capabilities are not adequate to deal with today's business problems quickly and optimally. SynQuest has decision-support engines, or internet-enabled systems, which support each one of the 12 principles. And do so optimally, in seconds.

Peter Klein gives an example. 'A customer wants to buy a car. So the salesperson goes through a configuration engine that looks at all the options specifics and the parts required to fulfill them. The engine then calculates the earliest date on which the custom car can be reliably delivered to the customer. Bear in mind that these custom orders include mostly components, such as bumpers, seats, wheels, and others, that must be obtained from suppliers at several tiers. However, customers will not wait for days to receive a probable delivery date. They expect an instantaneous answer. If customers have to wait, the salesperson will lose that order and possibly a customer for life, just with a click of a mouse.

'The new paradigm,' says Klein, 'is taking all these complex transactions and throwing them into a memory-resident program that – using complex mathematical techniques (algorithms), which are transparent to the user – can provide the best possible answers, in terms of the best reliable date to promise the customer.'

What the system has done is to place the customer order in an integrated planning system, which schedules it through the supplier, manufacturing and logistics facilities available and determines whether the requested delivery date can be realistically and profitably met. If it cannot be met at the list price, the system will calculate the minimum additional charge to ensure that delivery date is met without affecting the supplier's profit. Alternatively, the system offers the best possible alternative date without additional charge. All of this is calculated in seconds. So, the customer is given specific alternatives that involve price and service trade-offs, while the supplier protects its profits.

Klein believes 'the logistics suppliers, the people delivering the product to final consumer, are the critical element in the entire process. The UPS, FedEx or DHL fellow who drives up to the customer's house is the most important person in the chain, because that person provides the human interface in the transaction. That fellow is in reality a virtual employee of the supplier.'

PRINCIPLE IN ACTION
Titleist-FootJoy

THE CUSTOM GOLF BALL DIVISION of Titleist-Footjoy was sad-
dled with special orders that became worthless when they couldn't be
shipped on time.[5] To complicate matters, Titleist's IT group was reluc-
tant to unplug the legacy system because of a significant investment.

Under increasing pressure to streamline its antiquated ordering
process and improve on-time fulfillment, the Titleist division was des-
perate for a way out of this sand-trap. The winning stroke: SynQuest
Synchronized manufacturing software from SynQuest of Norcross,
Georgia, which allowed Titleist to augment its legacy system with a key
client/server ordering component instead of re-architecturing the
system from scratch.

'The quality of the ball and the artwork for the customization is very
important to the customer, but if we don't get it there in time for the
tournament, it really doesn't matter how good it is,' says Bill Frye,
Plant Manager at Titleist, in Fairhaven, Massachusetts. With the new
system in place, Titleist is able to increase customer satisfaction and
decrease turnaround time without a lot of expense and downtime for
system redesign.

Identifying the snag in the current system was easy – not enough information. Sales representatives would take orders on the phone, and based on their experience of past lead times, commit to a delivery date. Often, however, pertinent information – such as projects already in the works, current levels of manufacturing capacity or delivery dates of other large orders – was overlooked, since the data was accessible only to plant floor operators. By the time sales representatives were made aware of a potential problem, the new orders had already been promised. 'There was a "disconnect" and we had to find a way to share the information,' said Frye.

66by the time sales representatives were made aware of a
potential problem, the new orders had already been promised 99

A large portion of the critical information was stored on a legacy AS/400 order-entry system, which was accessed only by the sales representatives and plant managers. The rest of the data resided on the plant floor, with no mechanism in place to gather or share it throughout the company. Titleist IT group was not about to sacrifice the time and money it had poured into the AS/400 system. The group decided to maintain that as its primary order-entry, processing and tracking repository and supplement it with the SynQuest applications to manage the plant floor operations.

The SynQuest application, housed on four IBM P90 Pentium servers, is updated continuously by sales representatives and plant floor workers, who have been given access to the system via 11 Windows 3.1 client PCs scattered throughout the plant. Every hour changes to the orders in progress or status of the manufacturing systems are uploaded to the AS/400 order-entry system using the export-on-demand feature of SynQuest. The latter includes the necessary hooks to communicate with the back-end AS/400, but Titleist's IT department also wrote special remote program calls to pull status reports from the Pentium floor systems.

Because the system tracks the progress of each line item and gives real-time status of each component required to fill a customer's order, sales representatives can view the volume and projected workloads for the manufacturing plant and set order delivery with more accuracy.

While most custom orders differ in one way or another, sometimes basic components of different jobs can overlap – another area where SynQuest can help. By prioritizing work and batching similar jobs, operators spend less time performing non-value-added tasks, such as setting up or breaking down an operation. Improving time management along scheduling and prioritizing capabilities has allowed Titleist to compress manufacturing lead times by more than 50 percent, from 12 days to five.

One unexpected benefit to the dual AS/400/SynQuest system has been a new sense of ownership on the part of the plant workers, according to Frye. Traditionally considered to be at the low end of the manufac-turing totem pole, several hundred workers, who span three shifts, now have input into making and delivering the custom Titleist prod-ucts on time. 'There was real anxiety at the beginning, but now the employees see what a difference it is making,' he says.

Given all these improvements, thrifty golfers in the market for seconds on high-quality golf balls will have to look elsewhere – that's one market Titleist has no plans to dominate.

We chose this case study to show that while it's fine to reduce inven-tory costs, other aspects will need to be speeded up to replace the vacuum. Orders and information on all resources and inputs need to be available and fresh, not just at the factory floor but also to the sales-person who is in front of the customer. In order to execute this, all businesses involved from raw material stage to the retailer need to be integrated holistically in an ecosystem.

In the next case study, we show different angles, problems, issues and resolutions related to inventory and logistics.

SUPPLIER PROFILE

OpenSite Technologies Inc.

where dynamic commerce begins

FOUNDED IN 1996, OPENSITE TECHNOLOGIES[6] was the first company to offer packaged online auction applications. The company, whose headquarters is in Research Triangle Park in North Carolina, is an award-winning, dynamic commerce pioneer with partners across the world dedicated to selling and supporting OpenSite solutions. OpenSite is a leader in online auctions driving the dynamic commerce revolution.

OpenSite has received accolades and recognition from many industry organizations and publications, including 'Anaylst's Choice' by *PC Week* and 'Best of Show' for outstanding e-commerce applications by Fall Internet World in 1998 and again in 1999.

"branded online auctions are critical to long-term success, because they provide the ability to build brand equity "

OpenSite believes that 'Internet auctions provide powerful new tools for boosting an organization's bottom line, while building an online community'. It also says: 'Branded online auctions are critical to long-term success, because they provide the ability to build brand equity. A branded auction site creates loyal customers who come back for the goods you sell and the services you provide. By owning your own auction site, you can build a database of bidders and not just winners.'

Because moving quickly is a critical success factor in the e-commerce environment, the in-house development of auction software can be an obstacle. OpenSite offers a cost-effective, proven alternative to building your own auction software. With hundreds of auctions powered by OpenSite technology, the company holds a market-leading position for both small and large businesses.

Among its suite of products and services, it offers Dynamic Pricing Toolkit, Auction Now, OpenSite Auction 4.2, OpenSite Concierge Service, Professional Services and BidStream.com.

In May 2000, Siebel Systems, Inc. announced its acquisition of OpenSite Technologies, Inc. The pooled interests of both organizations amounted to $542 million. OpenSite products will be known as Siebel eAuction and will be deployed as a part of Siebel Systems' e-commerce offering. It seems economically sensible that organizations are dissolving into each other so that they can provide their customers with a more compelling offering.

INTERVIEW WITH SUPPLIER

'Marry the inventory of goods and the profile of individuals efficiently.'

David Aldridge, VP Europe, and Matt Rushton, Marketing Director

EVERYTHING IN AN ORGANIZATION is negotiable, says Matt Rushton.[7] It's all about automated inventory reduction and inventory control. Even auctions are about inventory management. Dynamic pricing is about managing your raw materials and components for a minimum price, a minimum inventory and managing out towards its life cycle so you don't then have a warehouse full of, say, old computers.

'A typical situation,' says Rushton, 'is the sale of advertising space. An ad rep rings you up on a Monday saying, we close on Friday, you buy a page every other month, why aren't you buying one this month? If he's a good salesman he'll ask what sort of price you would be prepared to pay. If no deal is struck at that point, the ad rep will call back at 2pm on Friday and renegotiate a better deal for you. Either he will give you a much lower price or he will give you a larger discount for two ads or even give you an editorial next month alongside your ad. On a website everyone is bidding for their own pages. So the editor or publisher can look at that closely and say, how much more revenue can I bring in now through advertising? Should they print another, say, 16 pages to get all the revenue from the advertisements? There is a straight decision then – income versus cost.'

'But it's not just about income and cost. There is also the connection between the life cycle of a product and the profiles of individuals who purchase it at different stages of the life cycle,' explains David Aldridge. 'The beginning of the life cycle is when you can't produce enough to satisfy the market. This is where the goods stores make a big promotion and charge a premium. Then you have the middle of the life cycle, where you are basically using various other tactics to generate volume, some form of sale and promotion, and when it reaches the end of the life cycle, you have to consider getting rid of the last amount of inventory. Now, let's look at the profiles of individuals. Car dealers and manufacturers manage the asset because they know that for instance you would rather have a two-year-old BMW for £250 a month than £350, and there's another guy, who lives in a council house, who is happy to take the six-year-old BMW for £50 a month. It's also about managing the profiles of individuals. It's matching the profile of the individual with the inventory that is being recycled. Without profiling you can't do it.'

❝it's matching the profile of the individual with the inventory that is being recycled ❞

He adds: 'Inventory will disappear.' Suppose Dixons [the electrical wholesalers] knew you were moving house and needed a new fridge, a new freezer, a new microwave, a new cooker, a new television, a new washing machine and a new dryer. They would target you today if they knew that. But they don't know that until you walk into the store and say that you have just moved house and you need whatever it is. They would probably sell you these items for a special bundle price.

On the business side, it's not just about managing; it's about managing efficiently. There's a lot of advertising for free markets in the *Financial Times*. At freemarkets.com, where you can go in and bid, it's business-to-business, procuring goods for your organization at a discount. Suppose you want a million steel tubes to make a bridge; if at 10 o'clock they were priced at $10 million, at 10.15 they might be $6 million.

'Dynamic pricing also makes your purchasing cleaner,' says Aldridge. 'We were working with an African client and one of the areas we worked in was supplying to government and government-related industry. You win a project and somewhere down the line the suppliers may have to pay backhanders. But governments are now looking at putting contracts on the web, specifying what they want, when they want it and how they want it and their terms. How do you take out the corruption? You can't.'

It is not just about disposing of inventory, nor just about reducing risk, it's about making money in times when there is shortage as opposed to foolishly giving things away at the normal price when people are prepared to pay a premium. Rushton provides two examples. First, a shopkeeper who knows there is a shortage of Delia Smith books and he knows that W H Smith and Waterstones have sold out. He can actually put the price up. The major retail chains can't because they can't do it through their computer systems. Second, there is a site being built today on transportation – because transportation is a big 'buy' business – where companies like UPS, FedEx and DHL are actually making a bid on the logistics of moving the goods for any company.

Timing is also critical in auctions, and opportunities certainly exist for those who seek it. Aldridge says. 'I go to QXL and buy our computers when we have a new member of staff. I know when QXL computers go at the cheapest point in time and I bid then. They used to have two auctions a day at one time and on Sunday nights too. The best bargain I ever got was when one of the England football matches was on, no one was bidding on anything, so I went out there and QXL had to sell that computer that night at a very low price.'

PRINCIPLE IN ACTION

Dexpo

THE DENTAL INDUSTRY IN THE UNITED STATES is highly fragmented, with 117,000 dental offices buying goods from 200 distributors and 1,000 manufacturers. In such a segmented industry, Dexpo[8] forms a cohesive community and creates an efficient market in which buyers gain purchasing power and sellers have better access.

Dexpo initially came to OpenSite for a traditional auction format to offer a full range of dental supplies and equipment. Dexpo immediately recognized the opportunity for a reverse auction to enable dentists to procure high-ticket equipment. With this capability, dentists post the manufacturer name and model number of the equipment they want to buy and distributors submit bids. All orders are turned over to dealers for fulfillment, so Dexpo does not disrupt the natural order of doing business.

'OpenSite's focus on responsiveness and on software quality is what attracted me in the first place and that's what keeps me with them today,' exclaims Jeffrey Goodman, CEO of Dexpo.

Dexpo is now turning its attention to aggressive marketing and giving dentists more reasons to visit. Plans call for online continuing education and bulletin boards – all in an effort to build an effective forum for dentists to communicate directly with manufacturers and to learn from industry experts.

66plans call for online continuing education and bulletin boards 99

We chose OpenSite Technologies because its software powers internet auctions which ultimately is about automated inventory reduction, control and management. To create and manage these auctions you need to build communities or ecosystems of buyers and sellers. In the Dexpo case study, OpenSite created an ecosystem for dentists and suppliers to dentists.

EXECUTIVE SUMMARY OF
PRINCIPLE 9

IN THE RECENT PAST, OBSOLETE OR DISTRESSED or simply overstocked goods would have been sold or scrapped. Today, internet auctions have revolutionized the world of inventory and logistics. Software is used to optimize strategic, tactical and operational management in an integrated fashion, to the benefit of all parties.

▶ To ensure your survival, you must have access to management tools that quickly provide you with the best solution to confront any set of circumstances, and the ability to respond to 'what if' questions in the most profitable manner.

▶ In networked business, ERP systems implemented in mainframes or client/servers are dying; their decision-support capabilities are not adequate to deal with today's business problems quickly and optimally.

▶ Customers will not wait for days to receive a probable delivery date. They expect an instantaneous answer. If customers have to wait, the salesperson will lose that order.

▶ If a requested delivery date cannot be met at the list price, the system will calculate the minimum additional charge to ensure that delivery date is met without affecting the supplier's profit. Alternatively, the system offers the best possible alternative date to offer the customer without any additional charge.

▶ The UPS, FedEx or DHL fellow who drives up to the customer's house is the most important person in the chain, because that person provides the human interface in the transaction.

▶ Dynamic pricing is about managing your raw materials and components for a minimum price, a minimum inventory and managing out towards its life cycle so you don't then have a warehouse full of unwanted goods.

▶ It is neither simply about disposing of inventory nor about reducing risk; it's about making money in times when there is shortage.

▶ Timing is also critical in auctions, and opportunities certainly exist for those who seek it. On Sunday nights or special national events such as football matches, when no one is bidding on anything, bargains can be had.

▶ You can't have a strategy in isolation. Remember, this is an ecosystem. There is a connection between the life cycle of a product and the profiles of individuals who purchase it at different stages of the life cycle. It's about managing and matching the profiles of individuals with the recycled inventory.

NOTES

1 'The transfer of energy,' **Eyewitness Guides Ecology**, Steve Pollock, Dorling Kindersley Ltd, 1993, p. 10.

2 BAA Heathrow, airport information, facts and figures, http:/www.baa.co.uk/domino/baa/baanet

3 http:/www.synquest.com

4 Interview with Peter Klein, Vice-President Europe, on December 6, 1999.

5 'Hole in One,' Aileen Crowley, **PCWEEK**, December 9, 1996, Ziff-Davis Publishing Company, LP 1996.

6 http:/www.opensite.com

7 Interview with David Aldridge, VP Europe, and Matt Rushton, Marketing Director, on January 17, 2000.

8 Case study – Dexpo: US dental industry.

PART 4

B2C
(BUSINESS TO CUSTOMER)

PRINCIPLE 10

SELLING SOFTWARE

personal
customer
selling
invent/log
supplier
buying
payment
security
network
system
planning
learning

E

12 1 2 3 4 5 6 7 8 9 10 11

STATEMENT OF **PRINCIPLE 10**

IN THE NATURAL WORLD YOU CAN OBSERVE how organisms help each other. Coral polyps are small marine animals that create limestone shells; these build up to massive structures called coral reefs. They are among the most productive ecosystems on Earth. The reef owes its wealth to a special relationship between corals and plants. Inside each polyp there are tens of thousands of single-celled plants called zooxanthellae, which supply the coral with additional energy through photosynthesis.[1] Similarly in business, visionary leaders, like coral polyps, build up business ecosystems through their special relationships with tens of thousands of their empowered employees, business collaborators and financial partners.

In our living example of Heathrow, although retail space only uses 12 percent of terminal space, it contributes more than 50 percent of BAA's total revenue. BAA is the world's number one travel retail specialist and pioneered the idea that airports must have a strong commercial side to be a success. BAA offers retail shops, tax-free shops, restaurants and online purchases. It's all about selling; it's all about commerce. Community and content are the rivers that bring the rich soil of customers to the sea of commerce.

Whether it's traditional all-day breakfasts in Garfunkel's, seafood salads at Caviar House Seafood Bars, extra-value meals at McDonald's, cappuccinos at Starbucks or a pint of ale at Wetherspoons, Heathrow offers a fair range of restaurants and bars. This has not happened by accident. Through consultation with food critic Egon Ronay, every item in the 140 restaurants, cafés and bars at BAA's airports is tested.

All four of Heathrow's terminals feature high street shops such as W H Smith, Hallmark, Boots, Dixons, HMV, Swatch, Hackett, Body Shop, Principles and Gap. Other familiar UK luxury brand names such as Holland & Holland, Harrods, Liberty, Mappin & Webb, Mulberry and Thomas Pink have also opened a branch shop. And continental fashion houses have joined the party, with shops such as Gucci, Hermes, Chanel, and Ferragamo.[2]

Whether you are one of the 140 restaurants, cafés and bars at BAA's airports or one of the high street shops with a presence at one of Heathrow Airport's terminals, you do not just rent floor space from BAA – it also offers its tenants a host of ancillary facilities that together make it a marketplace for customers.

Principle 10 encompasses selling software: software that helps selling. The internet has no unions, it has no night and day, and it has no statutory trading restrictions. It is a 24-hour-a-day, seven-days-a-week, 365-days-a-year, non-stop trading community. Past methods of selling have always had some form of restriction, either human, governmental, space or time, but the internet never closes.

> **if goods are promised and not delivered, the internet customer will not accept excuses but will go elsewhere**

In this salesman's dream, many things can go wrong. If goods are promised and not delivered, the internet customer will not accept excuses but will go elsewhere. Another common mistake is if the website is difficult to understand or navigate. Research shows that difficult sites, overloaded with graphics and slow to load on to the screen, turn off users.

Under this principle, we show only two pre-eminent examples, but there are many forms and components of selling software that could be exhibited, such as communication support tools or 'call me software', web authoring tools, web database tools, and front-end and back-end e-commerce suites. Other areas are affiliation software suppliers, examples of companies using affiliation programs, multimedia graphic design software, content publishing, and search engines, which link your site to the major search engines. It is not difficult to see how organizations can become paralyzed from the wide array of choices. This is why only a few organizations will end up offering a 'package' that will do many of these functions.

The desired result of selling software is to create a website that encourages people to visit, to buy and to be so delighted with a great experience that they return to buy again and again. The ownership is in the hands of the Sales and Marketing Directors. The key influencers are the Project Manager, the Finance Director and the Operations Director, who are involved to ensure the decisions are in line with the plans to buy goods and collect payment.

Just as BAA offers its tenants a host of ancillary facilities that together make it a marketplace for customers, on the internet space organizations such as INTERSHOP and Microsoft, featured in the following case studies, provide various grades of offerings to their customers.

SUPPLIER PROFILE

INTERSHOP

creating the digital economy

IN 1989, 19-YEAR-OLD STEPHAN SCHAMBACH was a physics student at Jena, a town of 100,000 in what was then known as East Germany. That year the Berlin Wall came down and, in an unrelated event, Schambach dropped his scholarly pursuits in favour of another passion: electronics and computers. He is now CEO of INTERSHOP Communications Inc.,[3] headquartered in San Francisco.

INTERSHOP Communications Inc is one of the world's leading providers of sell-side electronic commerce software for complete business-to-business and business-to-consumer solutions. With more than 100,000 licences sold worldwide, INTERSHOP customers include many of the world's largest telecommunications companies and commerce service providers (CSPs) such as: Deutsche Telekom, France Telecom, Bell South, Swisscom, BCE Emergis, MindSpring, PSINet and Ticketmaster Online-CitySearch. Many corporations have chosen INTERSHOP as their enterprise e-commerce application, including Bosch, Canon USA, Hewlett-Packard, Mercedes-Benz and NatWest.

Starting his business in an abandoned Protestant parsonage with five people, INTERSHOP was at one stage the best-performing stock on Frankfurt's Neuer Markt, soaring from its €50 launch in 1998 to €590 in first quarter 2000. Revenues skyrocketed 159 percent in 1999 to €46.3 million. With a market capitalization of about €7 billion, 24 offices and 650 employees globally, Schambach wants to be the 'the motor for the internet economy'. The company ranks third behind American leaders Open Market Corp and Broadvision Inc.

INTERSHOP has effectively divided its product sets into two product lines to support different business models – selling direct, selling indirect, enabling merchants and marketplaces. The first product line is called INTERSHOP 4, which incorporates INTERSHOP Hosting, Merchant and ePages. INTERSHOP Hosting and ePages are shared-server hosting solutions, which are sold in bundles of tens or hundreds to a service provider who then rents them out. INTERSHOP ePages allows CSPs and commerce communities to offer merchants highly deployable, low-cost, entry-level e-commerce websites with basic functionalities. INTERSHOP Hosting is the next step up for CSPs to offer more features and allows them to host multiple sophisticated storefronts on a single server, which translates into savings for the customer. INTERSHOP Merchant is a dedicated server solution that allows CSPs to provide maximum performance to high-traffic sites.

❝it is now the world's most powerful sell-side e-commerce solution❞

Schambach went upmarket with a next generation XML (Extensible Markup Language) and Java-based product called INTERSHOP enfinity, released in October 1999. This software is aimed at large companies, including Hewlett-Packard, and allows them to take orders from a host of new web devices such as mobile phones and Palm handhelds.

It is now the world's most powerful sell-side e-commerce solution, enabling enterprises to sell anywhere, integrate everything and protect investments through future-oriented technology.

'This new product puts INTERSHOP in the big leagues,' says David Truog, an analyst at Forrester Research.[4]

In the following interview, INTERSHOP Managing Director John Griffith shows how quickly the company grew exponentially and why it has such a powerful proposition.

INTERVIEW WITH SUPPLIER

'We've got a complete domination of the sell-side marketplace.'

John Griffith, UK Managing Director

IN FEBRUARY 1999, THERE WAS AN INTERSHOP get-together in San Francisco. John Griffith remembers. 'We had a blue sky session, where we tried to imagine what would be our vision in two years' time. One guy said INTERSHOP would spawn a hundred millionaires. Another guy sketched up a front cover of *BusinessWeek* magazine and put Stephan Schambach's head on it.'[5] Only a year later there were actually between 30 and 40 millionaires and Schambach's head was on the February 7, 2000 edition of *BusinessWeek*.

To understand INTERSHOP's value to companies such as Commerce One you actually have to look at the nature of the relationship between them. Commerce One creates a MarketSite; Commerce One will do a procurement environment, into which companies like Boots and Bass will come along and procure anything from pencils to bicycle wheels. If these companies go into that procurement environment and not enough sell-side content is in there, they will back away, saying this procurement environment is not fulfilling their expectations. So what Commerce One is compelled to do is to fill that procurement environment with as much content as it can.

It can do that in two ways. First, it can go out and ask those who want to put sell-side offerings into its MarketSite, and can do so using their technology; it can load up data and park that data within the Commerce One site. Second, it can go to the entire INTERSHOP community. It can say to the market leaders in sell-side content creation: take any INTERSHOP storefront data by means of what we call a MarketSite connector and drop that content and that data into the MarketSite. 'In this way, instantly multiplying not just the volume of content but also ultimately the value of the procurement environment. How?' asks Griffith. 'They can go back to Boots and say, we had 50 people in our procurement environment, now we've got 150,000 – thanks to INTERSHOP.'

❝the key thing is mySAP will be successful only on the quantity of sell-side content that it attracts ❞

Another example of the procurement environment is mySAP.com. Xerox has maybe 4,000 or 5,000 suppliers, of which only a small proportion are running SAP themselves, which poses a small problem. If SAP wanted to procure using a SAP-to-SAP connection, that would be fine. But as soon as it wants to procure using this wonderful mySAP.com procurement environment, from suppliers which are not running SAP, it would have the same problem as Commerce One. It can drag in its data and format it, but that's very retentive by nature. Or it can put on an INTERSHOP site at any level and make it work, so the sell-side of the SAP can go directly into the next environment. You can choose to put on a high-end INTERSHOP product or a middle-ground INTERSHOP product, may be even hosted by a third party. The key thing is mySAP will be successful only on the quantity of sell-side content that it attracts. If it only attracts other SAP companies, that's pretty poor.

Griffith concludes: 'Any of those procurement environments will have to seek the broadest and fastest providers of sell-side content they can possibly find and that's probably only going to come from the likes of INTERSHOP and Microsoft.'

The following case study shows INTERSHOP's enfinity in action.

PRINCIPLE IN ACTION

Cicada Music

CICADA[6] IS A PORTAL SITE for users to listen to live streaming audio, create custom CDs and download MP3 music files. A child of Octane Music, it was launched in February 2000. (As of mid-2000, Octane and Cicada merged into Classical.com.)

'Where there is a chip, there will be music' is the mantra for Roger Press, a former music industry executive who is tapping the internet to alter the way the world is listening to music. Press, now CEO of the UK internet start-up Octane Music, is not satisfied to offer 'just another' music retail site on the web as he eschews the travails and costs of bricks-and-mortar retailing to gain 24/7 access to a global clientele. 'Our mission is to free the world from the constraints of physical music collections. Wherever you are, we want to deliver your favorite music on to your desktop, into your car, even to your cell phone in real time.'

To achieve this ambitious goal, Octane, which owns an extensive library of jazz recordings and a catalog of classic music, is working on a portal site that ultimately will blend e-commerce with streaming audio, downloads of MP3 files, personalization and custom CD manufacturing.

PricewaterhouseCoopers seized the opportunity to become an early adopter of INTERSHOP enfinity and took up Octane's project as a real-world solution with tight deadlines and an eager consumer audience. 'Octane's undertaking provided the ideal testing ground for us to explore the potential of INTERSHOP enfinity because the site requires extensive integration with personalization and up-to-date retail features as well as cross-marketing and reporting,' said Mark Reed, Manager of Consulting Services at PwC. 'No other out-of-the-box product could deliver the flexibility and modular extensibility like enfinity. Developing a proprietary solution was not a viable option because the test site had to go live after only six weeks.'

❝with enfinity, the boundaries of e-commerce applications have been moved beyond the limits of traditional technology❞

With enfinity, the boundaries of e-commerce applications have been moved beyond the limits of traditional technology. The standard product handles common functions such as sophisticated product catalogs, shopping baskets and electronic payments. However, INTERSHOP offers much more. In Octane's case, enfinity's pipeline architecture has helped Marketing Director Alex Kovach translate his business ideas into the structure of the solution without extensive use of techno-speak. 'The graphical user interface and the drag-and-drop features of enfinity's Visual Pipeline Manager made it so easy to create and edit business flows while the site was still in development,' he said.

Most importantly, enfinity's flexibility allows Octane to change and modify business flows as market demands change and requires adaptation of the site's functionality. Octane's secure download of MPEG music files through a suite of pipelets is an example of the use of enfinity's business steps that are programed in Java to perform specific functions. Octane accepts payments through the CyberCash payment cartridge that is integrated with Barclay's ePDQ.

Octane's rush to market and the successful deployment of the test site within six weeks required a break with the traditions of project management and meant drawing from an array of resources. Retail Solutions

Centre, part of PwC based in the UK, and INTERSHOP R&D in Jena, Germany, assisted with customization and on-the-job training with the enfinity product. 'We were very impressed by the ability of the PwC and INTERSHOP teams to take on a very demanding challenge and deliver a working website within six weeks,' said Tim Lloyd, Director of Business Development at Octane. 'This would never have been possible without an advanced internet retailing product like enfinity, as it gave us a vital leg-up in the development race.'

While www.cicadamusic.com is viewed as the pilot project that helps gather valuable information about customer preferences, it has only a fraction of the features that will be available on the final site. 'The market is ready for MP3 and high-quality live streaming, especially now that high-speed internet access is becoming more affordable and commonplace,' Kovach explained. 'Deep and sophisticated personalization will be critical for our success and we are confident that enfinity's flexibility and openness for added functionality will go a long way toward keeping the site up to date to reflect changes in consumer behavior.' Cicada Music and Octane Music merged in mid-2000 to form Classical.com (www.classical.com).

What this case study shows is how INTERSHOP has been able to create a significant community or ecosystem by allowing market leaders in sell-side content creation to take any INTERSHOP storefront data and drop that content and data into the MarketSite, in this way, instantly multiplying not just the volume of content but also ultimately the value of the procurement environment. In the case of Cicada Music, it's like inviting existing shopping traffic in a captive mall to come and visit your new store.

SUPPLIER PROFILE

Microsoft Corporation

digital nervous system in action

FOUNDED IN 1975, MICROSOFT[7] is the world leader in software for personal and business computing. The company offers a wide range of products and services designed to empower people through great software – any time, any place, and on any device.

Based in Redmond, Washington, and with 35,000 employees across the world, Microsoft generated net revenues of $20 billion and net income of $8 billion in 1999 – a growth of 73 percent over the previous 12 months. In 2000 net revenues climbed to $23 billion and net income to just below $10 billion. More than 40 percent of Microsoft's employees work in research and development and another 45 percent in sales and support. The average reported age of its employees is 34.

E-commerce strategy
Microsoft has partners in four key areas of the internet and e-commerce marketplace, says John Noakes, Business Development Manager, BizTalk. 'First, we have internet service providers and independent software vendors (ISVs). They are companies that have applications to sell – examples would be SAP, Peoplesoft and J. D. Edwards. Second, we have development service companies (DSCs).

These are organizations that don't have applications but have skills, technical skills, systems design, systems architects, implementation and project management. They help design custom solutions and implement packaged solutions on Microsoft platforms. Third, we have systems integrators, such as Cap Gemini, Logica and CSC. Fourth, we have the Big Five consultancies, PwC, KPMG and Andersen Consulting.'

❝Microsoft is putting a lot of emphasis on BizTalk, which allows software to talk the language of business❞

Microsoft's e-commerce strategy can be summarized by three key words, says Noakes: build, integrate and promote. The *build* part of the strategy is about helping companies build a web presence. The suite of products that form the core Microsoft e-commerce platform are Windows 2000, SQL Server 7, Internet Information Server (IIS) and Commerce Edition. The *integrate* part is about taking that website and integrating it with your existing legacy or heritage systems and, more importantly, with your suppliers' systems and customers' systems. Microsoft is putting a lot of emphasis on BizTalk, which allows software to talk the language of business. BizTalk is a platform neutral framework, a set of rules and regulations using XML, a global standard owned by W3C, the World Wide Web Consortium. The *promote* part is about the role of the portal. You have built a website, you've integrated it with your suppliers, then and only then should you really think about promoting to the big wide world and be open for electronic commerce. If you haven't got your house in order, you are not going to be able to deliver.

Microsoft's core internet engine product is Commerce Server running on IIS. Noakes says there are three key words to describe Commerce Server: engage, transact and analyze. The *engage* part is about designing and building websites that help your organization engage with the customer, without ever having to talk with them – this area is about personalization, which is covered in Chapter 12. The *transact* part is about the ability to conduct online transactions in a secure and authenticated manner. The *analyze* part is about discovering answers to questions such as 'how often did I sell product x from page 32 of my website during the month of March between the hours of 10 and 12?' That kind of rich analysis of website traffic has to be just three or four clicks away.'

Microsoft.NET

In October 2000, Microsoft launched .NET. The purpose of Microsoft.NET[8] is to make information available any time, any place, on any device. The driving force behind Microsoft.NET is a shift in focus from individual websites or devices to new constellations of computers, devices, and services that work together to deliver broader, richer solutions.

The Microsoft.NET platform will fundamentally change the way that computers and users interact. By bringing employees, customers, data, and business applications into a coherent and intelligently interactive whole, .NET will allow businesses to benefit from radically increased efficiency and productivity (see Figure 10.1).

To get a sense of the opportunities that .NET will provide, let's look at today's situation. User information is principally a local phenomenon; if you log in from a different machine, your preferences, data, and applications are not accessible. Also, data for the same user across different applications and sites is difficult or impossible to automatically integrate into a single, coherent view for the user. Microsoft.NET promises to address these deficiencies. It will do this by realizing the vision of enabling access to a user's entire range of data and applications anywhere and from any device.

These changes will arise from a new generation of applications, created and connected by today's software developers using the .NET platform, with XML as an industry standard. Ultimately, this will allow developers to create programs that transcend device boundaries and fully harness the connectivity of the internet in their applications. Businesses

will thus benefit from radically increased efficiency and productivity, as
.NET brings employees, customers, data, and business applications into
a coherent and intelligently interactive whole. In short, .NET promises a
world of business without boundaries.

❝in short, .NET promises a world of business without boundaries❞

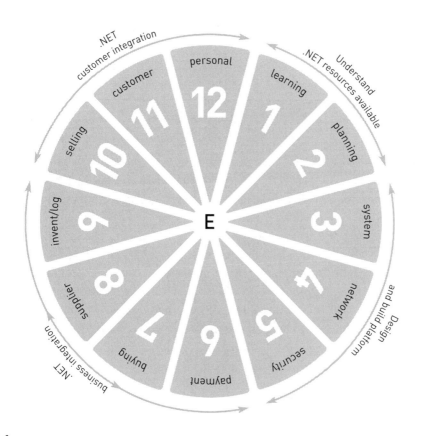

FIG 10.1

INTERVIEW WITH SUPPLIER

'Software is the key element in transforming the world.'

Neil Holloway, UK Managing Director

'WE PASSIONATELY BELIEVE that software will be the key driver
with regard to providing a better experience for business-to-business or
business-to-consumer, e-business, t-business, m-business or whatever
you want to call it,' says Neil Holloway.[9] 'The best way to describe next
generation window services is to look back 15 years,' he says. 'We took
a long-term bet on graphic user interface and what we actually did was
to build a platform for that and then we built other applications on top
of that, such as Word and Excel. If you move forward, it is clear people
will do business over the internet and that software will be delivered
as a service over the internet. What we need to do is build the right
kind of platform and services to deliver window services over the
internet through to multiple devices, whether that's a PC, a mobile
device or a TV.'

Andy Matson, Manager, E-commerce Group at Microsoft, illustrates
what Microsoft has been doing with the MS Office software package in
the recent past. 'If you look at the difference in Office over the last two
or three releases, and indeed with Office 2000, there's an enormous
amount of internet awareness within that package. You can author

natively in HTML and it publishes natively in FrontPage' HTML from Office. In PowerPoint, if you are searching for clip art and you are connected to the internet, PowerPoint will go to the web and search for items within the clip art database.' Microsoft is attempting to weave its software and community into the internet.

Microsoft's community is enormous. 'Millions of people write applications on top of Windows,' says Holloway. 'In the UK, there are probably about 400,000 developers and we have a very high market share with products like Visual Basic and Visual C, so you only need to take that and extrapolate it out worldwide. In fact, I would suggest that the biggest community there's ever been has been the Wintel community – Microsoft's Windows and Intel.'

> **"Microsoft has also created a whole new community in its ecosystem through its internet portal MSN "**

But Microsoft has also created a whole new community in its ecosystem through its internet portal MSN. This is sometimes reported as number one or number two in the UK for online service. It created 18,000 public communities in the first eight weeks after introducing MSN Web Communities, and 3 million users in two months when it introduced MSN Messenger Service. 'Nobody has a consumer portal like MSN,' says Matson. 'MSN competes not with Sun or Oracle but with AOL and Yahoo! Therefore it is in a different part of the company, with a different remit.'

MSN is aimed at the consumer, whereas bCentral is aimed at the small business customer. bCentral is a Microsoft service that allows businesses to get themselves online by building a store very simply by themselves or getting a partner to do it for them. It allows it to be promoted using link exchange, which has 75 percent coverage of the websites on the internet.

Microsoft's strength is certainly financial. 'We currently spend $3.8 billion in research and development, which puts us in the top five companies in the US. Next year we'll probably up that by about 20 percent, so that takes you to almost $5 billion,' says Holloway.

But that's not all. Another Microsoft strength is 'our ability to turn on a sixpence and we're not shy about doing u-turns,' says Matson.

Going back to John Noakes's, three key words about Microsoft's Commerce Server – engage, transact and analyze – you will see these three words in action in the case study below, which features Starbucks Coffee Company.

PRINCIPLE IN ACTION

Starbucks Coffee Company

STARBUCKS COFFEE COMPANY is the world's leading roaster and retailer of specialty coffees.[10] The company has more than 3,500 stores worldwide and posted revenues of $2.2 billion in fiscal year 2000. Like many popular brands, Starbucks Coffee Company launched a website to complement its retail presence. Loyal customers, as well as those who know of the Starbucks brand, go to www.starbucks.com to buy coffee products and gifts, and to learn more about the art of roasting and brewing coffee. The site also offers services such as the Starbucks 'Taste Matcher' tool, which interactively recommends specific coffee roasts and blends based on a customer's preferences. In the short time between the launch of Starbucks.com in July 1998 and the end of 1999, traffic had increased to the point that the site was experiencing approximately one million hits per day.

situation

Its old platform was no longer capable of meeting the company's strategic goals, says Jim Nystrom, Vice President of E-commerce for Starbucks. Successfully connecting with its customers over the internet makes them better customers in the stores. By leveraging the internet to extend its reach enables Starbucks to own coffee in the minds of the consumer, and regardless of location it creates a more satisfied and loyal customer. For example, there are people who buy coffee many times each week in their retail stores, but who still purchase ground coffee for home use at the grocery store. By making it convenient – even pleasurable – for them to purchase coffee for use at home over the internet, Starbucks can not only increase coffee sales but market other items that the consumer may not have considered purchasing at Starbucks, such as a new Barista coffee maker.

“Starbucks needed to deliver a richer, more
personalized experience for the user”

business challenge

Starbucks needed to deliver a richer, more personalized experience for the user. It needed to be able to identify patterns in customer behavior, make assumptions about the causes of those patterns, and then rapidly test those assumptions towards maximizing revenues and customer satisfaction, and in a manner that minimized downside risk. This would require the ability to implement targetted promotions, and to identify the correct customers for each promotion. It also needed an easy means to create, manage, and refine these promotions, one that could be used by its marketing staff in real time, and would not require development resources every time a change was needed.

solution

With six months left before the Christmas holiday season, Starbucks decided to upgrade to Microsoft Commerce Server 2000 and take advantage of the extensive 'out-of-the-box' e-commerce functionality it provided. Using pre-built components provided with Commerce Server 2000, such as the Targeting System, Catalog System and the Business Process Pipeline System, Starbucks would gain the new features it needed without several months of development time. New analysis features provided by the Commerce Server 2000 Business Analytics System would help Starbucks to better understand customer behavior and preferences by enabling it to extract and analyze site usage, purchase data, and results of promotions – with a very high level of detail and insight. New management features, such as the Commerce Server 2000 Business Desk, would provide the company's business managers with an integrated set of tools to access the reports and put this information to best use through rapid creation and refinement of targetted promotions, and the maintenance and continual enhancement of the site.

Before upgrading, the Starbucks team defined the project's vision and scope, analyzed both new and existing business requirements, and defined requirements for scalability, performance and functionality. In a parallel effort, developers familiarized themselves with Commerce Server 2000 and developed a tool using the Visual Basic development system to export the existing Starbucks catalog to XML, which could then be imported into the Commerce Server 2000 Catalog System by accessing the system's import features through the Business Desk. Planning to extend the data warehouse was also under way, in order to meet the reporting capabilities of Starbucks' business users.

closing the loop – driving rapid improvement Upgrading

to Commerce Server 2000 and SQL Server 2000 has resulted in benefits for Starbucks customers as well as the company's technical and marketing personnel. Thanks to the Commerce Server 2000 Profile and Targeting Systems, customers enjoy improved site performance and a better, more personalized experience. Starbucks enjoys decreased development costs and faster time to market due to the extensive out-of-the-box functionality provided with Commerce Server 2000. The Starbucks technical team is able to manage the site with less effort by configuring the Business Desk to provide business managers with self-service access to functionality that would have previously required development resources. This leaves developers free to focus on interesting, value-added tasks, such as improving site functionality.

Starbucks marketing personnel have also benefitted from the upgrade to Commerce Server 2000, in more ways than one. They now enjoy improved reporting and analysis through the Business Analytics System, and they have the capability to react to this data and close the loop in real time through the site-management capabilities of the Business Desk.

"it needed the ability to better communicate with customers in order to learn their preferences"

If they see that certain content is very popular, they can easily create a promotion tied to the content, knowing that they have the tools to monitor response and make incremental changes to the promotion. 'As part of our corporate culture, Starbucks encourages innovation, and we understand that innovation requires taking risks,' says Jim Nystrom. Commerce Server 2000 greatly improves the company's agility in these situations. Business Analytics enables it to monitor results in almost real time, and the Business Desk enables business managers to make rapid corrections or refinements until they're satisfied with the results. The level of integration enables them to close the loop extremely quickly, which minimizes any potential long-term negative impact.

business benefits Starbucks' primary motivation for upgrading to Commerce Server 2000 was to deploy a platform that would enable the company to meet its strategic goal – reaching out to customers via the internet and extending the Starbucks experience into the user's home or office. To do this, it needed the ability to better communicate with customers in order to learn their preferences, and the flexibility to use this knowledge to deliver a better customer experience. 'For Starbucks, the main benefit of moving to Commerce Server 2000 was being able to have a personal conversation with our customers – to determine what they want and then personalize the Starbucks experience to meet those needs,' says Nystrom. Once Starbucks understand their preferences on the individual level, it can use this knowledge to drive improvements to the customer experience across the company, whether via the internet or one of its retail stores.

Now that Starbucks has these extensive e-commerce capabilities, it plans to extend them to the company's retail store managers. Nystrom says: 'For example, if a store manager decides to bring in a jazz trio for a night, he can access our e-commerce platform via the Business Desk, identify users who have searched for a store in his area and have also purchased a jazz CD, and target these users with an offer inviting them to come to see the trio.'

We chose Microsoft because it is pre-eminent in 'selling software' and it runs an enormous organization, with tentacles in almost all business organizations across the world. It has achieved all this on the back of Windows and Microsoft Office. With its .NET strategy, Microsoft is embarking on an ambitious plan to provide software that will run your business from the internet at affordable rentals. Although it has not as yet assembled all the pieces, which may take up to the end of 2002 to complete, it is effectively saying it can deliver 'the pizza' or 12 principles to you via the internet, on a pay-as-you-go basis. If it succeeds, Microsoft will have transformed itself from an enormous organization into a super-ecosystem.

EXECUTIVE SUMMARY OF

PRINCIPLE 10

THE PURPOSE OF 'SELLING SOFTWARE' is to create a website that encourages people to visit, to buy and to be so delighted with a great experience that they return to buy again and again. It's all about selling; it's all about commerce. Community and content are the rivers that bring the rich soil of customers to the sea of commerce. 'Selling software' is the powerful current that drives the river down to the estuary. In the two case studies above, we have shown how the software currents are attempting to navigate the hard waters of buyers and customers.

▶ If companies go into the procurement environment and do not find enough sell-side content, they will back away, saying this procurement environment is not fulfilling their expectations.

▶ Any procurement environment will have to seek the broadest and fastest providers of sell-side content and that's probably only going to come from the likes of INTERSHOP and Microsoft.

▶ An e-commerce strategy must build, integrate and promote. For e-commerce to work, it must engage, transact and analyze. By *engage* we mean designing and building websites that help your organization engage with the customer, without ever having to talk with them – personalization. By *transact* we mean the ability to conduct online transactions in a secure and authenticated manner. By *analyze* we mean discovering answers to a host of questions derived from a rich analysis of website traffic, which helps you to understand your customers better.

▶ Successfully connecting with customers over the internet makes them better customers in your stores.

▶ The main benefit of a personal conversation with your customers is to determine what they want and then personalize the web experience to meet those needs.

▶ You can't have a strategy in isolation. Remember, this is an ecosystem. E-commerce alone will not work effectively unless your organization has developed a platform that will bring your employees, customers, shareholders, collaborators, data, and business applications into a coherent and intelligently interactive whole.

NOTES

1 'Riches of the reef,' **Eyewitness Guides Ecology**, Steve Pollock, Dorling Kindersley Ltd, 1993, p. 46.

2 Heathrow, airport information, facts and figures, http:/www.baa.co.uk/domino/baa/baanet

3 http:/www.intershop.co.uk

4 'Germany's Hot Star,' William Echikson, **Business Week**, E.BIZ, February 7, 2000, EB19.

5 Interview with John Griffith, UK Managing Director, on February 1, 2000.

6 INTERSHOP success stories: http:/www.cicadamusice.com 'PwC and INTERSHOP deliver sophisticated music website on enfinity'.

7 http:/www.microsoft.com/uk/ and http:/www.biztalk.org and interview with John Noakes, Business Development, BizTalk, on January 13, 2000.

8 Microsoft.NET Resource CD ROM National Hall, London Olympia September 28/29, 2000.

9 Interview with Neil Holloway, UK Managing Director, on January 28, 2000, and telephone interview with Andy Matson, Manager, E-Commerce Group, on February 4, 2000.

10 Case study – Starbucks Coffee Company http://www.microsoft.com/servers/net/Starbucks.htm

PRINCIPLE 11

CUSTOMER PORTALS

personal

learning

planning

system

network

security

payment

buying

supplier

invent/log

selling

customer

12
1
2
3
4
5
6
7
8
9
10
11

E

STATEMENT OF **PRINCIPLE 11**

IN THE ESTUARY, FRESH WATER from rivers enters the sea, creating a rich and fertile ecosystem that is almost as productive as a coral reef or a tropical rainforest. Most environments depend on plants to create a first energy source, but estuaries are fed by a constant supply of mud, silt, the remains of plants, and other organic material, or detritus, brought down by the rivers, which mixes with material brought in by the tides.[1]

In our world, the community is the estuary, where the rivers of content converge in the sea of commerce, creating a rich and fertile ecosystem.

Principle 11 embodies customer portals. A customer portal is rather like a supermarket through which a company sells. It is in effect another distribution channel. Yet when we look at portals such as Yahoo! and Amazon, they are evolving to the point where they are becoming the new 'global' public utilities or, put another way, the new information masters.

One of the trappings of a portal is that it builds a 'community' and requires members to register. In this way, it builds up a demographic record collated in a database that develops into a valuable asset for business to tempt advertisers and e-merchants. What makes portals attractive to retail consumers is their ease of use. Logging on to a portal on the internet is rather like opening up a catalog of products and services. The difference is that the catalog is huge, with lists of category choices in groups of generic subjects such as business, travel, entertainment, money, news, people, health and education, shopping, politics, home and family and much more.

Under each generic category you will find hundreds if not thousands of sub-categories to investigate and explore. By following a hierarchical route, you can hyperlink to millions of websites, which offer the product, service or information you are looking for. Portals use search engine technology to help speed through the maze. They become route maps, but in time, once you have selected your preferred portal, you will stick with it for pretty much everything. It will become a destination you will rarely leave as its presence moves with you on all devices – PC, TV, mobile phone, cable TV, bank ATM and so on.

❝portals use search engine technology to help speed through the maze❞

Back at Heathrow Airport, there are many communities. There is the community of BAA and then there is the community of each airline, the community of airline pilots, of stewards, of cabin crew, of aircraft technicians as well as communities of the airport-based employees. Each of these communities also has sub-communities. Take Swissair for instance – it has a community of customers, a community of employees and a community of shareholders.

BAA has a contract with the local communities in which it operates. It takes an active part in supporting them. It listens to its neighbors and addresses their concerns. It acts resolutely to minimize environmental impacts and acts positively as a good corporate citizen in the wider community.[2]

The airlines have their communities and sub-communities. You may recall the example of American Airlines given in Patricia Seybold's book, *Customers.com*, which we featured in our book *Battle of the Portals*. In 1997, American Airlines offered its frequent fliers special deals online and within a year it had in excess of 800,000 subscribers – what a community it now has!

Here's the difference between a customer portal and a supplier portal. A customer portal is a portal where like-minded individuals congregate, such as Amazon.com, Yahoo! and eBay. A supplier portal is a portal where suppliers congregate to obtain or deliver optimal prices, such as Covisint, E-Steel and PlasticsNet.

The desired result is to create a site that has many buying or interest features to it. The objective is to create a community that returns regularly and has a sense of belonging that reaches 'tribal' levels. The critical issue here is to capture customer data and use it to increase sales. The Sales and Marketing Directors own this principle and the Project Manager should also have a key influence over it.

Follow the wise words of Amazon CEO Jeff Bezos when planning your portal strategy. He says: 'Be a community builder, be a facilitator and be a networker.' It is critical to let your community network with one another, share ideas and information, and meet off-line as well as online.

In Chapter 10, Andy Matson described our next case study thus: 'Nobody has a consumer portal like MSN. It competes not with Sun or Oracle but with AOL and Yahoo!' Microsoft's MSN portal is number one or two in the UK for online service. It created 18,000 public communities in the first eight weeks after introducing MSN Web Communities, and 3 million users in two months when it introduced MSN Messenger Service.

SUPPLIER PROFILE

msn.co.uk

where do you want to go today?

MSN WAS LAUNCHED IN THE US AND THE UK in 1995 in conjunction with the launch of Windows 95. The portal site in the UK was launched in 1998. Microsoft's consumer internet service took the Christmas number one spot in the UK home internet market, according to a report by international research group NetValue, a measure of home internet use.

Not only was MSN number one in 'reach', the equivalent of advertising circulation, with 56.7 percent of the total internet population visiting its site, but msn.co.uk[3] came in at number five globally, making it the second top-performing UK player (29.3 percent). The top three of four internet domains were understandably US-based. Overall msn.com is the global number one.

NetValue measured the home internet audience, but MSN also leads the way in the total internet market, at work and in education. MSN's own figures for its combined business, education and consumer audience were 6.4 million for December 1999. Compared to 12 months before, when MSN had a total audience of 850,000, the UK arm of the world's most global internet service had increased at a rate of 752 percent.

MSN UK Director Judy Gibbons said: 'We put this success down to a number of key factors. One, the standard of our UK content, because we give people the material and services they want from 300 top media and internet companies including the FT, the BBC, The Telegraph Group, This is London, Yell and Amazon. Our content is updated and refreshed ten times a day, which is unique for a UK site. And a top editorial team including former BBC and heavyweight news editors and journalists monitors it.'

❝the company has also spent a lot of time and effort in making the site suit its customers❞

The company has also spent a lot of time and effort in making the site suit its customers. 'We're not "just a search engine" or "just an ISP". Our portal is active and changes on average four times a year in response to customers' feedback,' says Gibbons. It has invested millions in this and is in it for the long term. MSN is a global business in more than 30 markets, and in each of these markets it tailors content and services for that country. It knows the markets change every three months, so it changes with them. In November 1999, MSN featured on British national television and radio with an £8 million advertising campaign on the theme of 'Life's Great' with a view to increasing the number of visitors to its site.

what services are on offer?

▶ A single starting point for fast and easy access to the best information and services on the internet.

▶ Your own communications center offering free portable e-mail and fax services.

▶ A great new search tool with MSN Search.

▶ Customization and personalization facilities that allow you to create a home page relevant to you.

▶ Your own web communities, so that you can create your own website and online photo album with message boards, chat rooms and your favorite links.

▶ MSN Messenger to keep in touch with all your online contacts.

▶ Weather reports.

▶ Stock information.

▶ Live chats with celebrities such as George Michael, and live streaming media concerts such as Paul McCartney's return to Liverpool's Cavern Club.

▶ A vibrant shopping area with more than 35 retailers plus channels focussed on Property, Recruitment, Classifieds, Cars, Travel, News, Football, Business, Personal Finance, Entertainment, Learning and Computing.

▶ The MSN Gaming Zone with all the best online games from chess and backgammon to Age of Empires and Fighter Ace.

INTERVIEW WITH SUPPLIER

'The best of the internet in one place.'

Geoff Sutton, Programming and Revenue Group Manager

'THE KEY WAY FORWARD FOR PORTAL SITES on the internet is the understanding of users – figuring out what services and content they need, when they want it and how they want it delivered,' says Geoff Sutton.[4] Some prefer to browse and find websites and information that suits them at that time; others wish to go straight to what they want through accurate and swift search; yet others wish to be in contact with friends, family and business contacts through communications technology such as e-mail, Messenger and new devices. It's about personalizing the web for each individual.

Personalization and delivery is becoming more and more important. The fast adoption and development of services on mobile phones, televisions and other devices will make society more connected. 'When users think MSN, we want them to sense simplicity, user friendliness, accessibility and ubiquity. We want them to know that, with MSN, they can tap into the full power of the web anytime, anywhere, on any device. We call that the Everyday Web,' says Sutton, who believes that MSN makes day-to-day life more fun and liveable, empowering users with feelings of competence and control, and offering great, easy-to-follow content and design at every mouse click. Ultimately, the company wants people to consider MSN an absolute necessity for getting through each day productively and successfully. But who are these people? 'That is MSN's biggest challenge over the next year or so,' says Sutton, 'how we establish who our users are and how we really connect with them. I think we do have an idea of who they are. The number of female users is catching up with men, many are ABC1, and the demographics of MSN users are actually not far off the internet as a whole.'

From the business perspective, Sutton explains that MSN's partners are content providers, advertisers and retailers. 'Ours is a site of content aggregation, so we have 138 content providers. We make our money on advertising and we get a rental and a percentage on e-commerce transactions. We're trying very hard to build the revenue side of the business and to recover the huge sums invested, but there's always been the reach versus the revenue balance and to my mind the reach part is still the most important thing.' What's more, MSN is not really a stand-alone operation: it is part of the Microsoft ecosystem.

❝MSN and Microsoft provide retailers with a start-to-finish internet business solution❞

MSN and Microsoft provide retailers with a start-to-finish internet business solution. For instance, Sutton says: 'A retailer can come in at any point on this sort of site, whether it comes from building a website and hosting a website, promoting the website through link exchange or on MSN, or on our small business portal, bCentral. Microsoft has got a comparison engine, which we will be populating, building and promoting with as many retailers, small businesses and large ones into an electronic shopping area. One of the benefits we have is the technology part of Microsoft and MSN to create that environment and to bring the traffic we have and build on it.'

Traffic will come only if the security and trust issues are addressed. MSN's answer to these is its 'Passport', which is an authentication tool and wallet. 'If you go from one site to the next, whether it be a merchant site or site that needs an authentication, those sites that have Passport can identify that those customers are Passport holders and thereby provide the best shopping experience,' says Sutton.

We chose msn.co.uk because it is part of Microsoft's new ecosystem. However, Microsoft admits it does not know yet who makes up its community, mainly because it started its business first and on the back of that is now building a community. In the next case study, we show you how eBay built a community and business in unison.

SUPPLIER PROFILE

eBay

your personal trading community

EBAY[5] IS THE WORLD'S LARGEST personal online trading community. eBay created a market: efficient one-to-one trading in an auction format on the web. Individuals – not big businesses – use eBay to buy and sell items in more than 2,900 categories, including collectables, antiques, sports memorabilia, computers, toys, Beanie Babies, dolls, figures, coins, stamps, books, magazines, music, pottery, glass, photography, electronics, jewellery, gemstones, and much more. Users can find the unique and the interesting on eBay, everything from chintz china to chairs, teddy bears to trains, and furniture to figurines. As the leading person-to-person trading site, buyers are compelled to trade on eBay due to the large amount of content available. Similarly, sellers are attracted to eBay to conduct business where there are the most buyers. eBay provides more than 3.5 million new auctions and 400,000 new items every day.

the mission

eBay helps people trade practically anything on earth. The company was founded with the belief that people are honest and trustworthy, and believes that each of its customers, whether a buyer or a seller, is an individual who deserves to be treated with respect. It continues to enhance the online trading experiences of all constituents – collectors, hobbyists, small dealers, unique item seekers, bargain hunters, opportunistic sellers, and browsers. The growth of the eBay community comes from meeting and exceeding the expectations of these special people.

the history eBay was conceived as the result of a conversation between computer graduate Pierre Omidyar and his wife, an avid Pez™ collector (she owns a collection of more than 400), who said how great it would be if she were able to collect Pez™ dispensers and interact with other collectors over the internet. As an early internet enthusiast, Omidyar knew that people needed a central location to buy and sell unique items and to meet other users with similar interests. He launched eBay on Labor Day in September 1995 in order to fulfill this need.

Because of its active and thriving community, eBay has been the lucky recipient of several awards and distinctions, including:

► 'Forbes's Favorite Auction Site' (*Forbes*, December 1999)

► 'The New Establishment – The 50 Most Powerful Leaders in the Information Age' (*Vanity Fair*, October 1999)

► 'e.biz 25 The Most Influential People in Electronic Business' (*BusinessWeek*, September 1999)

► 'Winner of the Top E-Commerce Site' (Ziff-Davis, *PC Week*, *Interactive Week*, May 1999)

INTERVIEW WITH SUPPLIER

'It is the community that makes eBay what it is.'

Jennifer Mowat, Country Manager, eBay UK Ltd

'EBAY IS A PURE MODEL IN TERMS OF creating a marketplace for people to buy and sell,' says Jennifer Mowat.[6] What that means basically is that eBay does not buy anything itself to resell. Its focus is to create a clean and well-lit marketplace. In other words, it does not have any conflict of interest – it does not actually purchase goods that it sells on its site under its name.

eBay works on very thin margins, making money in two ways. First it charges listing fees, the fees that you pay to initially put an item on the site and which are waived in the UK as they grow to make it more enticing for buyers. Second is the final value fee, which are in fact success fees. If you successfully sell your item, you will pay eBay a very small percentage.

Because the margins are thin, overheads need to be low. The company's best support is its community of sellers and buyers. 'When you have a question, you go to our chat board, you say I am a newcomer and I would like to put up pictures, can someone help? Many people will explain to you what you need to do,' says Mowat. 'It is a very strong community and in a sense that is more powerful than what we do. We have a very strong customer support team, but we will never guess all the questions and we will certainly never guess all the answers. The power of the community, which today numbers over 10 million who actually use the site, is that it knows something about this site, they know where to put up their pictures and where to get other features that they can incorporate. They also know the best tips for when to trade and when not to, when to dig and when to stop digging.'

This is how an eBay auction works. If I am the owner of coins and I would like to sell them on eBay, I place a written description, add a picture so that you can see what I am selling, and set a starting price for my auction. I must also choose to set a reserve, which may be higher than the starting price, and I won't sell below that reserve. I can also choose the length of the auction; typically they run for about a week. You and potential buyers will be able to see what price the auction started at, what the current bid price is, and most importantly in terms of confidence, my user name and feedback rating.

❝to be able to do business on eBay, you must have a decent positive feedback ❞

The feedback rating is comments, both positive and negative, that people write about you on transactions that you have made in the past. To be able to do business on eBay, you must have a decent positive feedback. There are two types of feedback, standard, which is about you as a person, and transactional, in which item numbers must be quoted and the eBay system actually checks that the transaction has happened. 'At eBay, we believe that most people are honest and want to do repeat business, because it is unlikely that someone will be willing to destroy his or her reputation,' says Mowat. 'With negative feedback, people worry about buying from you. A good user may have 50 positive feedbacks and one negative, but that can't be helped and overall as a buyer that gives you confidence.'

There are two ways to bid. Either you bid progressively or you use a very interesting proxy bidding system. This means that you can actually determine how much you are willing to pay for this item. However, rather than make your bid, you request 'only implement my bid by the minimum I need to do' and anytime someone comes on to this site, you will automatically outbid them, which means you don't have to be watching the auction every moment and you need not overpay.

If you are successful in your auction, e-mails are sent out to both the buyer and the seller and you have three days to get in touch with each other. Normally, the buyer will send payment to the seller and as soon as the latter receives the payment, they send the goods to an address specified by the buyer.

In the event of theft or fraud occurring in an eBay sale, Mowat says: 'We work very closely with law enforcement agencies. We also have an automatic insurance policy for small to medium transactions, if goods are lost.' Today, the risk is very much on the buyer's side, but systems such as 'escrow services', which can be used for more expensive items, are useful. Escrow services are neutral third parties which will receive the monies from the buyer and the goods from the seller and only then despatch the goods to the buyer and the money to the seller.

❝selling and buying used or new goods was previously prohibitive and impractical❞

eBay realizes that 'it is the community that makes it what it is.' But there is no community without 'content'. And without community and content, there is no commerce. Selling and buying used or new goods was previously prohibitive and impractical. The need was always there, but the technology was not. What eBay has done is apply the internet to a business model that has quenched a natural need in the market and the result is that it has grown an ecosystem from nothing.

EXECUTIVE SUMMARY OF
PRINCIPLE 11

THERE IS NO COMMUNITY without 'content'. And without community and content, there is no commerce. The community is the
estuary, where the rivers of content converge in the sea of commerce,
creating a rich and fertile ecosystem. The case studies in this chapter
clearly show that to optimize your commerce, you need a solid community and continuous content to create your own ecosystem. Without
them, you had better look to join another ecosystem.

▶ A customer portal is rather like a supermarket through which a
  company sells. It is effectively a new distribution channel.

▶ One of the trappings of a portal is that it builds a 'community' and
  requires members to register. In this way, it builds up a
  demographic record collated in a database that develops into a
  valuable asset for business to tempt advertisers and e-merchants.

▶ What makes portals attractive to retail consumers is their ease of
  use. Logging on to a portal on the internet is rather like opening up
  a catalog of products and services.

▶ Portals use search engine technology to help speed through the maze. They become route maps, but in time, once you have selected your preferred portal, you will stick with it for pretty much everything. It will become a destination you will rarely leave as its presence moves with you on all devices – PC, TV, mobile phone, cable TV, bank ATM and so on.

▶ Traffic will come only if the security and trust issues are implemented.

▶ The power of the community is knowledge about what the community does, the best tips of the trade, and when to do things and when not to do them.

▶ You can't have a strategy in isolation. Remember, this is an ecosystem. The objective is to create a community that returns regularly and has a sense of belonging that reaches 'tribal' levels.

NOTES

1 'Where the river meets the sea,' **Eyewitness Guides Ecology**, Steve Pollock, Dorling Kindersley Ltd, 1993, p. 50.

2 Heathrow, airport information, facts and figures, http:/www.baa.co.uk/domino/baa/baanet

3 http:/www.msn.co.uk

4 Interview with Geoff Sutton, Programming & Revenue Group Manager, on December 10, 1999.

5 http:/www.eBay.co.uk; http:/www.eBay.com

6 Interview with Alexis de Belloy, Business Development Manager and Jennifer Mowat, Country Manager, eBay UK Ltd, on January 24, 2000.

PRINCIPLE 12

PERSONALIZATION

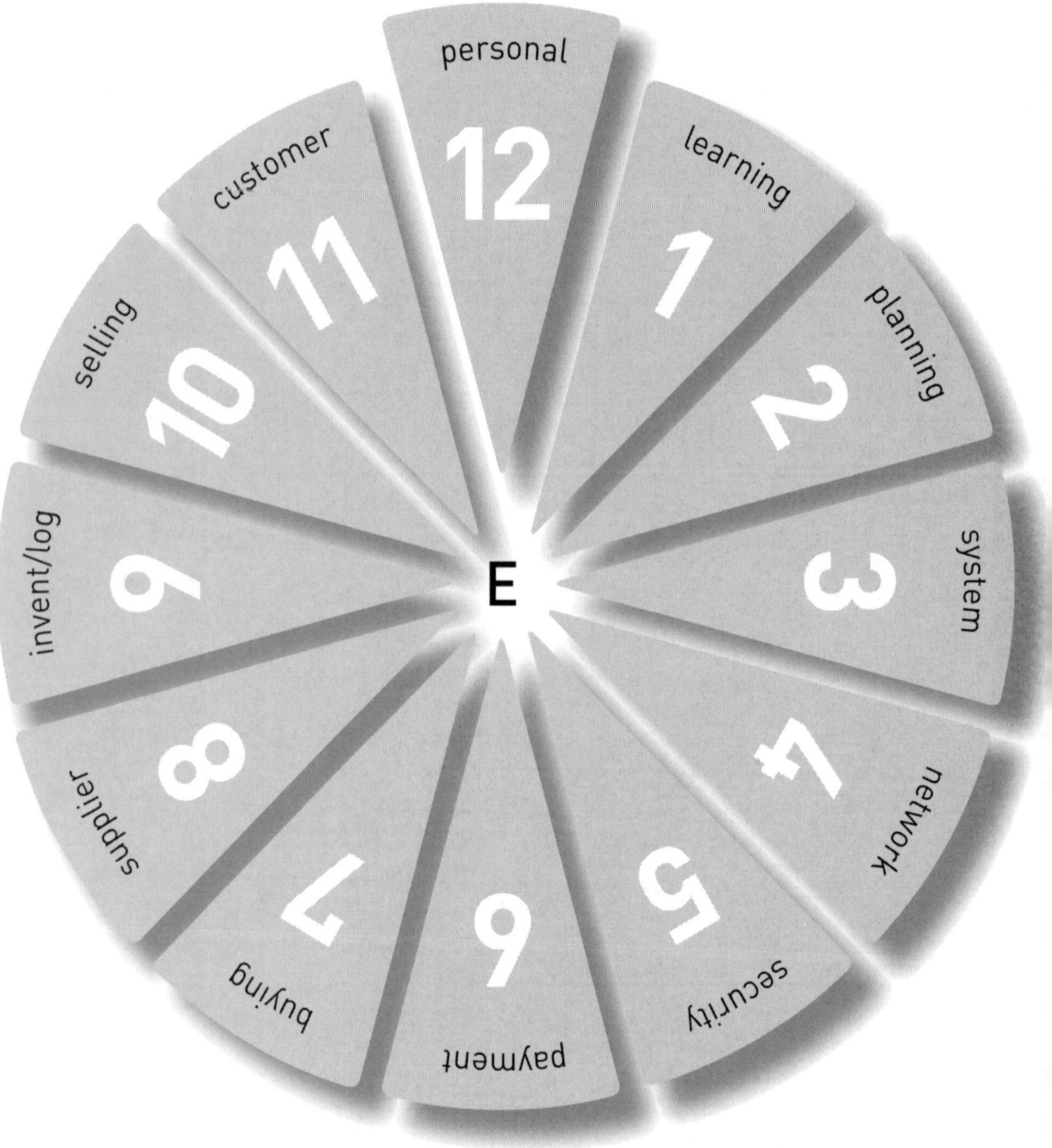
E
12
personal
1
learning
2
planning
3
system
4
network
5
security
6
payment
7
buying
8
supplier
9
invent/log
10
selling
11
customer

STATEMENT OF **PRINCIPLE 12**

EACH ANIMAL HAS ITS PERSONALITY. Despite the common distinctive feature of no limbs, snakes, which are closely related to lizards, have a wide variety of classifications: from anacondas to cobras, from pythons to rattlesnakes, from sea-snakes to vipers – each has a very different look, need and skills. Take the rattlesnake. It hunts its prey, the kangaroo rat, at night using heat-sensitive pits in its face. The rattlesnake's bite injects a powerful venom that will kill the prey quickly, but not immediately. Using smell receptors in its tongue, the snake follows its dying victim and then devours it. This method of killing uses the minimum amount of energy, which is a premium in the desert. The unique rattle in the tail is thought to have evolved as a warning signal to keep away larger animals that might trample it. Ironically, the rattlesnake is deaf and so is unable to hear its own sinister warning.[1] In the same way, for marketing to be effective, you need to research, study and know the habits, wants and needs of your customers. Like the snake, you must use your handicap to your advantage.

Don't make the mistake of treating your customer as a common snake. Find out what type of snake they are – cobra or rattlesnake – and then cater to their individual needs. People like to be treated with respect and consideration, yet they also like to belong to a group. This is where the internet has a powerful weapon in mass customization. Once customers have spent time personalizing services at a particular site, they are less likely to switch to competitors. With custom pages and other offerings, organizations can achieve superior communications with their customers, providing access to communication, constantly and instantly. They can also present a superior offering to their larger accounts. In time, this personalized offering to customers will move from desktops to all devices.

Airports and airline companies, like any retail business, need to personalize their offering to their customers. The belief is that the more personalized the service, the more likely it is that the customer will be pleased and therefore return for more of the same. The question is, at what cost, and can it be justified? In Chapter 11 we mentioned Patricia Seybold's example of American Airlines and how it increased its membership by providing personalized e-mails introducing special discounts, fares and savings. Next it added online transactions, booking your tickets electronically so that you could change them at the last minute if you wanted, and earning bonus frequent-flyer miles.

Principle 12 is about personalization, which means personalizing goods, products, services and information to an individual's needs and wants. Although the web is the technology of the future, paradoxically it also enables a return to a very old-fashioned value: personalized contact with customers. An internet site can be highly effective for monitoring and analyzing the buying habits of customers, customizing products and information to meet those habits, and quickly responding to queries and requests. Internet sites can build and enhance relationships with customers through 'personalization'. This is the personalization of the electronic relationships with your customers, suppliers and employees.

Why go to all this trouble? The simple answer is that in the past, the marketing strategy was one-to-one, which meant seller sold to buyer. The internet has reversed the relationship and created the one-from-one relationship, which means buyer buys from seller. Therefore, the better the sellers understands the buyers, the better they can serve them and so retain their custom. An e-commerce company can harness the power of personalization by harvesting customer profiles. Then it can generate offers that it can send down the e-mail route – called push technology – to software that helps manage internet relationships.

❝the power of personalization lies in its ability to create loyalty❞

The power of personalization lies in its ability to create loyalty. By allowing an e-commerce company to create dedicated pages for a specific customer, it builds an environment where the customer comes back time and time again and the experience becomes unique to that individual. The seller gathers information on his customer, personalizes the service, gathers and adds new information, personalizes it again, in a virtuous cycle, much like Amazon does on its website. As a result, the customer is less likely to switch to a competitor. In business-to-business terms the custom page enables a company to improve its communication and provide access to specialized information 24 hours a day. Also, the ability of a company to provide a custom offering to its top accounts is central to the goal of cementing relationships and maximizing the benefit of an e-commerce business.

The desired result of this principle is to create such an exemplary service in such an easy and addictive environment that it reduces the chances of your customer going elsewhere. The Marketing Director owns this principle and the Sales Director is a key influence.

Under this principle, the following software tools are covered: push technology, filtering software, intelligent agent software, targetted marketing services software, purchase identification software, internet relationship management software, matchmaking software and free e-mail.

In the following case study, we feature Autonomy Corporation which, like the rattlesnake, will seek, find and consume its information prey.

SUPPLIER PROFILE

Autonomy Corporation

knowledge management and new-media content solutions

AT THE HEART OF AUTONOMY'S[2] software is the ability to analyze a document, extract the ideas from the text and determine which are
the most important. This is achieved using proprietary pattern matching
technology developed by researchers from Cambridge University.
Because Autonomy's technology can derive meaning in a piece of text, it
can also profile users by analyzing the ideas in the documents they read
or produce. These profiles are then used to deliver personalized information, create communities of interest and, in knowledge management
applications, identify colleagues with useful expertise.

Dr Michael Lynch, a world-renowned expert in the field of adaptive
pattern recognition, founded Autonomy Corporation in March 1996.
Headquartered in San Francisco, Autonomy has offices in Boston,
Dallas, New York, Washington DC, Cambridge, Paris, Munich,
Frankfurt, Milan, Brussels, Amsterdam, Rome, Stockholm, Oslo and
Sydney. The company maintains close ties with Cambridge University,
where Dr Lynch originally developed Autonomy's technology.

Dr Lynch is also CEO of Cambridge Neurodynamics, a private company
which was founded in the early 1990s. Dr Lynch applied his PhD

research and technology – about matching and recognition of patterns (facial, fingerprint and behavior) – to the needs of the police investigative market.

Spun out of Neurodynamics in 1996, Autonomy Corporation was able to raise more than $15 million in venture funding thanks to Neurodynamics' track record and Autonomy's breakthrough technology and market potential. On July 10, 1998 the company went public on the EASDAQ exchange, achieving a valuation of $165 million. The initial public offering (IPO) raised close to $35 million and was more than seven times oversubscribed. In November 1999, Autonomy's valuation reached $1 billion. By March 2000, it had exceeded $7 billion. More than 200 companies worldwide use Autonomy's software, including British Aerospace, Lucent, Alcatel, Reuters, WorldOnline and PricewaterhouseCoopers.

business benefits

For corporate information portals, Autonomy has a suite of 'enterprise and knowledge management' products which:

▶ allows users to easily access relevant information through easy-to-navigate directories or natural language queries

▶ profiles employees so users can identify colleagues with relevant skills and knowledge

▶ delivers personalized information that helps employees stay on top of industry and competitive developments.

For online publishing companies and retailers, Autonomy has a suite of 'networked business solutions' products which:

▶ add depth and breadth to sites without having to hire scores of employees to tag and link existing and third-party content

▶ attract and retain online consumers through highly personalized information services

▶ add stickiness to sites by creating communities of people with similar interests

▶ add value to advertisers and sponsors by targetting ads and promotions to those individuals most likely to be interested.

❝people on the move do not have the time to browse, rather they need personalized information delivered to them automatically❞

Autonomy also has products for the wireless world. Its I-WAP™ has been specifically developed to address the limitations of today's wireless information delivery. People on the move do not have the time to browse, rather they need personalized information delivered to them automatically. This includes business intelligence, share price announcements and sports results. Autonomy's existing products, such as Portal-in-a-Box™, and Autonomy Update™ are now available with an additional WAP-compliant interface module, enabling users to access information at any time, wherever they are.

In the following interview, we offer an analysis of how knowledge management works.

INTERVIEW WITH SUPPLIER

'Understanding how organisms function.'

Neil Macehiter, Technology Solutions Director

IN THE PAST, KNOWLEDGE MANAGEMENT within an organization had focussed on putting large *structured* data warehouses together and then having power tools that would allow you to get the information out. But the assumption was that you knew the question you wanted to ask.

Today, we have masses of *unstructured* information. In a typical organization, the ratio of unstructured to structured is about ten to one, with unstructured information doubling every 12 months, according to META Group, a leading US research and consulting firm. Let alone the answer – we don't know what the exact questions are. Traditionally, you posit a question, look at what you get back and then rephrase the question, says Neil Macehiter.[3] With Autonomy, you get a result back that causes you to navigate down a particular path. Autonomy is an incredibly powerful technology: it provides a sophisticated means of navigating content and delivering highly personalized content.

For example, say you wanted to fly to Turkey on the 15th of August from Gatwick Airport at 10.47. You browse through a brochure on Turkey, see that it mentions a particular place, and find something that sparks your interest – say hang-gliding. So you then revert to different sources. What people actually like about the internet is getting to information quickly: in this case to be presented with a holiday and a suggestion of six similar holidays. Personalization is all about interacting with the content. Autonomy gains an understanding of what you are interested in and then uses that to target you.

How does the Autonomy engine work? It goes out and fetches content. It has these things called 'spiders', says Macehiter. You say to Autonomy, go to www.ecademy.com/news, navigate down three levels, grab any content, avoid anything with the following words, and bring back into the engine automatically. Autonomy is extending its capabilities so that it can have an intelligent information service that delivers exactly the right information to you exactly when you need it, no matter where it happens to be: on the web, on your hard drive, in your electronic mail, from people you know. Essentially, it unites your world, as it understands the content in your browser, in your e-mail or in your office productivity applications, and automatically delivers links to related information. In contrast, the traditional approach is to stop what you are doing, log on to your web page and then go back to what you were doing with your document.

❝there are two sides to knowledge management in an organization ❞

There are two sides to knowledge management in an organization. There is the content and there are the people. 'People, and the shared interest communities, are just as valuable as content, and in the Ecademy's case more so, in terms of what they know,' says Macehiter. For example, when Java emerged, it was all about making web pages dance around. There was a need for people to have examples of little applets that would show how Java could be used. At gamelan.com people would just go and they would publish things that were really useful for this site. They wouldn't charge anyone for it; they would just do it. The community built up and people started communicating with each other. There was a need and people were enabled to contribute. Newsgroups are not dissimilar.'

Commerce is the result of content and community, says Macehiter. 'I may never have gone to the Ecademy if I hadn't read your book [*Battle of the Portals*]. I found it in the offices of Simmons & Simmons, the law firm, picked it up and started reading it. It was amazing. I ordered a copy of it from your website. This is how I got into the Ecademy. It wasn't because I knew it existed but because of content, which I received as part of my community. The key to successful commerce sites is to deliver the best of breeds on content, community and commerce.'

In the next section, you will see the need, solution and benefits of why British Aerospace deployed Autonomy's Portal-in-a-Box™.

PRINCIPLE IN ACTION

British Aerospace and Portal-in-a-Box

RESEARCH CONDUCTED IN 1999/2000 shows that digital information is doubling in UK businesses every two years. The employee time spent trying to access it equates to £17 billion annually in the UK alone.

The internet and intranet were designed to facilitate the retrieval of information, but they are entirely reliant upon keyword searches and manual indexing – an arbitrary, unreliable and costly way of unearthing information. There is an alternative, however. Using Autonomy's knowledge management solutions, companies can automatically interpret and categorize enterprise information, which can then be personalized and delivered to the most relevant users through an internet/intranet portal. This is the approach behind Autonomy's Portal-in-a-Box product, which was tested so successfully in the British Aerospace (BAe) trials.

After a three-month competitive trial, British Aerospace successfully deployed Autonomy's Portal-in-a-Box solution to automatically manage and deliver personalized, relevant business information across its corporate communications and virtual university departments.[4]

This report describes the benefits of the technology, and how the results of the trial led to BAe's adoption of Portal-in-a-Box for rollout across the entire organization – 48,000 employees.

the client

British Aerospace is the fourth largest defense and aerospace company in the world, and the leading player in this market in Europe, with an order book of $8 billion per annum. With ongoing international collaborative programs involving 29 nations, BAe needs to keep its staff up to date and informed.

the need

BAe identified the following corporate information needs:

▶ to be able to automatically organize information from more than 300 internet sites, the company's entire intranet, many heavyweight databases and 12,000–15,000 live newsfeed stories per day, and personalize the delivery of that information to each user, *automatically*, without costly manual intervention

▶ to eliminate duplication of employee effort by alerting employees to existing relevant information

▶ to proactively deliver information to users as they go about their everyday business, thus dispensing with the need for search

▶ to build teams through virtual communities of interest, automatically putting users with related or mutual interests in contact with each other, and utilizing the company's greatest asset – its people.

the solution

While BAe already had a conventional intranet structure in place, the use of an intranet as an information-sharing tool for a wide range of data and operational tasks necessitated a different technological approach.

BAe chose to trial Autonomy's Portal-in-a-Box product, which automatically categorizes, tags and hyperlinks large volumes of information, eliminating costly, labour-intensive, manual processes. In addition, Portal-in-a-Box automatically generates real-time user profiles, based on the pages users visit and the documents they publish. Both these techniques are used to personalize the information delivered, whether this is breaking news, relevant documents elsewhere on the intranet, or the contact details of other people in the company whose interests and expertise match those of the user.

> **"Portal-in-a-Box is an off-the-shelf, rapidly installed solution, which brings immediate business benefits to users "**

Portal-in-a-Box is an off-the-shelf, rapidly installed solution, which brings immediate business benefits to users. At the same time, it is customizable and scalable, to meet the precise needs of organizations of all sizes. Like all Autonomy's technology, Portal-in-a-Box is powered by a pattern matching technology, which is based upon two fundamental principles – Bayesian Inference and Shannon's Information Theory. This pattern-matching technology identifies, understands, and extracts the ideas expressed within digital documents, and is able to locate documents containing similar information. The technology is able to understand information which is completely unstructured; there is no need for it to be tagged or ordered into fields.

the benefits

An average company of 1,000 employees can waste up to £2,500 each day as its staff spends valuable time in often fruitless searches for information. In an organization the size of BAe, this is a potentially enormous annual figure. Portal-in-a-Box can dramatically reduce this expense by actively putting staff in contact with the information which is most likely to be of use to them. At BAe, this has been shown in the following ways:

▶ employees within BAe enjoy instant access to relevant information and business intelligence, delivered to them in a fully personalized form

▶ documents previously circulated in disparate forms at BAe – hard copy, HTML, e-mail text, word-processing files, etc. – are now grouped into directories based on an automatic understanding of their content. This concentrates similar resources in the same repository

▶ users are alerted to information which can serve their needs, and are automatically linked into appropriate interest communities

▶ the Virtual University, BAe's intranet-based training initiative, can create a personalized development syllabus for each employee, based on automatic profiling of their expertise and areas of interest.

Ian Black, Head of Corporate Communications and Public Affairs, says: 'BAe decided that the concurrent demands for both the management and provision of information required a sophisticated, intelligent approach to knowledge management. The technology selected also had to meet the challenge of capturing and sharing the organization's hidden intellectual capital – a challenge that traditional technologies have consistently failed to meet.'

the future

British Aerospace estimates that the implementation of Autonomy's Portal-in-a-Box technology has the potential to significantly reduce the time spent by employees attempting to locate information and will deliver rapid return on investment. This level of return is not common to all the vendors in the knowledge management market, prompting Ian Black to comment that Autonomy is 'head and shoulders above the competition' when it comes to corporate knowledge management solutions.

Through these departmental pilots, Autonomy harnessed BAe's corporate information and ensured that the company enjoyed a significant return on investment when the system was rolled out across the entire organization.

Why did we choose Autonomy? Its background in matching and recognition of patterns – facial, fingerprint and behavior – makes it a perfect organic thinking organization. Even information must live in an ecosystem – a knowledge ecosystem. In an internet-enabled world, there is little value to 'isolated silos' of information. For information to have value it must reach the individuals who have the greatest need for it. For that to happen, information must reside in the correct silos and be easily retrieved and fetched to the seeker's desktop. There is an urgent need for this in an organization like BAe, which has to organize more than 300 internet sites, many heavyweight databases, and up to 15,000 live news-feeds per day.

In our next case study, Vignette Corporation enables internet businesses to reach more prospects, attract and retain new customers, and increase overall customer satisfaction.

SUPPLIER PROFILE

Vignette Corporation

e-business ideas that turn on your brain

VIGNETTE CORPORATION[5] (NASDAQ: VIGN) is the leading supplier of e-business applications for building online businesses. Vignette's products enable internet businesses to reach more prospects, attract and retain new customers, increase overall customer satisfaction, and raise the total purchase per online visit.

The name Vignette means a short graceful literary essay or sketch, but the true story, according to European Marketing Manager Rebekah Menezes (see p. 354) is that when they went out looking in the dictionary for a name with 'net' in it, they got to the letter V before they found anything that hadn't been registered.

In January 1999, Vignette had 50 customers with 50 employees worldwide, turning over about $50 million. Now it has more than 600 customers, 1,100 employees, and revenues of more than $100 million. In its IPO in February 1999, it went out at $19 a share and the company was valued at $2 billion. A year later, in January 2000, its valuation stood at $16 billion; by year-end it was down to $5 billion. In spite of the dot com market carnage, its market capitalization has grown two-and-a-half times since the IPO.

In just under five years, Vignette has grown to 1,100 employees throughout the US, Europe, Asia and Australia, all fixated on bringing practical networked business insights to problem solving and making every implementation successful. It has built a substantial customer base, with more than 600 customers in key vertical markets, including financial services, telecommunications, retail commerce/travel, media/publishing, high-tech manufacturing, healthcare and automotive.

66the V/Series equips businesses with a single view across multiple customers, partners, products and interactions 99

The company's flagship networked business solution, the V/Series product line, is the only complete networked business platform that provides the business insight, rapid business reconfiguration and integration across multiple touch-points required for networked business success. Introduced in April 2000, the V/Series platform incorporates and expands on Vignette's StoryServer and other products. The V/Series equips businesses with a single view across multiple customers, partners, products and interactions, giving companies the ability to maximize and measure the return on investment of all their online relationships and initiatives.

history

Founded in 1995 and headquartered in Austin, Texas – President George W. Bush country – Vignette has risen to become the industry leader in networked business applications. Its founders, Ross Garber and Neil Webber, began Vignette with a market-based approach by cold-calling the senior executives of pioneering networked businesses to learn about their technical and business challenges. By listening to them, Vignette was able to develop quickly into one of the most successful providers of content management solutions. This market-driven philosophy has been evident from the StoryServer products and now in the V/Series platform.

Others soon recognized Vignette's vision. As a private company, Vignette received $36.1 million in funding, which was the largest venture investment in an Austin-based software company at that time. Investors include Austin Ventures, Sigma Partners, Amerindo, Adobe Ventures LP, Charles River Ventures, Attractor Investment Management, Morgan Stanley Dean Witter, Hambrecht & Quist, CNET: The Computer Network, JGE Capital Management, Olympus Partners, Partech International and Goldman Sachs Private Investment Funds.

customers

Vignette customers are companies which are serious about doing business online. They are Global 2000 and dot com companies which understand that survival depends on the ability to use the internet to establish and preserve customer loyalty. A record 125 new customers chose Vignette during the fourth quarter 1999.

Vignette's leading customers read more like a list of fund investments and include American Express, Amway, AT&T, Bank One Corporation, Checkout.com, Chicago Tribune, Compaq, CNET, CSB Broadcasting, DaimlerChrysler, DHL, Direct TV, Dun & Bradstreet, E!Online, First Chicago, First Union Corporation, Guardian Newspapers, Hollywood Online, IPC Magazines, IntelliQuest, JavaSoft, Le Monde, Mecklermedia, Merrill Lynch, National Semiconductor, New Media Magazine, New York Life, Nokia, PC World Online, phone.com, The Royal Bank of Canada, Seagate, Siebel Systems, Simon & Schuster, Sportsline USA, Sybase, Tandy Corporation, Time Inc., New Media, Time Warner Roadrunner, Travelocity, Upside, US West Communications, Volvo, Whole Foods Markets and ZDNet.

INTERVIEW WITH SUPPLIER

'It is the relationship that rules.'

Rebekah Menezes, European Marketing Manager

'VIGNETTE POWERS 12 OUT OF THE TOP 20 SITES with the highest traffic,' says Rebekah Menezes.[6] 'And the reason we are very successful is because we consider our customers' success to be our success. In terms of international customers, Nokia is probably one of the best examples of a truly global site. All content is localized into at least ten languages, anything from Finnish to German to Chinese.' Vignette powers its site but it doesn't actually host it.

E-business is not just about selling. 'We don't just think about enabling a transaction, but through personalizing content to each individual user, we aim to develop a relationship with that person online,' says Menezes. To do that you need to understand the content and understand the interests of the individual on the receiving end of that content. For example, if you look at *Guardian Unlimited* sites, the content is tagged in such a way that you can differentiate between news, various sports and entertainment items. Suppose every time you went on to a *Guardian* site, you were interested in sports and in boxing in particular, the site would enquire whether you knew Mike Tyson was going to be fighting in the UK next weekend, and whether you would like to buy tickets.

Menezes advocates considering the personal perspective. 'When you meet somebody for the first time, you don't tell them too much information about yourself. So when you go to a site and they ask you 10 or 20 seemingly personal questions, you think, why should I give them this information? What value am I going to get out of it?'

Vignette takes this human relationship psychology into account from the first phases of a customer relationship cycle. For instance, when someone new comes on to a site, the first thing Vignette does is ensure the site looks good by personalizing the content according to the browser the person is using, their country of origin and the language they speak.

'At the next level we would then observe you as you move around the site anonymously,' continues Menezes. 'There is nothing sinister about it, it just enables us to understand more about the type of content you would like to see, with a view to engaging your attention for longer.'

❝Vignette can draw on and understand what it is that attracts or fails to attract the user❞

In order to understand customers better, Vignette invested in a company called Bizrate.com, which provides valuable anonymous data by tracking how long somebody spends (at a site) before clicking somewhere else. With this anonymous data, Vignette can draw on and understand what it is that attracts or fails to attract the user. Menezes believes that in order to be really effective you have to match this knowledge with content, and that's what Vignette enables a networked business to do.

All this cannot work without committed employees. Organizations generally pay lip service to their 'most important asset' – their employees – but do not follow it up with action. This is not the case with Vignette. The company has an investment fund program for employees, which it opened in 2000 with $50 million. That money is invested in companies such as Bizrate.com and 'we get 50 percent of the profits. It works in a similar way to share options, which vest over four years and have proven a great incentive to people,' says Menezes. 'I had never managed people before I came to Vignette and I manage about 12 people now. I want every one of them to be the best that they can ever be. Ross Garber [one of the founders] is probably the most inspirational person I have ever worked for in my career.'

PRINCIPLE IN ACTION

Atevo Travel

ATEVO TRAVEL (www.atevo.com)[7] is a full-service online travel site that integrates content, commerce and community to offer one-stop shopping for time-crunched customers. Headquartered in Birmingham, California, Atevo Travel has carved its niche in the online travel arena by delivering what it has coined as a 'thoroughgoing context' to help users enjoy and maximize their travel-planning experiences. Atevo Travel is committed to providing customers with convenient reservations services, along with a wide variety of travel content and forums for community interaction.

meeting the needs of an online community

Atevo Travel launched its online travel website in 1997, using a system developed internally. While the site was functional, Atevo Travel found that to remain ahead of the industry, anticipate customers' needs, and accommodate its growing partner base, the site would have to provide fresh, interactive and personalized content. The company was searching for a solution to streamline development, shorten maintenance time, and provide a scalable environment for growth. After reviewing a number of vendors, Atevo Travel believed Vignette offered the right combination of technical functionality, content management and relationship management features to serve all its customers.

advancing technology through smart relationships

Atevo Travel had a few options for implementing the new solutions. It could integrate the Vignette software with the internally developed system, or re-engineer the entire site using Vignette. Ultimately, it decided to use Vignette as the foundation for its site, which was relaunched in March 1998. 'Vignette was the most powerful solution for supporting our growing business needs. The transition was seamless and offered a more flexible environment,' said Hyun Shin, Chief Operating Officer at Atevo Travel.

❝Vignette is a hugh factor in Atevo's ability to meet online travelers' needs with great efficiency and agility❞

According to Shin, Vignette is the centrepiece to help deliver the content needed online. Vignette is a huge factor in Atevo's ability to meet online travelers' needs with great efficiency and agility. The implementation period lasted four and a half months, which included learning the TCL development language, developing the new site and rolling out a full product, which was 33 percent faster than Atevo Travel had originally planned.

Atevo was certain Vignette would help it better manage and accelerate its content development processes, minimize site maintenance and maximize technical resources, said Shin. It was especially impressed with the caching functionality because it allowed Atevo to better manage dynamically generated pages and save its customers time when loading pages.

The scalable Vignette platform enables Atevo Travel to offer comprehensive destination information for cities, states, countries, and national parks; practical news, tips, and advice; lively feature articles and travel recommendations; maps, photos, and other travel-related features. It also allows the company to create innovative features such as Your Travel Page, a free personal travel page, and Travellers' Exchange, an extensive set of message boards to provide interaction with fellow travelers.

Using Vignette, Atevo Travel was also able to create individual partner sites. As customers log on to the Atevo Travel site, they view co-branded partner pages that are cached. Serving these pages is much faster and enables Atevo Travel to support high traffic to its site during peak travel seasons. 'We have been so satisfied with the flexibility of Vignette that many times we recommend that our partners evaluate Vignette's product offerings,' said Shin. Atevo Travel has created co-branded partner pages with *Nando Times, Earthlink, Minneapolis-St. Paul Star Tribune, The Arizona Republic,* and *Milwaukee Journal Sentinel.*

the results

With Vignette, Atevo Travel quickly became a comprehensive online travel resource rather than just a cyber-travel agency. Since the launch of its reengineered website, it has successfully built partnerships with companies such as GTE.net, Discover Card, Planet Direct, Nando Media, *New York Post* and *Via Nova Destination* magazine. According to Shin, Vignette has played a pivotal role in generating increased interest and worldwide business. Atevo Travel has also experienced increased employee productivity, easier online maintenance, and a more streamlined development process. Shin says the Vignette solution helped minimize overall site management time by 33 percent.

moving forward

Atevo Travel's business goals include leveraging its investment in Vignette to offer improved customer service through increased personalization. To better address specific customer interests, Atevo Travel will capitalize on the lifecycle personalization services, which capture user information non-intrusively. The company also plans to target and secure more online customers worldwide. 'We have remained a Vignette customer because we share Vignette's vision of using the web to closely manage our relationship with customers to provide an integrated online solution for their needs,' says Shin.

So, you would not be wrong to say that Atevo remains in the Vignette ecosystem.

So why did we choose Vignette? Apart from being a leader in this principle, Vignette is a powerful ally to have in your ecosystem. It nurtures the online relationship with your customer and, Rebekah Menezes says, 'It is the relationship that counts.' Why? Because it cements the community in your business organization and delivers the commerce that sustains the ecosystem.

EXECUTIVE SUMMARY OF
PRINCIPLE 12

PERSONAL SERVICE IS AS OLD as the human race. Personalization is the electronic manifestation of personal service. Although the web is the technology of the future, paradoxically it also enables a return to a very old-fashioned value: personalized contact with customers, who may also be employees, shareholders or suppliers. E-business or e-commerce is not just about selling. It's about developing relationships with customers and stakeholders online.

▶ The internet is a powerful weapon in mass customization. Once customers have spent time personalizing services at a particular site, they are less likely to switch to competitors

▶ With custom pages and other offerings, organizations can achieve superior communications with their customers, providing access to communication, constantly and instantly.

▶ An internet site can be highly effective for monitoring and analyzing the buying habits of customers, customizing products and information to meet those habits, and quickly responding to queries and requests.

► In the past, the marketing strategy was one-to-one, which meant seller sold to buyer. The internet has reversed the relationship and created the one-from-one relationship, which means buyer buys from seller. Therefore, the better the sellers understand the buyers, the better they can serve them and so retain their custom.

► The ability of a company to provide a custom offering to its top accounts is central to the goal of cementing relationships and maximizing the benefit of an e-commerce business.

► Companies waste enormous amounts of money when employees spend valuable time in often fruitless searches for information.

► Intelligent software allows users to easily access relevant information, profile employees so users can identify colleagues with relevant skills and knowledge, and deliver personalized information that helps employees stay on top of industry developments.

► Intelligent software automatically personalizes the delivery of information from multiple sources to each user. It can eliminate duplication of employee effort, it can proactively deliver information to users, and it can build teams through virtual communities of interest.

► You must take 'human relationship psychology' into account on websites – greeting people in their language, ensuring the site looks good, clean and simple to navigate. Not probing, but allowing the customer to take the lead in asking the questions.

► You can't have a strategy in isolation. Remember, this is an ecosystem. The objective is to deliver to the consumer a product, service or information which is second to none. Without a rich database of customers, there is no business, let alone a networked business.

NOTES

1 'Surviving in arid lands,' **Eyewitness Guides Ecology**, Steve Pollock, Dorling Kindersley Ltd, 1993, p. 40.

2 http:/www.autonomy.com and an Autonomy CD entitled **Making Sense of Information**, which included company information, product and service information and numerous case studies.

3 Interview with Neil Macehiter, Technology Solutions Director, on November 19, 2000.

4 Case study – British Aerospace and Portal-in-a-Box.

5 http:/www.vignette.com and Vignette e-business series Book II, **Success Through Understanding**.

6 Interview with Rebekah Menezes, European Marketing Manager, on January 20, 2000.

7 Case study – Atevo Travel.

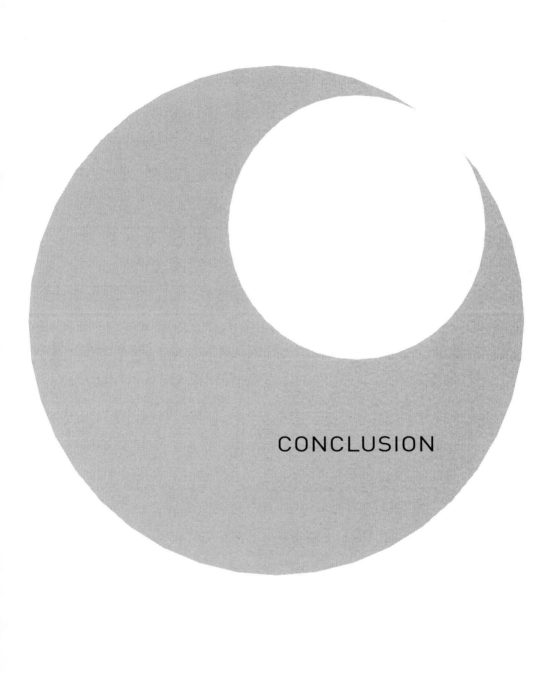

CONCLUSION

'If you are planning for a year, sow rice;
If you are planning for a decade, plant trees;
If you are planning for a lifetime, educate people.

Chinese proverb[1]

THE DELIBERATE CULTIVATION OF CROPS changed every-
thing, enabling human beings to increase the productivity of the land
and escape the tyranny of the food chain. This single development
makes humans ecologically different from all other species. It opened
up the possibility of a tremendous population increase and has
changed the face of the Earth itself.[2] Today, the deliberate cultivation of
electronic relationships is changing everything, enabling human beings
to increase the productivity of their mind and escape the tyranny of
'supply chain' thinking.

Economic growth is a function of connectivity; the more connected we
are, the more economic growth we produce. The connectivity has been
achieved through technology and if technology is the engine, then
finance is the fuel. When things change so swiftly, what we know quickly
becomes obsolete. The business world we live in today is changing dramatically and as a result it will affect our social and personal lives too.
Economics, finance, law, and education will all change. In fact, everything from aviation to zoology will not be spared. We need to be flexible.
We need to be adaptable. We need to learn constantly just to stay afloat.
But to excel at what we do, we will need to do more than just learn. We
need to learn to enjoy 'learning'. If we are not riding the wave of change,

we will find ourselves beneath it. We are compelled to increase our connections and become more connected both online and off-line.

the airport analogy
We have shown each principle in action in the living example of London Heathrow Airport. We have also shown the relationship of each principle with all the other principles. Heathrow Airport is an ecosystem. This illustration reveals and confirms that the process is not a linear one. The result is not a linear process of 12 but an organic and symbiotic process of 144 (12 × 12). The 12 principles are all tied together. If one Principle or aspect is adjusted, there will inevitably be a ripple effect throughout the business ecosystem. For your business it is the same. You need not only be aware but constantly vigilant. If you change one aspect, it will ripple through your organization.

❝the more the relationship grows between each principle, the more improvement there is in the performance of each ❞

The more the relationship grows between each principle, the more improvement there is in the performance of each, through the feedback loop. To help us understand these connections, even though they are organic and interconnected, we break them down so that we can map the stakeholders or communities on to the 12 principles (Figure C.1).

▶ *The community of shareholders*, which we call B2S or business to shareholders, is the domain of the Chief Executive Officer and Chief Knowledge officer and covers primarily *Principles 1 and 2.*

▶ *The community of employees*, which we call B2E or business to employees, is the domain of the Chief Information Officer and covers primarily Principles 3, 4 and 5.

▶ *The community of businesses*, both in supply chains and as sales feeders, which we call B2B or business to business, is the domain of the Chief Operations Officer and Chief Financial Officer and covers primarily *Principles 6, 7, 8 and 9.*

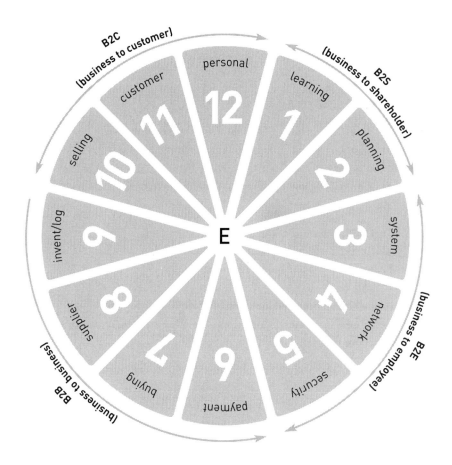

FIG C.1 Stakeholder communities

▶ *The community of customers*, which we call B2C or business to customer, is the domain of the Chief Marketing Officer and covers primarily *Principles 10, 11 and 12*.

However, these are not rigid groups because ecosystems, whether natural or business, do not have borders. They are fluid, they are flexible, and they are fundamental. Every enterprise is linked to many communities and many supply webs. Because ecosystems are fluid and transparent, it is therefore imperative that organizations have a clear and transparent message to all their stakeholders and a clear under-standing of where they fit in their own ecosystem – one website to cater for all these stakeholders' viewpoints and needs.

our message to shareholders

Any reputable organization must have a community of shareholders, online and off-line, which we call B2S. The Chief Executive Officer and Chief Knowledge Officer are the members of the board who should take primary responsibility for this community and as a result manage primarily *Principles 1 and 2* – learning and planning.

But shareholders also need to ask questions in order to better assess an organization. What business ecosystem does the organization in which you are investing inhabit and what is its role? How can the organiza-tion enlarge its ecosystem so that it can ensure survival and secure its place in the ecosystem, or will it work to be part of someone else's ecosystem? Are mergers and acquisitions the only remaining way to grow a business or is there a new avenue?

The key to the answers lies in the questions. *Explore* research compa-nies; *speak* to investment houses and venture capitalists; *listen* to recruitment organizations; *discover* university courses and E-Commerce training workshops; *consult* internet law firms and ask the right ques-tions; *question* and seek advice from tax specialists and accountants. An organization is more likely to succeed if, with proper planning from professionals, it reconfigures its entire business strategy so that the full advantages of the internet are integrated into its existing business.

You cannot have a strategy in isolation. You need to understand that every aspect in an organization is affected and they all need to be transformed in a holistic way. You need to introduce a three-dimen-sional or 360 degree approach to questioning in organizations.

our message to employees

Organizations must form a commu-nity of employees, online and off-line, B2E. The Chief Information Officer is the member of the board who takes primary responsibility for this community and as a result manages primarily Principles 3, 4 and 5 – system software evaluation, network evaluation and security.

Learning the 12 principles will not only improve your understanding of networked business but also increase the marketability of your profile of skills to recruiters. You should combine learning on the job and taking a sabbatical to study networked business. Learning is not harnessing only your intellect but also your emotions. In this way, you will ensure that you are absorbing not just the information but also the experience. The key to learning is questioning; answers are a dead-end, unless they move you to more questions.

Remember, this is an ecosystem. It is far more than just working closely with your partners or colleagues. Just look at the EDS case study in principle 4, where 1,200 employees were transferred from Rolls-Royce to EDS. You must be prepared to be transferred or, even better, elect to be transferred so that you can cross-fertilize your ideas with your hosts.

Studies have shown that 80 percent of a purchasing specialist's job is spent on administration. The paper has become their job rather than what their job should actually be. Does that ring true for your job? Don't be afraid to push at the limits. Increase your knowledge on the new technology and assess how it may help you do a better job. Don't wait for your employer to help you and offer things on a platter. Go out there and be proactive; your employers will reward you, and if they don't, your new employers will.

The employment terrain is changing. Even your immediate boss does not really understand what is going on. The cultural change is the hardest challenge for traditional businesses to meet. The success of this transformation is dependent on the whole process changing simultaneously, which is why the CEO must take control of the whole process. The CEO needs savvy and reliable officers when the clarion calls for change. You can't have a strategy in isolation. Remember, this is an ecosystem. Make sure you unleash your ideas like a virus among your friends and colleagues[3] and that your name is clearly connected to it.

our message to businesses

All organizations have a community of businesses, partners or suppliers, online and off-line, which we call B2B. The Chief Operations Officer and Chief Financial Officer are the members of the board that take primary responsibility for this community and as a result manage primarily *Principles 6, 7, 8 and 9* – internet payments, buying, supplier portals, and inventory and logistics.

Businesses have already experienced the benefits of the internet. They have seen massive savings by moving their procurement to the electronic network. According to Scient, the US e-business systems innovator, the transformation so far has been in the *departments* and *enterprises* and is now moving into the *markets*. Within the next few years, it will have touched all *industries* and all *economies*.[4] But by then, every organization will have been transformed: merged, acquired or liquidated. Ultimately, we believe that the real battle for attention will begin when businesses cannot catch the attention of their customers and the cost of doing so becomes prohibitively expensive.

❝businesses have already experienced the benefits of the internet ❞

Just as with shareholders, organizations need to reconfigure their entire business strategy so that the full advantages of the internet are integrated into their existing business. In this way, they can build a seamless flow from supply webs to customer relationship management, but the internal systems must be in place first. Building a networked business or any business involves risks.

To take no risk at all is the greatest risk. A fundamental part of managing risk is the creation of evidence. Without the paper trail created in the real world, legal recourse online can be impossible. Non-repudiation services create complete and signed digital receipts for commercial online transactions. Once the security issue is addressed, an organization needs to take calculated risks to become a leader in its sector. It must establish itself at the epicentre of its supply web, a supplier portal, which even if it does not control, it will certainly have a significant influence over. Yet this portal is not just about price, nor about simply reducing procurement costs: it is about quality of suppliers and service. The supplier community must also have access to management tools (software) that quickly provide it with the best possible solutions to confront any set of circumstances from the manufacturing to distribution to delivery.

From the delivery point, it's about a personal conversation with the customer to determine what they want and to personalize the web experience to meet their needs. With custom pages, organizations can achieve superior communications with their customers, suppliers, shareholders and employees. The ability of a business to provide a custom offering to its top accounts is central to the goal of cementing relationships and maximizing the benefits. The ability of a business to provide intelligent software to its employees to make them cost- and time-efficient is central to keep them on top. Finally, at delivery, the fellow who drives up to the customer's house is the most important person in the web, because that person provides the human connection to the organization.

On e-commerce delivery, US management guru Peter Drucker makes three insightful comments. First, in most businesses today, delivery is considered a 'support' function. Under e-commerce, delivery will become the one area in which a business can truly distinguish itself. It will become the critical 'core competence'. Second, for the first time in business history, e-commerce separates selling and purchasing. Selling is completed when the order has been received and paid for; purchasing is completed only when the purchase has been delivered and actually not until it satisfies the purchaser's want. And whereas e-commerce demands centralization, delivery has to be totally decentralized. It needs to be local, detailed, and accurate. Third, in traditional business structures, selling is still seen and organized as a servant to production or as a cost centre that *sells what we make*. In the future, e-commerce companies will *sell what we can deliver*.[5]

To convert your business to a networked business is complex, difficult and expensive. You will eventually be compelled to do it, because all your competitors will have done it. Ultimately, it is a zero sum game, because everyone else will have done it. Then and only then will every-one's attention turn to harvesting communities with rich databases of consumers. 'E-commerce represents a full-frontal assault on business organization theory. The hard part is for business leaders to make a commitment to reconceptualize their business model, and that is hard, hard work,' warned IBM chairman Louis Gerstner in December 2000.

our message to consumers
All organizations have a community of customers (consumers), online and off-line, which we call B2C. The Chief Marketing Officer is the member of the board who should take primary responsibility for this community and as a result manage primarily Principles 10, 11 and 12 – selling software, customer portals and personalization. In the old industrial economy, each person's labour power was considered a form of property that could be sold in the market-place. In the new, networked economy, selling access to one's day-to-day living patterns and life experiences, as reflected in purchasing decisions, becomes a much sought-after intangible asset, says Jeremy Rifkin of Wharton Business School. Converting a relationship into a commodity and creating communities marks a turning point in the way commerce is conducted. To belong is to be connected to the many networks that make up the new global economy. Being a subscriber, member or client becomes as important as being propertied. In other words, it is access rather than ownership that increasingly determines one's status in the coming age.[6]

“it is the access' that has given consumers 'control' on the web ”

It is this 'access' that has given consumers 'control' on the web. Organizations are finding it harder and harder to influence consumer choice because of the proliferation of the media and the mushrooming cost of attempting to maintain the same influence. Businesses cannot sell to consumers, but consumers can buy from them, any time, any place. Consumers must surf and become familiar with the internet. They should participate in auctions, where they can learn tips such as bidding at times when the great majority of people are watching a national sport or event. Consumers must experience purchasing from the web to get a feel of what it's like to shop online. Although the internet is a technology of the future, it has enabled a return to old-fashioned values of personal contact and community spirit.

Businesses are looking at their customers in a new light. In the recent past, they spent more money chasing new customers instead of pampering their existing ones, who brought in more revenue and cost less to maintain. Now they see the lifetime value of each customer as a valuable income stream and so we have 'lifetime customer relationships'. As a result, businesses will use the web to follow consumers' behavior, track their purchases, finances, lifestyles, dietary choices, health, clothing, leisure and travel pursuits. This need not result in the insidious environment that some commentators have pictured. Continuous feedback allows businesses to anticipate and service customers' needs on a constant, open-ended basis. In this new economic environment, the consumer is left with little time, a barrage of new methods of communication – mobiles, e-mails, PDAs (personal digital assistants) – and continuous learning. The situation is stressful and unlikely to improve unless we change our mind-set. We need to look at learning as a pleasurable, life-long series of experiences that enhances our well-being.

While education is serious business, that doesn't mean that educational experiences can't be fun. The term 'edutainment' was coined to connote an experience straddling the realms of education and entertainment. Nothing is more important, more abiding, or more wealth creating than the wisdom required to transform customers. And nothing will command as high a price. In the budding transformation economy, the customer is the product. The individual buying the transformation essentially says, 'change me'. Transformations will become scrutinized, lionized and criticized – but not commoditized.[7]

our message to governments
Governments too can be transformed through the ballot box. We have not covered any form of governments in this book because they do not sit in the 'ecosystem' arena. They sit above ecosystems: their place is in the 'biome'. But

because governments exercise power and influence on business ecosystems, we are compelled to show how their situations will impact on businesses. Governments are wiring themselves electronically, albeit at a slower pace than their commercial 'ecosystem' constituents.

> **governments are wiring themselves electronically, albeit at a slower pace than their commercial 'ecosystem' constituents**

Collecting taxes has become so onerous and unenforceable that we believe governments will seek to delegate tax collection powers to business ecosystems. Peter Willey, head of Ernst & Young's personal tax division in the UK, said: 'The system has become so complex. If it continues, it will collapse. Self-assessment has been written for tax collectors, not taxpayers.' The Inland Revenue is halfway through a £2 billion ten-year development program for an online filing system, which is now considered a disaster. Only 32,000 tax returns have been filed over the internet, out of a target of 600,000.[8]

Although the situation in the US is remarkably better than in the UK, it still leaves a great deal to be desired. In 2000, 30 million Americans submitted their tax returns online. The biggest attraction of electronic filing is the rapid refund, which takes about two weeks, whereas those who file by mail will not see their refund for two or three months. By 2007, the IRS expects online returns to increase to more than 55 million, out of a current US population of 275 million, and this figure is expected to increase to 300 million by 2010. To convert less than 20 percent of the population to online tax returns within ten years is not impressive progress or an economically viable option.[9]

In the United States, President George W. Bush's administration has pledged to concentrate on two issues: to increase education and reduce taxes. In early 2001, the *Wall Street Journal* highlighted an interview with Bush's new Treasury Secretary Paul O'Neill, recognizing him as a long-time advocate for replacing the income tax with a consumption tax. According to the article, O'Neill wants to push for a national discussion. He said: 'If we don't have a conversation about the truth of this stuff, how are we ever going to change it?'[10]

Clearly, governments (Inland Revenue and IRS) must have 'conversations' with their citizens, communities, stakeholders, and business ecosystems. In the course of these conversations, if they listen well, governments may actually discover that people are fed up of filling in complicated tax forms. Perhaps the voting individuals may actually prefer to pay a higher consumption tax if they can forego all the other taxes – income, capital gains and inheritance. There are clearly many other issues that must be addressed, such as how the poor will cope with a higher consumption tax. Undoubtedly there will be endless questions raised and endless solutions proposed. Ultimately, the answer will be found at the intersection of politics and economics. How much will it cost to administer the tax system? And what is politically acceptable to a democracy? We believe that collecting taxes will fall on organizations, and it will not be unreasonable for them to take a percentage of the taxes as their payoff, before forwarding the balance to the government.

Even governments will have to accept that in the new economy, 'letting go' or delegating their powers to organizations actually gives them more control and paradoxically empowers and transforms the citizens. Democracy is enhanced, not reduced. If governments are to be effective and efficient, they will open 'conversations' with citizens, communities, stakeholders and business ecosystems, find out what is the most palatable and most efficient way to collect taxes, then proceed to implement their findings. They will need to rethink the entire tax system holistically, realizing that therein lies the opportunity for enhancing democracy not just through the method of taxation but also through the creation of electronic voting. By not listening, governments will not function and will atrophy. By listening to their constituents, who are being transformed, governments can in turn transform themselves.

a just cause

For an individual, this transformation can come to life only when there is a cause. A cause is an ideal, principle or belief in the name of which people band together to do something. A cause is bigger than a business or an organization; it goes beyond growth, profits, or even personal wealth accumulation.[11] A cause is *not* a cause-related marketing campaign. A cause gathers a host of organizations or ecosystems to want to work together. Just imagine a flock of birds and picture how sometimes they show a remarkable cohesion. The most characteristic migratory formation of geese, ducks, pelicans, and cranes is a 'V' formation, with the point tuned in the direction of flight. This is 'ecosystem' in action.

A cause generates an emotion in all stakeholders – customers, employees, suppliers, shareholders and governments – that impels them to want to own a share in the cause. A cause puts meaning into commerce. This will become an organizational imperative in the new economy for three reasons. First, organizations can no longer throw money to capture customers inefficiently. Second, the internet compels organizations and the markets to become transparent and to behave with integrity or else lose value. Third, individuals are suffering from 'time famine', relentless change, and a spiritual vacuum.

So what will a cause do for ecosystems? When cultivating pearls, the nucleus of a pig toe shell is inserted into the pearl oyster; to protect itself from this irritant, the oyster secretes multiple layers of nacre which after two or three years becomes the pearl.[12] Our proposition is that a cause is like an irritant that compels an organization to secrete the necessary ingredient to organically grow its communities of stakeholders: customers, suppliers, employees and shareholders. Our proposition is encapsulated in the French proverb:

> 'Vision without action is hallucination.
> Vision with action is a cause.' [13]

Where causes bind people together spiritually, web services unite them electronically. Unlike websites that you visit – think of visiting restaurants – web services are services that come to you – like home deliveries. If websites are like reading a book, web services are like a two-way conversation. The way web services work is that the moment you log in, on any device, with a single user name and password, those web services are available immediately at your beck and call – much like the 'electronic butler' we described in *Battle of the Portals* (1999).

NOTES

1 Chinese proverb – CSFB report **e-Learning: Power for the Knowledge Economy**, by Gregory Cappelli, Scott Wilson and Michael Husman, released on March 2000, http:/www.csfb.com/news/2000/february_29a_2000.html. p. 6.

2 'Human ecology,' **Eyewitness Guides Ecology**, Steve Pollock, Dorling Kindersley Ltd, 1993, p. 58

3 **Unleashing the Ideavirus** by Seth Godin, Do you Zomm, Inc., Dobbs Ferry, NY, 2000.

4 Extracted from slides given at a Scient presentation to Ecademy members at Russell Hotel in London in March 2000.

5 'Can e-commerce deliver?' Peter Drucker, **The World in 2000**, an **Economist** publication, p. 122.

6 **The Age of Access: The new culture of hypercapitalism where all life is a paid-for experience**,' Jeremy Rifkin, a fellow at Wharton School Executive Education Programme, **Industry Standard**, March 20, 2000.

7 **The Experience Economy: work is theatre and every business a stage**, B. Joseph Pine II and James H. Gilmore, Harvard Business School Press,1999, p. 90, 172 and 206.

8 **Tax System on Brink of Collapse**, Sarah Toyne, **Sunday Times**, London January 28, 2001.

9 **Uncle Sam: zap it to me**, Genia Jones, **Industry Standard**, Special reports, grok, Financial Services, February–March 2001.

10 http://www.fairtax.com – **Wall Street Journal**, New York, January 29, 2001.

11 **Leading the Revolution**, Gary Hamel, Harvard Business School Press, 2000, p. 248.

12 **How to be a pearl expert; the process of cultivation**, Mikimoto
http://www.mikimotoamerica.com/expert.shtml

13 **Vision without action is hallucination**. Unattributed French proverb.

INDEX